Barcode in back

MW01122320

Humber College Library
3199 Lakeshore Blvd. West
Toronto, ON   M8V 1K8

Studies in Childhood and Youth
Series Editors: **Allison James**, University of Sheffield, UK, and **Adrian James**, University of Sheffield, UK.

Titles include:

Kate Bacon
TWINS IN SOCIETY
Parents, Bodies, Space and Talk

Emma Bond
CHILDHOOD, MOBILE TECHNOLOGIES AND EVERYDAY EXPERIENCES
Changing Technologies = Changing Childhoods?

David Buckingham, Sara Bragg and Mary Jane Kehily
YOUTH CULTURES IN THE AGE OF GLOBAL MEDIA

David Buckingham and Vebjørg Tingstad (*editors*)
CHILDHOOD AND CONSUMER CULTURE

Tom Cockburn
RETHINKING CHILDREN'S CITIZENSHIP

Sam Frankel
CHILDREN, MORALITY AND SOCIETY

Allison James
SOCIALISING CHILDREN

Allison James, Anne Trine Kjørholt and Vebjørg Tingstad (*editors*)
CHILDREN, FOOD AND IDENTITY IN EVERYDAY LIFE

Nicholas Lee
CHILDHOOD AND BIOPOLITICS
Climate Change, Life Processes and Human Futures

Manfred Liebel, Karl Hanson, Iven Saadi and Wouter Vandenhole (*editors*)
CHILDREN'S RIGHTS FROM BELOW
Cross-Cultural Perspectives

Orna Naftali
CHILDREN, RIGHTS AND MODERNITY IN CHINA
Raising Self-Governing Citizens

Helen Stapleton
SURVIVING TEENAGE MOTHERHOOD
Myths and Realities

E. Kay M. Tisdall, Andressa M. Gadda and Udi Mandel Butler (*editors*)
CHILDREN AND YOUNG PEOPLE'S PARTICIPATION AND ITS
TRANSFORMATIVE POTENTIAL
Learning from across Countries

Afua Twum-Danso Imoh and Robert Ame
CHILDHOODS AT THE INTERSECTION OF THE LOCAL AND THE GLOBAL

Hanne Warming
PARTICIPATION, CITIZENSHIP AND TRUST IN CHILDREN'S LIVES

Karen Wells, Erica Burman, Heather Montgomery and Alison Watson (*editors*)
CHILDHOOD, YOUTH AND VIOLENCE IN GLOBAL CONTEXTS
Research and Practice in Dialogue

Rebekah Willett, Chris Richards, Jackie Marsh, Andrew Burn and
Julia C Bishop (*editors*)
CHILDREN, MEDIA AND PLAYGROUND CULTURES
Ethnographic Studies of School Playtimes

Studies in Childhood and Youth
Series Standing Order ISBN 978–0–230–21686–0 hardback
(*outside North America only*)

You can receive future titles in this series as they are published by placing a
standing order. Please contact your bookseller or, in case of difficulty, write to us
at the address below with your name and address, the title of the series and the
ISBN quoted above.

Customer Services Department, Macmillan Distribution Ltd, Houndmills,
Basingstoke, Hampshire RG21 6XS, England

Children and Young People's Participation and Its Transformative Potential

Learning from across Countries

Edited by

E. Kay M. Tisdall
University of Edinburgh, UK

Andressa M. Gadda
University of Strathclyde, UK

and

Udi Mandel Butler
The International Center for Research and Policy on Childhood, Brazil

palgrave
macmillan

HUMBER LIBRARIES LAKESHORE CAMPUS
3199 Lakeshore Blvd West
TORONTO, ON.   M8V 1K8

Selection, introduction and editorial matter © E. Kay M. Tisdall, Andressa M. Gadda and Udi Mandel Butler 2014
Individual chapters © Respective authors 2014

All rights reserved. No reproduction, copy or transmission of this publication may be made without written permission.

No portion of this publication may be reproduced, copied or transmitted save with written permission or in accordance with the provisions of the Copyright, Designs and Patents Act 1988, or under the terms of any licence permitting limited copying issued by the Copyright Licensing Agency, Saffron House, 6–10 Kirby Street, London EC1N 8TS.

Any person who does any unauthorized act in relation to this publication may be liable to criminal prosecution and civil claims for damages.

The authors have asserted their rights to be identified as the authors of this work in accordance with the Copyright, Designs and Patents Act 1988.

First published 2014 by
PALGRAVE MACMILLAN

Palgrave Macmillan in the UK is an imprint of Macmillan Publishers Limited, registered in England, company number 785998, of Houndmills, Basingstoke, Hampshire RG21 6XS.

Palgrave Macmillan in the US is a division of St Martin's Press LLC, 175 Fifth Avenue, New York, NY 10010.

Palgrave Macmillan is the global academic imprint of the above companies and has companies and representatives throughout the world.

Palgrave® and Macmillan® are registered trademarks in the United States, the United Kingdom, Europe and other countries.

ISBN 978–0–230–34867–7

This book is printed on paper suitable for recycling and made from fully managed and sustained forest sources. Logging, pulping and manufacturing processes are expected to conform to the environmental regulations of the country of origin.

A catalogue record for this book is available from the British Library.

A catalog record for this book is available from the Library of Congress.

Typeset by MPS Limited, Chennai, India.

Contents

List of Figures and Tables

Figures

Tables

Acknowledgments

The network that led to this edited book was funded by The Leverhulme Trust. Further support for the network and engagement has been provided by the British Academy, the Economic and Social Research Council (RES-451-26-0685, RES-189-25-0174), the European Research Council and the Royal Society of Edinburgh.

The authors and publishers wish to thank the following for permission to reproduce copyright material:

Children's Institute, for permission to use material from a previously published chapter, in L. Jamieson, R. Bray, A. Viviers, L. Lake, S. Pendlebury and C. Smith (eds) *South African Gauge 2010/2011* (2011).

United Nations International Children's Fund, for Figure 1.1, from R. A. Hart *Children's Participation: From Tokenism to Citizenship* (1992).

Save the Children, for Figure 1.2, from P. Treseder *Empowering Children and Young People Training Manual: Promoting Involvement in Decision-making* (1997).

John Wiley and Sons, for Figure 1.3, from H. Shier 'Pathways to Participation: Openings, Opportunities and Obligations', in *Children & Society*, 15(2) 2001.

Notes on Contributors

Carine Le Borgne is a doctoral researcher at Edinburgh University. Her research is exploring the implementation of children and young people's participation rights, based on the practice of two children's rights organizations, one in Scotland (UK) and another in Tamil Nadu (South India). She worked for four years for Asmae (a French NGO working for underprivileged children) as child rights and child participation advisor. She previously worked in the Philippines, India and Egypt for Asmae. She also worked for the Children and Family Department at the local government in France at the beginning of her career.

Udi Mandel Butler's research has been mainly with children and young people living in a context of urban poverty in Rio de Janeiro, in particular those living on the street and in the *favelas*. His recent work has engaged with young people's perceptions of and engagement in public action in Brazil (NGOs, social movements, cultural groups and community organizations). On this theme, he has also conducted collaborative projects, through writing and photography, with young activists living in Rio's *favelas*, in association with CIESPI (the International Center for Research and Policy on Childhood) in Rio de Janeiro where he is a research fellow. Udi was a lecturer in Visual Anthropology at the Institute of Social and Cultural Anthropology, Oxford University, where he is now a research associate.

Andressa M. Gadda is a research associate at the Centre for Excellence for Looked After Children in Scotland (CELCIS), at the University of Strathclyde. Her research has mainly focused on the experiences of 'looked after' children and young people and the social care system in Scotland. She is particularly interested in the socio-historical constructions of childhood, the relationship between protection and control, poverty and discrimination. Andressa has a PhD in Social Work from the University of Edinburgh.

Sandy Halliday, a chartered engineer, has worked in building research, training and policy guidance and as project advisor for local and national government and private clients for over 25 years. She initially worked as a research manager developing UK policy and disseminating information on passive design, resource efficient, clean technologies and benign processes, products and materials. She founded Gaia Research (1996) to develop sustainable solutions for the built environment. Sandy's work extends to research, policy guidance, brief development, community consultation and interdisciplinary education. Sandy has published extensively including the *Green Guide to the Architect's Job Book* and *Sustainable Construction*. See www.gaiagroup.org.

Patricia Henderson is Senior Lecturer at Rhodes University in the Department of Anthropology. Her research interests include medical anthropology, the anthropology of children and youth and the anthropology of performance and creativity as social critique. Her theoretical interests include phenomenology and embodiment. She was a principal researcher at the Children's Institute, University of Cape Town during the period when the initial work toward this volume was done. One of Henderson's most recent publications is a monograph entitled, *A Kinship of Bone: Aids, Intimacy and Care in Rural KwaZulu-Natal* (2012), for which she won the Vice Chancellor's book award for 2013 at Rhodes University.

Rachel Hinton is a social anthropologist with particular expertise in the field of refugees and education. She currently works for the Department for International Development (DFID) as a social development advisor and manager of the Education Research Team. She is responsible for commissioning research that will inform education programming in developing countries. Since joining the DFID, she has worked on countries as diverse as Albania, Bangladesh, Bosnia, Ghana, India and Nepal, contributing to public expenditure reviews, country assessments, policy analyses and evaluations of policies and programs. She is the co-author of the book 'Inclusive Aid' that examines power and relationships in the new aid environment. Rachel has a PhD in Anthropology from Cambridge University.

Lucy Jamieson is Senior Advocacy Co-ordinator for the Children's Institute, University of Cape Town. She has a Masters in Democratic Governance focusing on children's participation in legislative processes. Lucy is a social justice and children's rights advocate; she works and publishes on the involvement of children in civil society advocacy in policy and law reform. She coordinates civil society advocacy campaigns and networks at national level, such as the Children's Bill Working Group, and initiated a number of projects to ensure that children participated in both the design and implementation of the Children's Act.

Howard Liddell (1945–2013) founded Gaia Architects in 1984 following a professorship (Oslo) that also gave rise to his co-founding of Gaia International. Through nearly 30 years of practice he has established his international reputation as a leader in ecological design, sustainable masterplanning, building biology and community architecture. He specialized in assisting community groups to convert aspirations into real projects. He achieved recognition for architectural design, energy conservation and environmental design. He was recognized as a vibrant and inspirational mentor and speaker and much sought after for training. He is the author of *Eco-Minimalism: The Antidote to Eco-Bling*. See www.gaiagroup.org.

Drew Mackie trained as an architect and planner and has worked in community regeneration for almost 30 years assisting community groups all over the UK. He has designed many games for government, local government, community and corporate clients and is a past Chairman of the International Simulation and Gaming Association (ISAGA). He founded Gaia Planning with the late Howard Liddell and provides the Urban Design input to the EcoCity projects, working with the children to create urban places while thinking about who uses them, at what time and for what purpose.

Cathy McCulloch is Co-Director and Co-Founder of Children's Parliament in Scotland. With a background in Community Education, Cathy has worked in rural and city locations over the past 30 years. Her management experience has focused mainly on organizations working with children, Black and Minority Ethnic (BME) communities and families. She has led each of the EcoCity projects that have taken place around the UK since the original project in 1992. In her current post as Co-Director of Children's Parliament, she is responsible for a range of programs focusing on children's effective engagement and participation with a strong focus on children's human rights.

Helen Meintjes is trained in Social Anthropology and Senior Researcher at the Children's Institute, a child policy research and advocacy unit based at the University of Cape Town. Her research has focused primarily on the nature and provision of formal and informal care for children in the context of the AIDS epidemic in South Africa. She is one of the founders of the *Abaqophi bakwaZisize Abakhanyayo* children's radio project in rural Kwazulu-Natal.

Colin Morrison is one of the founding members and Co-Director of The Children's Parliament. Colin's professional background began in teaching and then moved to community-based youth social work and children's play. His professional practice was largely in the voluntary sector. In addition to work at the Children's Parliament Colin is also a partner in the social research company TASC (Scotland).

Shirley Pendlebury is Professor Emeritus at the University of Cape Town (UCT) and currently a senior scholar associated with the School of Education at UCT. Much of her contribution towards this volume took place while she was Director of the Children's Institute, a multidisciplinary child policy research and advocacy institute at UCT. Social justice, inclusion and democracy in education have been recurring themes in her research, publications and conference presentations.

Marcelo Princeswal is a PhD candidate and has a Masters in Public Policy and Human Development from the State University of Rio de Janeiro (UERJ). He has a Psychology degree from Universidade Federal Fluminense (UFF) and is a consultant at the International Center for Research and Policy on Childhood (CIESPI) in partnership with PUC-Rio, where he has participated in several research projects. He has also worked with social movements in the field of education and training policy.

Saima Saeed is Associate Professor at the Centre for Culture, Media and Governance (CCMG), Jamia Millia Islamia, New Delhi, India. She has over 12 years of work experience spanning across media industry (television news, documentaries and non-news genres), media teaching and research. She has been teaching at CCMG since its inception in 2007. She is an alumnus of A J K Mass Communication Research Centre, Jamia Millia Islamia, New Delhi and Lady Shri Ram College for Women, University of Delhi. Her research interests include news studies, media and democracy, media and the margins, minorities and children, political communication and the dynamics of transnational media and globalization. Her recent book *Screening the Public Sphere: Media and Democracy in India* (2013), published in Routledge, Francis and Taylor Group, expounds an original social theory of media by positing four concepts – citizenship, public knowledge, criticality and power – as central to an understanding and evaluation of contemporary journalistic practice, ownership patterns and content, while framing the role and relationship of television news with regard to democracy and development.

Savyasaachi is Professor of Sociology at the Jamia Millia Islamia University in New Delhi. He has worked in the fields of political ecology, indigenous people, development, social movements and conservation architecture. Savyasaachi has been a visiting scholar at the School for International Training in Boston (USA) and at the National Institute of Design in Ahmedabad (India). He is the editor of *Between the Earth and the Sky: The Penguin Book of Forest Writings* (2005).

Kelly Teamey's research has been in the fields of education and international development, looking broadly at varying conceptualizations and practices of education and how they relate to international development policy. Of particular interest are alternative approaches to education and literacy, primarily amongst local and community nongovernmental organizations and social movements. She has carried out fieldwork in Pakistan, India, Bangladesh, Brazil, Mexico and Lebanon. Kelly has a PhD in Educational Research from King's College London and is currently a freelance researcher after several years working as a lecturer at the University of Bath, UK.

E. Kay M. Tisdall is Professor of Childhood Policy at the University of Edinburgh. She is Programme Director of the MSc in Childhood Studies (http://www.sps.ed.ac.uk/pgtcs) and Co-Director of the Centre for Research on Families and Relationships (http://www.crfr.ac.uk). She has worked practically on promoting children and young people's participation in legislation and policy, as well as developing a related research program.

List of Abbreviations

ACRWC	African Charter on the Rights and Welfare of the Child
ICTs	Information and communication technologies
ILO	International Labour Organization
MST	Movement of Landless Workers
NGO	Non-governmental Organization
UNCRC	United Nations Convention on the Rights of the Child
UNDP	United Nations Development Programme
UNICEF	United Nations International Children's Fund

1

Introduction: Children and Young People's Participation in Collective Decision-making

E. Kay M. Tisdall, Rachel Hinton, Andressa M. Gadda and Udi Mandel Butler

Over the past 20 years, children and young people's participation in decision-making has become part of international, and often national, policy rhetoric. Participation activities have grown apace. These range from bringing children and young people to the international stage – for example, in person to the United Nations (UN) General Assembly Special Session on Children in 2002 or virtually at the International Labour Organization (ILO) and the III Global Conference on Child Labour in 2013 – to the (re)formation of institutional structures – for example, national children's and youth parliaments, pupil councils in schools and youth forums in local government. Activities also include a host of one-off projects and events, such as conferences, arts-based installations and YouTube clips. Toolkits have proliferated, providing examples of how to engage children and young people productively. Practice has developed, so that participation facilitators use a range of methods – from social media, to 'creative' methods like murals or role play, to more traditional consultation and research techniques – to elicit children and young people's views on matters that affect them. Never before have there been such formal support of children and young people's participation and so many attempts to make it a reality.

Children and young people's participation is not new. A historical lens provides numerous examples, from the 1911 children's strikes in England, to youth councils forming post-World War II in such countries as Australia and Germany (Beaumont, 2014), to children and young people protesting against apartheid in South Africa (see Chapter 8). The current legal and policy emphasis on children and young people's participation has been inspired by the United Nations Convention on the Rights of the Child (UNCRC), which was adopted by the UN General

Assembly in 1989. The UNCRC is the most ratified human rights convention in the world (only two State Parties have not ratified it). States that ratify the Convention have the responsibility to safeguard those rights and must submit regular reports to the UN Committee on the Rights of the Child. The legal impact of the UNCRC within a country depends on each country's legal structure, as well as what efforts each country has made to legally incorporate the UNCRC within its laws and legal framework (Lundy et al., 2013).

Article 12 of the UNCRC was novel in giving children the specific right to have their views considered. The text of Article 12(1) is:

> State Parties shall assure to the child who is capable of forming his or her own views the right to express those views freely in all matters affecting the child, the views of the child being given due weight in accordance with the age and maturity of the child.

Article 12 is not radical in giving children self-determination; it is balanced by other key principles like Article 3, which treats children's best interests as a primary consideration in all actions concerning children. The UN Committee on the Rights of the Child (2009, para 9) distinguishes between the right of the child to be heard as an individual and the right of children to be heard as a group. It is the latter right, the right of children to be heard collectively, that this book concentrates upon.

Article 12 and its associated articles relating to the freedom of expression and information (Article 13), access to appropriate information (Article 17) and freedom of association (Article 15) have galvanized governments, non-governmental organizations and others to encourage children and young people's participation. Yet, participation has faced many challenges. Repeatedly, and across contexts and countries, children, young people and adults report common frustrations:

- raising expectations of impact, without sufficient transparency about the intentions of the participatory process or the difficulties in shifting existing power structures;
- focusing on process rather than impact, so that children and young people may have positive experiences of involvement but their views have little to no impact on decision-making;
- adult systems and adult behavior failing to adapt in ways that enable meaningful participation with children and young people;
- failing to recognize heterogeneity within groups of children and young people;

- over-consulting some children and young people, whilst other children and young people are not invited to give their views; and
- limiting children and young people's agendas, so that their issues and concerns are not addressed. (See for example Hinton, 2008; Lansdown, 2011; Percy-Smith and Thomas, 2010; Tisdall, 2014).

For those who support children and young people's participation, the questions become how to move past these common frustrations, to articulate new ways of taking forward children and young people's participation, to provide other possibilities that might translate the policy rhetoric into social reality.

While there has been considerable scrutiny of participatory methodology and discussion about the suitability of these methods with particular groups of children and young people, there has been considerably less theoretical development and cross-cultural learning. Further, reflections and debate can be rooted within specific disciplinary boundaries. To that effect, a network was formed through the Centre for Research on Families and Relationships, bringing together academics and practitioners from four countries – Brazil, India, South Africa and the United Kingdom (UK) – to try and learn across academic disciplines and theories and across these countries.

This book represents learning from the network and its activities. Network members found themselves reflecting on the phrase 'transformative participation', as wording that might differentiate between the all-too-familiar participation forms with their common frustrations, and participation that would meet the aspirations of the UNCRC – or more. For some network members, such as those immersed in the UK literature and practice, the pairing of 'transformative' with 'participation' was new, leading to questions of what 'transformative' means, how it can be understood, how one can identify participation that is transformative and what did 'transformative participation' lead to? For other network members, the pairing was more familiar, as having a long-standing and contested history within development studies (discussed in Chapter 2), but largely applied to adults rather than children and young people. The concept of 'transformative participation' thus became an organizing and debated feature for this book.

Below, the network's origins and development are outlined and the four country contexts briefly compared. The introduction then considers the definition(s) of participation and the prevalent typologies within the children and young people's literature. The chapter concludes by outlining the subsequent chapters in this book and their respective individual and collective contributions.

Origins of the cross-country network

In 2006, academics from Brazil, India, South Africa and the UK met in Edinburgh for a seminar entitled *Theorising Children's Participation: International and Interdisciplinary Perspectives.*[1] The seminar drew on theorizations from social capital, development studies, governance and governmentality, to challenge children and young people's participation (see *International Journal of Children's Rights* 16(3) 2008). The mixing of perspectives was helpful in at least three ways: first, bringing together examples and discussions between majority and minority worlds, which had tended to be separated in the literatures and discussion networks; second, learning across disciplines and theoretical frameworks; and, thirdly, having cross-country conversations. The network wanted to find and recognize theorizations from a diversity of countries and contexts, rather than privileging minority world theories primarily written in English. The network wished to engage with academics, practitioners and children and young people working in their own contexts, with their own ways of viewing and enacting children and young people's participation.

The Leverhulme Trust subsequently funded the network, 'Theorising Children's Participation: Learning across Countries and across Disciplines' from 2009 to 2011. Cross-country exchanges facilitated engagement with children and young people with experience of participation, practitioners and academics. There were three exchanges, each involving field visits, discussions and an intensive seminar drawing in local practitioners and academics. The exchanges were in Cape Town, South Africa (2009), Rio de Janeiro, Brazil (2010) and Delhi, India (2010). Further information about the exchanges and publications resulting from these can be found at the website.[2]

The four countries involved have marked contrasts – as well as similarities. All were involved initially because they had active forms of children and young people's participation but notable distinguishing features. For example, in Brazil, grassroots activities run alongside municipal and state level formal initiatives, such as children's participative budgeting and children's parliaments. In India, participation activities range from local groups of indigenous minorities, to collective advocacy of child laborers at an international level. In contrast,

Bray (2003) and Moses (2008) argue that, in South Africa, children and young people are involved largely via bottom-up, community initiatives rather than governmental strategies. Yet South Africa's Constitution contains clear statements of children's rights. Service, government and non-government organizations in the UK have vigorously sought to promote children and young people's participation, often through top-down consultations and structural institutions such as pupil councils in schools and Youth Parliaments (Hill et al., 2004). All four countries have ratified the UNCRC: three early on (Brazil in 1990; the UK in 1991; and India in 1992) and South Africa slightly later, in 1995.

The comparisons and contrasts continue, when looking at the socio-economic profiles of each country. Even though Brazil, India and South Africa have made rapid advances in terms of economic development over the past 10 years (Malik, 2013), Table 1.1 shows that their gross national income per capita is still considerably lower than that of the UK.

The aggregate numbers mask inequalities across the population, as demonstrated by the population percentage living below the international poverty line in Table 1.1. All four countries have high levels of income inequality (for the UK, see Cribb et al., 2013).

Table 1.1 Economic indicators for Brazil, India, South Africa and the UK

	Brazil	**India**	**South Africa**	**UK**
GNI per capita (US$) 2010*	9,390	1,340	6,100	38,540
Percentage of population below international poverty line of US$1.25 per day, 2000–2009**	4	42	17	—

— Data not available for the UK during the period specified in the column heading.

* Gross National Income (GNI) is 'the sum of value added by all resident producers plus any product taxes (less subsidies) not included in the valuation of output plus net receipts of primary income (compensation of employees and property income) from abroad. GNI per capita is GNI divided by midyear population. GNI per capita in US dollars is converted using the World Bank Atlas method.' (UNICEF, 2012, p. 115).

** The percentage of population below international poverty line of US$1.25 per day is 'Percentage of the population living on less than US$1.25 per day at 2005 prices, adjusted for purchasing power parity. The new poverty threshold reflects revisions to purchasing power parity (PPP) exchange rates based on the results of the 2005 ICP.' (UNICEF, 2012, p. 115).

Source: UNICEF (2012, p. 112–115).

As Table 1.2 demonstrates, population-wise India is by far the largest of the four countries, with over one billion people in 2011. Brazil is a distant second, while South Africa and the UK are more similar (50,460,000 and 62,417,000 respectively).

Table 1.2   Population of Brazil, India, South Africa and the UK in 2011

	Brazil	India	South Africa	UK
Total Population (thousands)	196,655	1,241,492	50,460	62,417
Population under 18 (thousands (Percentage of total))	59,010 (30.0%)	448,336 (36.1%)	18,045 (35.8%)	13,153 (21.1%)
Population under 5 (thousands ((percentage of total))	14,662 (7.4%)	128,542 (10.4%)	4,989 (9.9%)	3,858 (6.2%)

Source: UNICEF (2013).

India also has the largest number and proportion of children and young people under 18 and under 5 of the four countries included here. Brazil and South Africa have 30.0 percent and 35.8 percent respectively of their population aged under 18, while the UK has only 21.1 percent. Thus, the UK is the outlier in having a smaller proportion of children and young people within its overall population, compared to Brazil, India and South Africa.

There are also stark contrasts between these counties when considering key health and education indicators for children, as shown in Table 1.3.

For example, infant and under-5 mortality rates (U5MR) differ widely between the countries – from a high of 61 per thousand U5MR in India to a low of 5 per thousand U5MR in the UK. For the three countries for which data on school net attendance ratios were available, Brazil has the highest primary school net attendance at 95 percent of all primary school aged children. India and South Africa have similar primary school net attendance ratios for both male and female primary school aged children. Secondary school net attendance ratios are considerable lower than primary school net attendance ratios in all three countries. This is particularly the case for female secondary school attendance

Table 1.3 Child health and education indicators for Brazil, India, South Africa and the UK

	Brazil	India	South Africa	UK
Infant mortality rate* (under 1) 2011	14	47	35	4
Under-5 mortality rate** (U5MR) 2011	16	61	47	5
Primary school net attendance ratio*** (%) 2007–2011****, male	95	85	80	–
Primary school net attendance ratio (%) 2007–2011****, female	95	81	83	–
Secondary school net attendance ratio (%) 2007–2011****, male	74	59	41	–
Secondary school net attendance ratio (%) 2007–2011****, female	80	49	48	–

— Data on school attendance were not available for the UK during the period specified in the column headings.
* Infant mortality rate is the 'probability of dying between birth and exactly one year of age expressed per 1,000 live births' (UNICEF, 2013).
** Under-5 mortality rate is the 'probability of dying between birth and exactly five years of age expressed per 1,000 live births' (UNICEF, 2013).
*** Net primary and secondary school enrolment ratios are 'the number of children enrolled in primary or secondary school who belong to the age group that officially corresponds to primary and secondary schooling, divided by the total population of the same age group. The main sources of this data are the Demographic and Health Surveys and Multiple Indicators Cluster Survey' (UNICEF, 2013).
****Data refer to the most recent year available during the period specified in the column headings.
Source: UNICEF (2013).

in India and South Africa, where net attendance ratios drop to less than 50 percent of all secondary school aged females. Although there is no comparable data available for the UK as a whole the Scottish Government reports that in 2010–2011 attendance stands at just under 95 percent of all primary school aged children; whilst secondary school attendance stands at just over 91 percent of males and just under 91 percent of females secondary school aged children (Scottish Government, 2011).

Since 1990 the United Nation Development Programme has published its annual Human Development Reports in a push towards thinking about and measuring development in a new way – one which focused on the impact of development on individual lives rather than merely economic growth. For that purpose, the Human Development Index (HDI) was developed. The HDI is a composite measure of health, education and income indicators that ranks a country's progress according to these key indicators. This ranking is often used as a benchmark of a country's development (Suryanarayana et al., 2011). Of the four countries included here, in 2012 the UK is the only one to rank amongst the countries with *very high human development* (UN Development Programme, 2013). Brazil's rank is amongst the countries with *high human development*, whilst South Africa and India are ranked amongst the countries with *medium human development*.

Thus, each country has its own socio-economic context, its particular profile for children, young people and their families, and ensuing development and policy challenges. Each country has its own form of governance and government, and this effects the intersections of institutions within and outwith government to address such development and policy problems. All four countries are similar in having a liberal democracy, although each with its own history, development and tensions with dynamics of inequality and marginalization centered around such characteristics as class, caste, ethnicity and gender. This resonates with children and young people's participation, as participation is frequently justified as training children and young people in democratic skills and for future political engagement and instilling a commitment to democracy. Each country chapter presents the political and socio-economic context and reflects on the implications for children and childhood generally and children and young people's participation in particular.

Children and young people's participation

Perhaps because it is such a popular term, 'participation' has many and varied definitions. Within children and young people's participation literature, Hart is a seminal author. In 1992, he defined participation as 'the process of sharing decisions which affect one's life and the life of the community in which one lives' (p. 5). This definition usefully emphasizes participation by children and young people in their everyday lives and communities. What Hart's definition lacks is an emphasis on impact.

Article 12 of the UNCRC requires this impact: children and young people's views should be given 'due weight' in all matters that affect them. Lundy (2007) proposes four interrelated elements, to understand Article 12:

• Space: children must be given the opportunity to express views
• Voice: children must be facilitated to express their views
• Audience: the views must be listened to
• Influence: the views must be acted upon, as appropriate. (p. 933)

She defines the 'right of audience' as 'a guaranteed opportunity to communicate views to an identifiable individual or body with the responsibility to listen' (p. 237). 'Influence' goes beyond listening to having the potential for change.

While 'participation' is not used within the UNCRC text, the UN Committee on the Rights of the Child describes participation in this way:

> This term has evolved and is now widely used to describe ongoing processes, which include information-sharing and dialogue between children and adults based on mutual respect, and in which children can learn how their views and those of adults are taken into account and shape the outcome of such processes. (2009, p. 3)

In its General Comment, the Committee emphasizes particular aspects of Article 12's wording and accompanying implications. Children should be supported to participate – and they may well need information to clarify their views and assistance to express them. Children's participation should not be undermined by unhelpful and inaccurate ideas of their capacity. For example, a child should be presumed to have the capacity to form a view and it is not up to the child to prove this capacity. The right to express a view has no age threshold and children need not to have comprehensive knowledge to be considered capable. Children should have feedback on how their views have been taken into consideration.

Early on, typologies have been extremely influential in promoting children and young people's participation. Hart (1992) adapted Arnstein's ladder of citizen participation for children and young people. Hart's ladder of children's participation has eight rungs (see Figure 1.1). The bottom three (manipulation; tokenism; and decoration) are categorized as non-participation. The remaining top five represent varying levels of children's engagement in the decision- making process.

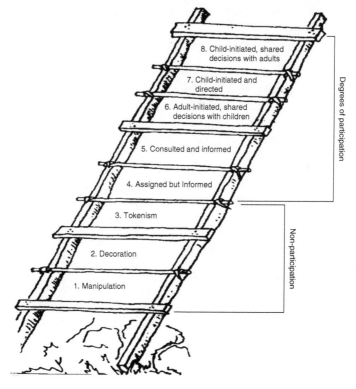

Figure 1.1   Hart's ladder of participation
Source: Hart (1992, p. 8).

Hart's 'ladder of participation' differentiates one-off engagements (such as children and young people being invited to adult-dominated conferences) from processes where children and young people have greater decision-making powers. Critics have lamented the linear nature of the ladder (Reddy and Ratner, 2002) and the impression that the goal is to reach the highest rung (Sinclair, 2004). The ladder implies that power rests either with children and young people, or with adults, as though it is a zero-sum game: in other words, for someone to gain power, another must loose (Lukes, 2004). Hart (1992, p. 11) himself cautions that his ladder should not be used as 'a simple measuring stick of the quality of any programme'. Malone and Hartung (2010) argue that the ladder's pervasive influence is partly due to its time of publication – when the emerging field of children's participation had a void of 'intellectual capital'. While it has served well for practitioners in the field, it is problematic in its hierarchical and overly simplistic nature.

Recognition of the ladder's limitations has led to the creation of other models – many of which are based on the ladder itself. For example, Treseder (1997) rearranged the levels of participation into a non-hierarchical circle (see Figure 1.2).

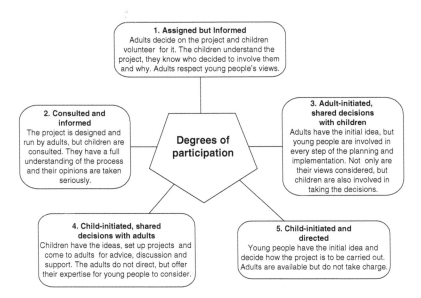

Figure 1.2   Treseder's model of degrees of participation
Source: Treseder (1997, p. 10).

Treseder's model is similar to Hart's, in assessing the degrees to which children initiate participation. Treseder adds the dimension of institutional context to his model. He argues that children may need the support of organizations to be empowered to participate more actively than being consulted and informed.

Shier (2001) highlights degrees in his pathways to participation model (see Figure 1.3). His model is based on five different levels of obligation, taking the reader through a series of questions about how children are being engaged and the degree to which the environment provides openings or opportunities for further engagement. This model incorporates an assessment of what Arnstein referred to as 'roadblocks'. Level 1 begins with children being listened to, Level 3 is children's views are taken into account (noted as the minimum to meet the UNCRC) and Level 5 moves to shared power and responsibility for decision-making.

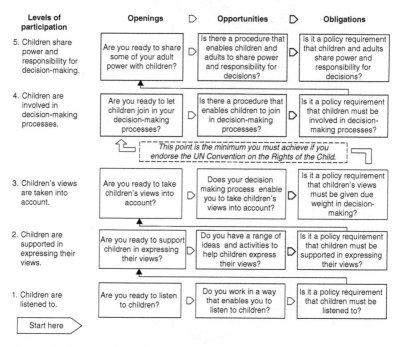

Figure 1.3 Shier's pathways to participation
Source: Shier (2001, p. 111).

The terms 'openings' and 'opportunities' usefully distinguish between a willingness to operate at a certain level and the actual ability to do so. The 'opportunities' only occur when the appropriate resources, skills knowledge and institutional structures exist to operate at that level. This requires stakeholders to assess the power relations and institutional barriers to each level of participation.

Lansdown (2001) differentiates between three types of engagement (consultancy, participation and self-advocacy) that have ascending control by children and young people. This typology explicitly recommends assessing the political economy for change. Different approaches are required in different contexts, such as political violence, where adult engagement can ensure children and young people's safety (Hart et al., 2004).

Together, these typologies widen the debate on how to operationalize institutional commitment to children and young people's right to participate, as established by the UNCRC. The typologies have been powerful tools to document the lack of children's participation in a range of forums. Although the more recent models have embraced institutional contexts, the influence of sociocultural contexts on the openings and opportunities has yet to be understood adequately. Johnson (2011) goes some way to do this, in her Change-Scape model. Building on her evaluations of participatory activities in the UK and Nepal, Johnson (2011) draws out issues of culture, politics and policy and the physical environment. Along with such external forces, she identifies internal forces within the institution as well – confidence, capacity and commitment. These articulate with Shier's model above. To translate children and young people's views into change, she notes the importance of mechanisms – building capacity, communication, confidence, collaboration and children's evidence. She titles her Change Scape model as 'Conditions for transformational change and change in services to improve children's wellbeing' (2011, p. 583). She thus is clear about what transformation is for – to improve children's wellbeing – but, drawing on the familiar use of the term in development studies literature (see for example 2011, p. 578), she does not critically consider its meaning further in this article and instead considers transformation at individual, organizational and societal levels. For the network, and this book, then the questions remain about the definition, identification and purpose of 'transformative participation'.

How children and childhood is constructed, within a particular context, is interlinked with their participation in decision-making. The 'new' sociology of childhood has drawn attention to the social constructions of childhood: 'A child's immaturity is a biological fact: but how this immaturity is understood and how it is made meaningful is a cultural one' (James and Prout, 1990, p. 7). Conceptualizations about children and childhood influence practices and approaches towards them. The still dominant minority world view of children as vulnerable and in need of protection significantly restricts which children can participate (for example, young children are often excluded from research because they are deemed to be unable to give their informed consent) and how and when they can participate (for example, children are often asked for their views on topics set out by adults and their engagement is sought after a project's aims and objectives have been determined) (Malone and Hartung, 2010). Lansdown (2010) writes:

> [it] is worth bearing in mind that the vulnerability of children derives, in some part, not from their lack of capacity, but rather, from

their lack of power and status with which to exercise their rights and challenge abuse. (p. 19)

Even within comprehensive texts, such as Cornwall and Eade's 'buzzwords' book (2010), the focus on children or young people is limited. This reflects the broader marginalization of children and young people in institutional decision-making processes, even within spaces that are (supposedly) critically reflexive about power inequalities. Of all the different types of marginalizations (gender, race, and sexuality) brought to the forefront, age is often overlooked.

Within the minority world, socialization theories (for example, Parsons' theories) and child development (for example, understandings of Piaget) led to adults being seen as mature, rational and competent whereas children were viewed as 'less than fully human, unfinished or incomplete' (Jenks, 1996, p. 10). Qvortrup (1994) makes the connection between the social construct of childhood as 'human becomings' rather than 'human beings', and the ensuing exclusion of children:

adulthood is regarded as the goal and end-point of individual development or perhaps even the very meaning of a person's childhood. They are however revealing for the maybe unintended message, which seems to indicate that children are not members or at least not integrated members of society. This attitude, while perceiving childhood as a moratorium and a preparatory phase, thus confirms postulates about children as 'naturally' incompetent and incapable. (p. 2)

The human investment model builds on this valuing of children as human becomings: to invest in children now is to ensure their future contribution to society as adults, both economically and socially (Lister, 2003). If children are only seen as 'human becomings' or societal investments, then they are not perceived as citizens presently. Further, they do not even have rights because they lack rationality, they lack competence, they need protection not autonomy, and they must be socialized into 'good citizens' (see for example Phillips, 1997; Purdy, 1992).

Yet, a critical approach can also be applied to the 'new' constructions of childhood as social actors, exercising agency. These constructions are themselves specific configurations of power/knowledge (Smith, 2012). Drawing on Foucauldian ideas, Smith argues for strong parallels between the rise of the 'competent child' and the significance placed on responsibility and self-reliance by neoliberal approaches to government (see also Gallacher and Gallagher, 2008; James, 2007; Prout 2005;

Punch and Tisdall, 2012). In neoliberal societies, risk and responsibilities once deemed social have become individualized; individuals must take responsibility for becoming 'good citizens' worthy of inclusion in mainstream society. The 'participating child' becomes part of the 'self-maximizing, entrepreneurial subject of neoliberal and advanced liberal thought' (Smith, 2012, p. 30). Rather than being liberating, participation becomes a new form of domination as it justifies increased surveillance and regulation of children and young people. For example, recognizing children and young people as social actors facilitates the measurement and management of childhood and youth. Thus, the (re) conceptualization of childhood does not necessarily represent a 'break' with the past but the continuation of governmentality, to draw upon children and young people's capacity to self-regulate.

Qvortrup (1994) writes of the familialization of childhood, that children's rightful place is within the private family sphere (albeit children in fact are ever-increasingly institutionalized in early years and school settings). The interacting roles between parents, children and the state continue to be a productive analytical lens in general, and for children and young people's participation in particular. The family context can powerfully determine the extent of children and young people's participation. It is not unsurprising that children with limited adult control, such as street and working children, have led to some of the more successful child-controlled initiatives (see Chapter 6). Lunberg et al. (2009) argue that children and young people acquire a level of autonomy about their own activities at rates that vary depending on their own traits and abilities, the preferences and resources of their parents, and their environment.

Children and young people's participation, then, is challenging for a host of 'traditional' ways of conceptualizing children and childhood, parents and parenthood, and adults and adulthood. Participation challenges how children and young people are perceived in their communities and how they are addressed in governance and policy. Children and young people's participation is radical, arguably, in its requirement for intense and widespread cultural and institutional change: 'to be most effective, participation requires widespread changes in political and institutional structures, as well as in attitudes, values and cultural practices' (Inter-Agency Working Group on Children's Participation, 2007, p. 7). Children and young people's participation thus has multiple potentials for transformation. It may instill individual transformation, for children, young people and/or adults. While children and young people's participation may be influenced by constructions of childhood, participation in turn influences how children and childhood are constructed – as well as adulthood and parenthood, families and communities. Children and young people's participation may require the transformation of political and institutional structures but also may create new ways of governance and legitimacy.

'Transformative participation' thus became of interest to the network, picking up from claims within development studies (see Chapter 2) and offering potential for addressing the challenges of children and young people's participation. But this requires a sustained consideration of what is meant by the term and to examine if and what ways children and young people's participation can be transformative. This led to the agenda for this edited book.

Subsequent chapters

The next two chapters present theoretical ideas that explore what 'transformative participation' might be for children and young people's participation. The claims for transformation have a lengthy history in development studies and Chapter 2 (Teamey and Hinton) reviews these. The chapter returns to the foundations of participation and critical pedagogy, with ideas developed by Freire in rural communities in Brazil, and considers transformative learning more broadly. The growing literature on 'indigenous ways of knowing' suggests ways of learning, knowing and connecting for 'transformation'. Chapter 3 (Savyasaachi and Butler) continues with this critical look at top-down theorizations of participation, by considering participation's minority world history. The chapter considers how participation can be 'decolonized', to allow for pluralistic possibilities of participation through listening to stories, histories, values, practices and concepts at local levels. Together, these chapters question the standardized understandings and uses of 'participation', to open up new possibilities based on learning, relationships and listening.

Chapters 4 to 10 bring together a country overview and a case study example, for Brazil, India, South Africa and the UK. The authors of each country chapter were asked to address three tasks: to discuss critically the socio-economic and policy context for children and young people's participation; to consider how childhood is constructed and the implications thereof for participation; and to identify possibilities for, evidence and possible understandings of transformative participation. Each country team identified a case study example; a relevant author was then approached to write up the case study. Case study authors were asked both to be descriptive – what was the case study – and analytical – what could be considered transformative, in what ways, what evidence did they have for this, and what potential lessons could be learned. Authors were asked to include the views of children and young people, where possible.

With this template, Chapter 4 (Butler and Princeswal) takes a genealogical view, drawing out through this historical approach the moments that imposed specific challenges in Brazil, which in turn led to forms of participative organization and mobilization. The subsequent case study (Princeswal and Butler) draws out children and young people's involvement in the Landless Movement (MST), which has developed its own pedagogy and ways of participating that bring together children, young people and adults.

Chapter 6 (Saeed) draws together cultural resources to understand childhood in India and the current challenges facing children there, to consider the range of policy and activities for children and young people's participation. The case study involves *Arunodhaya*-Centre for Street and Working Children, a non-governmental organization working to address child labor for over 12 years. Drawing from two sets of evidence, Le Borgne discusses potential aspects of transformation for individuals, the organization and society, as well as ongoing barriers to participation.

Chapter 8 (Pendlebury, Henderson and Jamieson) traces children and young people's claims to public space in South Africa, through the last years of apartheid and into the formation of the democratic state. The chapter examines discrepancies between the principles of participatory democracy in the South African Constitution and *de facto* ways in which respect, power and participatory efficacy are linked to age and position in everyday life and in formally regulated public spaces. The chapter explores possibilities for transformative participation, drawing on children and young people's political and creative practices rooted in history and specific changes taken place in the state. The case study (Meintjes) on *Abaqophi BakwaZisize Abakhanyayo* children's radio project shows how tapping into local and popular radio media enables children to ask questions and to voice their views, in ways acceptable to communities that would otherwise expect children to show customary practices of (silent) respect.

Chapter 10 (Tisdall) completes the country reviews, with a consideration of UK policy and three trends within children and young people's participation activities that provide potential for transformative participation. The case study (Morrison, McCulloch, Mackie, Halliday and

Liddell) discusses the EcoCity process created by Gaia Planning and the Scottish non-governmental organization Children's Parliament. The EcoCity process engages children and adults over a five-day period, in redesigning their community.

The book draws together its lessons in the conclusion, authored by Butler and Teamey. Here, key themes across the chapters are discussed. The conclusion ends by considering future possibilities for conceptualizing children and young people's participation that have both practical and theoretical implications. The case studies presented suggest the need for further research to understand the impact of political contexts and social constructions of childhood on children and young people's spaces to participate. We are still a long way from understanding the drivers of change to enable children and young people's active contribution in society.

The writing, editing and re-editing of the book has shown both the collective learning from the network over time and the continued value of 'rubbing together' different ideas, disciplines and perspectives from various parts of the world. For example, the network has come together in recognizing a remarkably similar list of challenges for children and young people's participation (see earlier in this chapter), the need to consider the 'adult side' of participation (the role of adults, especially in achieving impact from participation) as well as children and young people's involvement, and to (re)consider the role of 'creative' activities as participation and their potential for transformation. The network continues to debate definitions and goals of participation, transformation and transformative participation. Following the ideas of decolonization, stepping back and listening discussed in Chapter 3 and returned to in the concluding chapter, the book represents a respectful listening to differing perspectives, some of which come together in collective cross-disciplinary and cross-cultural understandings and others that are yet to be resolved, raising provocative issues for further engagement.

Note on terminology

Throughout the book, 'children and young people' is typically used, following young people's preference in some countries to be referred to as the latter. Broadly, 'children and young people' refers to children up to the age of 18, following the definition within the United Nations Convention on the Rights of the Child (Article 1); though in some cases (such as in Brazil) the term 'young person' may well extend to those up to their mid-twenties.

Further, this book tends to use the terms 'majority' and 'minority' world rather than other pairings, such as Third or First Worlds, Global South and Global North, or underdeveloped/developing and developed countries. This acknowledges that the 'majority' of population, land mass and lifestyles is located in the former, in Africa, Asia and Latin America, and thus seeks to shift the balance of world views that frequently privilege 'western' and 'northern' populations and issues (Punch, 2003). This terminology is not without its problems. This dichotomy ignores disparities within each category and similarities between certain countries, across the two categories. Further, as previously noted, Brazil and India have been described as 'rising powers', in terms of their economic and other strengths. South Africa has particular contrasts in its socio-economic contexts due to its recent history, making it unusual within the African context. Thus a division between two categories has disadvantages for the countries considered in this book. Nonetheless, the terms 'majority' and 'minority' worlds are sometimes a useful device to bring out comparisons and contrasts, and to recognize the hegemony of minority world concepts, policies and constructions.

In regards to both sets of terminology, authors have been invited to move from this default position, should they feel justified in doing so, and direct quotations and formal terms use the original terminology.

Notes

1. This initial seminar was funded by the British Academy, with additional support for the academic exchange coming from the Royal Society of Edinburgh.
2. See www.crfr.ac.uk.

Bibliography

Beaumont, A. (2014) *New Directions for Participation and Governance*, Unpublished PhD dissertation (Sydney: Macquarie University).

Bray, R. (2003) 'Who does the housework? An examination of children's working roles in the context of household and community dynamics', *Social Dynamics*, 29(2), 95–131.

Cornwall, A. and Eade, D. (eds) (2010) *Deconstructing Development Discourse: Buzzwords and Fuzzwords* (London: Oxfam).

Cribb, J., Hood, A., Joyce, R. and Phillips, D. (2013) *Living Standards, Poverty and Inequality in the UK: 2013* (London: Institute of Fiscal Studies).

Gallacher, L. and Gallagher, M. (2008) 'Methodological immaturity in childhood research?' *Childhood*, 15(4), 499–516.

Hart, J., Newman, J. and Ackermann, L., with Feeny, T., (2004) *Children Changing Their World: Understanding and Evaluating Children's Participation in Development* (London: PLAN UK/PLAN INTERNATIONAL).

Hart, R. A. (1992) *Children's Participation: From Tokenism to Citizenship* (Florence: UNICEF International Child Development Centre).

Hill, M., Prout, A., Davis, J. and Tisdall, K. (2004) 'Moving the participation agenda forward', *Children & Society*, 18(2), 77–96.

Hinton, R. (2008) 'Children and good governance', *International Journal of Children's Rights*, 16(3), 285–300.

Inter-Agency Working Group on Children's Participation (2007) *Minimum Standards for Consulting with Children*, http://plan-international.org/about-plan/resources/publications/participation/minimum-standards-for-consulting-with-children/.

James, A. (2007) 'Giving voice to children's voices: practices and problems, pitfalls and potentials', *American Anthropologist*, 109(2), 261–272.

James, A. and James, A. (2004) *Constructing Childhood* (Basingstoke: Macmillan).

James, A. and Prout, A. (eds) (1990) *Constructing and Reconstructing Childhood* (London and New York: RoutledgeFalmer).

Jenks, C. (1996) *Childhood* (London: Routledge).

Johnson, V. (2011) 'Conditions for change for children and young people's participation in evaluation: 'Change-scape', *Child Indicators Research*, 4(4), 577–596.

Lansdown, G. (2001) *Children's Participation in Democratic Decision-Making*, UNICEF, http://www.unicef-icdc.org/publications/pdf/insight6.pdf

Lansdown, G. (2010) 'The realisation of children's participation rights'. In B. Percy-Smith and N. Thomas (eds) *A Handbook of Children and Young People's Participation: Perspectives from theory and practice* (London and New York: Routledge).

Lansdown, G. (2011) *Monitoring and evaluating children's participation*, http://www.crin.org/resources/infoDetail.asp?ID=25809&flag=report.

Lister, R. (2003) 'Investing in the citizen-workers of the future: transformations in citizenship and the state under new labour', *Social Policy & Administration*, 37(5), 427–443.

Lukes, S. (2004) *Power: a radical view*, Second edition (London: Palgrave Macmillan).

Lunberg, S., Romich, J. and Tsang, K. P. (2009) 'Decision-making by children', *Review of Economics of the Household*, 7(1), 1–30.

Lundy, L. (2007) '"Voice" is not enough: conceptualising Article 12 of the United Nations Convention on the Rights of the Child', *British Educational Research Journal*, 33(6), 927–942.

Lundy, L., Kilkelly, U., Byrne, B. and Kang, J. (2013) *The UN Convention on the Rights of the Child: A study of legal implementation in 12 countries*, http://www.unicef.org.uk/Documents/Publications/UNICEFUK_2012CRCimplentationreport.pdf.

Malik, K. (2013) *Human Development Report 2013: The Rise of the South: Human Development in a Diverse World*. New York: UNDP.

Malone, K. and Hartung, C. (2010) 'Challenges of participatory practice with children'. In B. Percy-Smith and N. Thomas (eds) *A Handbook of Children and Young People's Participation: Perspectives from Theory and Practice*, (London and New York: Routledge).

Moses, S. (2008) 'Children and participation in South Africa: an overview', *International Journal of Children's Rights*, 16(3), 327–342.

Percy-Smith, B. and Thomas, N. (eds) (2010) *A Handbook of Children and Young People's Participation: Perspectives from Theory and Practice* (London and New York: Routledge).

Phillips, M. (1997) *All Must Have Prizes* (London: Warner Books).

Prout, A. (2005) *The Future of Childhood*. (London: RoutledgeFalmer)

Punch, S. (2003) 'Childhoods in the majority world: miniature adults or tribal children?', *Sociology*, 37(2), 277–295.

Punch, S. and Tisdall, E. K. M. (2012) 'Exploring children and young people's relationships across Majority and Minority Worlds', *Children's Geographies*, 10(3), 241–248.

Purdy, L. M. (1992) *In Their Best Interest? The Case against Equal Rights for Children* (Ithaca and London: Cornell University Press).

Qvortrup, J. (1994) 'Childhood matters: an introduction'. In: J. Qvortrup, M. Bardy, G. Sgritta and H. Wintersberger (eds) *Childhood Matters: Social Theory, Practice and Politics* (European Centre, Vienna: Avebury).

Reddy, N. and Ratner, K. (2002) *A Journey in Children's Participation*. The Concerned for Working Children, http://www.pronats.de/assets/Uploads/reddy-ratna-a-journey-in-childrens-participation.pdf.

Scottish Government (2011) *Summary Statistics for Schools in Scotland, No. 2*, http://www.scotland.gov.uk/Publications/2011/12/06114834/18.

Shier, H. (2001) 'Pathways to participation: openings, opportunities and obligations', *Children & Society*, 15(2), 107–117.

Sinclair, R. (2004) 'Participation in practice: making in meaningful, effective and sustainable', *Children & Society*, 18(2), 106–118.

Smith, K. (2012) 'Producing governable subjects: images of childhood old and new', *Childhood*, 19(1), 24–37.

Suryanarayana, M. H., Agrawal, A. and Prabhu, K. S. (2011) *Inequality adjusted Human Development Index for India's States* (New Delhi: United Nations Development Programme).

Tisdall, E. K. M. (2014) 'Addressing the challenges of children and young people's participation: considering time and space'. In: T. Gal and B. Faedi Druamy (eds) *International Perspectives and Empirical Findings on Child Participation* (Oxford: Oxford University Press). (Forthcoming)

Treseder, P. (1997) *Empowering children and young people training manual: promoting involvement in decision-making* (London: Save the Children UK).

UN Committee on the Rights of the Child (2009) *General Comment No. 12 The right of children to be heard*, http://www2.ohchr.org/english/bodies/crc/docs/AdvanceVersions/CRC-C-GC-12.doc.

UN Development Programme (2013) *Human Development Index*, http://hdr.undp.org/en/statistics/hdi, date accessed 20 December 2013.

UNICEF (2012) *The State of the World's Children 2012: Children in an Urban World*, http://www.unicef.org/uganda/SOWC_2012-Main_Report_EN_13Mar2012.pdf.

UNICEF (2013) *Statistics and Monitoring*, http://www.unicef.org/statistics/index_step1.php?sid=a3c70d2dfa4b545be4e61f8432431563, date accessed 5 December 2013.

Wyness, M. (2013) 'Children, Family and the State: Revisiting Public and Private Realms', *Sociology*, online June 10, 2013.

2
Reflections on Participation and Its Link with Transformative Processes

Kelly Teamey and Rachel Hinton

Introduction

This book explores the question of when and how children and young people's participation can be understood as transformative. Yet, this begs a host of questions – When are transformative forms of participation the actual aim? Transformative for whom? What are different ways that we can understand transformational processes and, in particular, how they involve participation? Why does participation so often *not* translate into the transformative experience expected?

Participation, as it emerged in the 1960s and 1970s, had its radical roots in social movements. These social movements sought to create social relationships that could transform oppressive institutional relationships of power. The process of creating these spaces can be considered transformative in a variety of ways, which this chapter explores. Thus, 'participation', as it was understood and valued, was intertwined with 'transformation' – the two were inseparable. Hickey and Mohan, in their introduction to *Participation: From Tyranny to Transformation?* claim:

> the proper objective of participation is to ensure 'transformation' of existing development practice and, more radically, the social relations, institutional practices and capacity gaps which cause social exclusion. (2004, p. 13)

Participation, as a form of intervention, may have originated with the quest for autonomy, citizenship, political rights and voice. However, many writers and practitioners have argued that 'participation' has also been co-opted as a process to enable those with power to maintain the status quo – through quelling political opposition (Rahnema,

1992; Vengroff, 1974) or co-opting those seeking spaces of political and cultural freedom into mainstream processes. Participation as a truly transformative process seems to have become increasingly lost the more institutionalized and 'top-down' participation spaces have become. This chapter explores ways to understand how and when *participation supports and precipitates transformative processes* for individuals and communities. In particular, we have sought to integrate understandings and descriptions of participation and transformation that are coming from writers, thinkers and practitioners that have tended to be sidelined by the mainstream. Other, less explored worldviews can broaden our imagination of possibilities into how we can understand, and enact, transformative processes of participation.

Definitions of transformation are as varied as they are widespread and enduring. We might begin by considering transformation as a fundamental part of any living being (human and non-human), for any age, particularly as we continually experience change in many different forms – physical, emotional or geographical. However, different types of transformation might render huge shifts for how we experience our daily lives, especially with regard to embedded practices of exclusion.

Should we perceive transformation as a noun (a prescribed endpoint), a verb (an ongoing process) or an adjective (describing a noun such as a person, community, event or situation)? When there is ambiguity in the use of the term and a lack of transparency in the intentions, those involved can have different expectations. The dilemma is how to reconcile such differing perspectives and expectations, particularly when involving children and young people.

With this in mind, the chapter explores writings and perceptions of 'participation' and 'transformation', and different ways in which each has evolved. The chapter begins with a language and terminology discussion, charting the emergence of 'participation' within the development field, from its association with social movements and critical pedagogy in the 1960s and 1970s, to its dominance in the development industry today. It reviews critiques of participation that are only more recently being considered in the adult as well as children and young people's fields. In addition, it reviews the alignment and connection that participation has with transformation.

Next, the chapter returns to foundational work of participation and transformation within learning and critical pedagogy, exploring the ideas developed by Paolo Freire, Ivan Illich and others. The chapter then considers transformative experiences more broadly within social movements, communities of practice and indigenous ways of knowing. With the current emergence of international indigenous social movements, there is a growing literature that provides new ways of knowing, learning and connecting for participation and transformation.

The chapter ends by asking us to explore a series of questions. These help us reflect more deeply on how different frameworks can constrain or enable opportunities to consider participation as a transformative process for children and young people.

The power of language

The language and words we each choose to use are never neutral. Participation is a recurring 'buzzword' of the development industry. In an Oxfam publication, Cornwall and Eade (2010) explore key terms, or 'buzzwords', in international development discourse that illustrate the power of language, terms and words. Terms such as 'participation', 'citizenship', 'partnership', 'empowerment', 'gender', 'sustainability' and 'governance' can typically be found in any genre of international development writing (from grassroots organizations and non-governmental organizations, to donor organizations and academic institutions). Yet, these terms carry different meanings and sets of values within different organizations and communities.

The concepts and language of international development are often defined by the cultural worldviews of bilateral and multilateral donor agencies – and are most often articulated in English. It is not just *what* is said (the words that are used). Additional significance lies in the *way* things are said and the meanings and values attached to particular terms and the agendas behind them (Chouliaraki and Fairclough, 1999; Cornwall and Brock, 2005a, 2005b; Cornwall and Eade, 2010; Fairclough, 1989, 2003). Devaki Jain's brief review inside the cover page of Cornwall and Eade's 2010 edited publication, *Deconstructing Development Discourse: Buzzwords and Fuzzwords,* describes its contribution as:

> a dissection of how vocabularies trap us ... These terminologies are the underbelly of the modernisation project which has shackled and burned holes into the aspirations and potential of countries of the South. (2010)

A healthy questioning of the terminology and rhetoric used, as well as the frames of reference, including its sets of values adhered to, can uncover understandings and possible reconfigurations that were previously unimagined.

The language, terms and words prioritized within any policy process influence the inclusion of some individuals and communities over others. Relations of power become crystallized within language and the choice of words. Words create certain realities within which some issues become identified as important, while others are never named, let alone addressed. 'Participation' is one of those words that have become commonly used, influential in including and excluding certain groups, issues and solutions.

For many, the task of participation was not to become involved in institutional relationships and norms as they were but, rather (individually and collectively), to transform 'cultural, political and economic structures which reproduce poverty and marginalization' (Leal, 2010, p. 91). Being outside oppressive institutional relationships and norms was advocated as necessary since development could only be achieved when 'humans are being themselves, when they possess their own decision-making powers, free of oppressive and dehumanizing circumstances' (Freire, 1970, p. 29). Participation was therefore a way to challenge the status quo and was conceptualized as a transformative process and practice.

A brief history of participation

As briefly mentioned in the introduction, in the 1960s and 1970s, the initial rise of 'participation' coincided with social movements – particularly in how they related to transformative processes. Paulo Freire was a key figure during this time, helping to propel ideas and practices of emancipatory pedagogy as related to participative practices of transformation. Freire's goal was not a fixed transitive form of participation (orientated toward a particular goal or outcome – see Rahnema, 1992), development or poverty alleviation, but 'the transformation of the cultural, political and economic structures which reproduce poverty and marginalization' (Leal, 2010, p. 91).

By the 1980s, participation became an essential 'ingredient' in the development industry. Community participation was perceived as an important attempt to listen to beneficiaries' views and better understand cultural differences. In part, this was a response to past failures in international development where externally designed interventions had failed when applied without sufficient attention to the social, political and cultural contexts of local communities. In practice, adults, young people and children were typically not distinguished and differences were conflated into a single 'view'. Work with children and young people, and tools to ensure their voices are heard, have been the focus of several publications (Johnson et al., 1995; Percy-Smith and Thomas, 2010).

Chambers (1983) is particularly well known for having developed 'bottom-up' and *representative* participation approaches (see also White, 1996), particularly with those who risked being excluded from more formal consultations and research. Methods were developed that sought to be cost- and time-effective, using less structured data collection procedures such as timelines and group mapping rather than highly structured surveys (for example, Chambers, 1981). Often the visual data provided a powerful tool that enabled information and findings to be communicated readily to decision-makers. The evidence generated from such 'bottom-up' approaches, which sought to capitalize on local knowledge and expertise, aimed to influence the design of new programs and policies.

Through the 1990s, these methods were reformed and developed into Participatory Rural Appraisal (PRA), with associated methods 'toolkits'. Large development agencies, including the World Bank, promoted PRA to be used alongside more quantitative data collection methods (Norton, 2001). Methods were enshrined in development manuals and an industry grew up around them.

As methods proliferated, the term 'participation' came to be used with limited reference to a wider range of meanings, such as those portrayed in White's influential 1996 article, which usefully makes a distinction between four forms of participation.

- **Nominal participation** is for display, with 'top-down' interests wanting legitimation for decisions, while 'bottom-up' interests seek inclusion.
- **Instrumental participation** is to achieve a particular end. 'Top-down' interests may consult local people as an efficient and cost-saving exercise; for the local people, such consultation is a demand or cost on them.
- **Representative participation** can provide 'bottom-up' interests with 'voice' in decision-making. For 'top-down' interests, this can lead to better decision-making and thus more sustainable and effective results.
- **Transformative participation** is both a means and an end. For both 'top-down' and 'bottom-up' interests, the aim is empowerment.

We can perceive each of these forms differently during the historical evolution of 'participation' within the development field. Although participation might have begun with the intention of being a truly transformative process and practice, this has been watered down in various ways to be more often integrated as *nominal, instrumental* and *representative* as White indicates, because of the widespread use of 'participation' as an 'essential ingredient' of development intervention that is often not well-considered nor defined.

White's model helps us to begin to explore the ways in which participation has been created, critiqued and co-opted. Conceptually and in practice, in the development industry the dominant aim of 'participation' has tended to be for improving services and governance rather than as a mode for transformative processes and practice. Listening to the views of service users, for example, would make the resulting services more effective (Needham, 2003). Strengthening civil society and enabling citizens to speak out would increase the accountability, and, ultimately, the legitimacy of governments and institutions (Clark, 1995; Edwards and Hulme, 1996).

In 2000, the World Bank launched the *Voices of the Poor* report, which exposed the realities and complexities of poor people's lives and the need for contextual understanding. Participation was advocated for developing policies that would result in change for the most marginal groups, including for children and young people. The report authors argued that:

> Fostering such partnership processes requires a dual focus on actions that, on the one hand, improve state capacity to grasp poor people's needs and the poverty impacts of public policies, and on the other hand, strengthen poor people's capacity to mobilize, articulate and defend their interests, and hold governments accountable. (Narayan et al., 2000, p. 487)

Participation was therefore conceived not only as a means to develop policies but also as a means to 'empower' those at the margin to mobilize, articulate and defend their rights (Narayan et al., 2000). Further, the state had to have the capacity to respond, leading to an accompanying focus on strengthening government and governance (see Gaventa, 2004). Yet, too often such institutional responses were missing, and the selective use of participatory outcomes further solidified institutional relations and norms, rather than challenging institutions to become transformative spaces.

Throughout its history in development, 'participation' and its associated activities have been subject to criticism. As early as the mid-1970s, writers (for example, Freire, 1970; Illich, 1970; Vengroff, 1974) argued that 'participation' was being co-opted to enable those with power to maintain the status quo. With the 'mainstreaming' of participation across so many dominant agencies and sectors, Rahnema (1992) and Leal (2010) argue that participatory development has distorted participation from its transformative historical roots to preserve the status quo. Leal particularly ties the ascendance of the participation 'buzzword' with the promotion of neoliberalism by the World Bank and the International Monetary Fund, during the implementation of Structural Adjustment Programs around 'third world' debt. Essentially, participation became a way to control dissent, to co-opt people into the existing dominant order.

Debates also emerged about the danger of 'evangelical' proliferation of PRA methodology (see Gaventa, 2004). Critics highlighted examples of poor quality data collection, viewed as extractive rather than transformative (for example, Cooke and Kothari, 2001). Vengroff (1974) argued that emphasizing self-help and local participation in developing services can be doubly disadvantageous, in diverting demands from the state to local initiatives, while simultaneously increasing support for the current regime. Cornwall (2008), writing over 30 years later, notes that the emphasis of such self-help and *representative* forms of participation can instead frustrate citizens who feel the state has not fulfilled its obligations, thus leading to resistance rather than support.

Despite the supposed focus in later decades on governments' capacity to fulfill obligations, too many activities concentrated on engaging people and too little on ensuring accountability and impact (Cooke and Kothari, 2001; Hart, 2008). As Leal (2010) argues, there has been an emphasis on participation *techniques* rather than the *meaning* of participation, so that power and political problems are translated into technical problems that the existing order can easily accommodate.

The concept of 'empowerment' has often been used with the aim of bringing together the concepts of participation and transformation. Similar to participation, 'empowerment' has become a key buzzword within the development industry; in fact it has been cited as the most commonly used term in the development language (Cornwall and Brock, 2005a). The task of defining empowerment is as equally challenging to that of 'participation'. For example, Ibrahim and Alkire (2007) have identified a list of 32 different definitions of empowerment. Empowerment often brings together ideas of developing personal competencies and abilities, in order to express views and make choices, with opportunity structures, so that society and institutions are responsive to such views and choices (see Samman and Santos, 2009). White (1996) uses the term 'empowerment' to describe *transformative* participation in her distinction of four forms of participation. In her article, White writes:

> The idea of participation as empowerment is that the practical experience of being involved in considering options, making decisions, and taking collective action to fight injustice is itself transformative. It leads on to greater consciousness of what makes and keeps people poor, and greater confidence in their ability to make a difference. (p. 8–9)

These descriptions of 'participation' and empowerment' encourage us to believe in their close connection to 'transformation'. Yet we can also become caught up in the myth that there is a simple and automatic linear process, one leading to the other. Writers such as Majid Rahnema, one of the many authors in *The Development Dictionary*, push us to explore otherwise, by reflecting on the various, sometimes contradictory, characteristics 'participation' can take within a single context. Rahnema (1992) distinguishes between four processes of participation:

- **Intransitive – Transitive:** Transitive forms of participation are, by definition, oriented towards a specific goal or target. By contrast, in its intransitive form, an individual lives the partaking process without any predefined purpose. Therefore, while one (for example, an individual) is listening, loving, creating, or fully living one's life, one partakes without necessarily seeking to achieve a particular objective.
- **Moral – Immoral:** Participation acquires a moral aspect, according to the ethically defined nature of the goals it pursues. It is generally associated with moral or desirable goals and, as such, given a positive connotation. It seldom comes to mind that the act of partaking may apply to evil or malicious purposes.
- **Free – Forced:** Participation tends to be perceived as a free exercise. This perception conforms neither to the meaning of the word, nor to the way in which it is translated into practice. For, more often than not, people are asked or dragged into partaking in operations of no interest to them, in the very name of participation.
- **Spontaneous – Manipulated:** In manipulative forms of participation, the participants do not feel they are being forced into doing something but are actually led to take actions which are inspired or directed by centres outside their control. (p. 127)

In spite of such critique, Rahnema and many others (for example Cornwall, 2008; Freire, 1970; Illich, 1970; Leal, 2010) continue to see the transformative potential of participation. The most widespread call is for participation not only to include, but to go beyond, the local, to recognize and address the social, economic and political contexts that shape, constrain and can provide opportunities for transformation (see Hart, 2008). The next section of this chapter explores this widespread call toward transformation and how learning is a fundamental part of any transformative process.

Exploring connections between participation, transformation and learning

Transformation is fundamentally a learning process and experience. If the earlier intentions of participation were to create transformative spaces, to do so requires a great deal of deep and critical learning – both about one's own self and also about the world around us, the world that we interact with on a daily basis. Rahnema (1992) helps us to understand this distinction by describing true transformation as both 'inner' (personal) and 'outer' (social). In accordance with Rahnema's logic, transformative experiences are simultaneously subtle and momentous, 'inner' (within one's self) and 'outer' (from one's self toward others) processes. Yet – how can we understand these processes of *inner* and *outer* transformation? How are they connected? How do we know when and where these processes of transformation occur?

A variety of theoretical and conceptual models has been created in the attempt to capture the key components of transformative processes. These theories and models predominate in the education and pedagogical literature, within the fields of adult education but also schooling and non-formal education for children and young people. Theories and models of transformation are also closely associated with writings on social movements and are recently gaining ground in the international development field.

Common across the literature on transformation are prescriptive, formulaic or linear models, suggesting 'what it takes' (or 'what learning it takes') for transformation to occur. Transformation is often depicted as an idealized 'end-point' (through *transitive* participatory processes as Rahnema explains). However, the process and experiences of transformation, the ways in which transformative experiences are sustained or continue to change, are not well understood. Representing transformation through a conceptual and linear model is a challenge, particularly because experiences of transformation are subjective and are often part of an ongoing process that is difficult to capture in a static form. Learning that is transformational tends not to occur in schools or other formal education contexts (Illich, 1970; Orr, 1992; Prakash and Esteva, 1998). This is not to say that transformation for a child or young person cannot or should not happen in a school but, more often than not, the institutional constraints associated with schooling do not allow for transformative learning experiences to occur. Illich, in fact, has argued that it is through schooling that societal norms do not change; rather they are reproduced as institutionalized social norms and values: 'School is the advertising agency which makes you believe that you need the society as it is' (1970, p. 79). Illich's entire intellectual and lived project was fundamentally about transcending and transforming institutional norms and expectations, within bureaucratic forms of all types (i.e. education, health and religion). He has described *true* learning environments that are free of institutional rigidity as 'unhampered participation in a meaningful setting alive with spontaneity, flexibility and creativity' (Illich, 1970, p. 44). This quote also signifies the importance of Rahnema's distinctions of intransitive and free forms of participation. An increasing number of educators and grassroots organizers have sought explicitly to provide spaces for transformational learning – to lessen hierarchy, and experiment with different forms of horizontal leadership and alternative pedagogy that are often reflective of Illich's description of a true learning environment (Esteva, 2010, 2012).

Yet, within these learning environments, experiences of transformation are not always easy; they may be a painful process. Transformative experiences can be *positive* too: for example offering and/or inspiring the establishment of new relationships that become more egalitarian, less hierarchical. Simultaneously, however, transformative experiences can be *negative* and/or *painful* as they might clash with cultural and social norms and leave individuals and/or communities with a different type of alienation. Transformative experiences are rarely either wholly good or bad.

Freire offers important insights on these discrepancies. From working on adult literacy projects with landless rural communities in northeast Brazil in the late 1950s and 1960s, he developed ideas that education can and should be a means of empowerment and transformation of oppressed individuals and groups. However, he was not just referring to 'education' as schooling. Rather he was referring to learning in its deepest sense that could lead to inner (personal) and outer (social) transformation.

Freire focuses on the relationship between the 'oppressed' and the 'oppressor' (1970, 1997, 1998; Freire and Macedo (2001)). This binary is not fixed, or unequivocal, with the oppressed all too often becoming the oppressor themselves. Individual critical reflection and collective action are thus essential, through a pedagogical process to learn how to transform injustice. For Freire, the aim is not only to teach literacy skills on how to read and write 'the word'; rather, and more importantly, the objective is to establish and engender critical skills to read 'the world' in one's local and broader context. This wider form of 'reading' and literacy emphasizes the ability to ask (and answer) critical questions about *why power relationships are structured as they are, how they historically came to be that way,* and *how action can be taken to change and transform* these relationships and structures.

Freire argues that transformation occurs when individuals of any age reach a deeper, more nuanced understanding and critical consciousness (also known as *conscientização*) of themselves and the historical, cultural and political relations that make up their world. Au explains:

> Freire's liberatory pedagogy revolves around the central idea of 'praxis' and seeks to be a pedagogy that enables students and teachers to be Subjects who can look at reality, critically reflect upon that reality and take transformative action to change that reality based upon the original critical reflection, thereby deepening their consciousness and changing the world for the better. (2007, p. 13)

These portrayals of transformation are primarily positive. The predominantly celebratory nature of transformative experience means that negative consequences, personally and socially, are often overlooked. Freire, though, notes that transformative experiences can be alienating and profoundly disorienting and thus neither comfortable nor convenient. Deeply transformative processes can open up other, alternative ways of understanding and being with the world, which might be in contrast with cultural and social norms. These experiences can be simultaneously empowering and disempowering, depending particularly on the levels of support that community relationships offer.

Freire's ideas of transformation and transformative learning are both personal (individual) and social (collective) (similar to Rahnema's distinction between 'inner' and 'outer'), with personal and social transformation being mutually reinforcing processes. Freire describes transformational processes occurring as individuals and communities move through different phases of consciousness. This begins with a *naïve consciousness*, to a *transitive consciousness*, and finally to a *critical consciousness* that enables (and empowers) individuals and communities to organize themselves and participate in transforming their daily experiences. Letting go of painful memories and oppressive experiences often requires facing pain, suffering or *naïve consciousness*. The period of *transitive consciousness*, which Freire argues is essential to the transformative process, has been described as 'the depth or descent into the dark night of the soul' (Dirkx, 2000, p. 249). Freedom from victimization, though, can bring about a new confidence or *critical consciousness*.

It is often easier to go through these transformative processes within a supportive community of like-minded individuals. Personal and social transformation tends to reinforce each other. But what makes up a supportive community – especially one that enables personal and social transformation? Lave and Wenger (1991) offer their conceptual framework of 'communities of practice' which can help us to understand further what characterizes a supportive community.

The 'communities of practice' framework focuses on the transformative power of community identity. Members of a community, they argue, are bound together by what they do and by what they have learnt through their mutual engagement in shared activities. Thus, the transformative experience of becoming part of a 'community of practice' involves identity development, both personally and socially.

Lave and Wenger define a 'community of practice' as having characteristics of a *joint enterprise* (understood and continually re-negotiated by its members), that produces a *shared repertoire* of communal resources (routines, sensibilities, artifacts, vocabulary, styles and so on), and that members have developed over time through relationships of *mutual engagement* that bind members together in a social community. Membership within these communities is for whomever participates and contributes to the practices within the community.

A variety of imaginative communities of practice has emerged from Freire's theories to navigate through the difficulties of conscientization processes. For example, Augusto Boal (1995, 2000) conceived of the 'theatre of the oppressed' or 'forum theatre', for children, young people and adults, as an opportunity to role-play experiences of oppression within groups, engage in critical dialog about the processes being enacted, and strategize about appropriate forms of political action in response. The ethos of 'theatre of the oppressed' is that 'everyone has the right to speak, everyone has the right to question and everyone has the right to be listened to' (Houston et al., 2001, p. 292). Forum theatre seeks to create solutions to problems, through the provision of a non-formal learning space in which debate might take place. Forum theatre is one of the tools of deep learning that is used as a participatory mechanism for inner (personal) and outer (social) transformation. Forum theatre is also reflective of a true learning environment that Illich has described.

Although Freire is revered for his theories and pedagogical practice of *conscientização*, his ideas have also been criticized for being linear and dualistic (separating humans from the place and context within which these transformative processes occur) (Bowers, 2005; Smith, 2003). Bowers (2005) argues that Freire's views of liberation and oppression focus on social structures, whereas other cosmologies and worldviews are focused on the notion of oneness and interconnectedness with the world around them (human and non-human alike) as depicted through indigenous ways of knowing.

Graham Tuhiwai Smith (2003), an indigenous *Maori* scholar, for example, argues that Freire takes a formulaic and linear approach between 'consciousness', 'resistance' and 'critical action', proceeding from one stage to the next, through a prescriptive (transitive) formula toward critical consciousness and transformative action. Instead, Smith (2003) draws on *Maori* cosmology (way of engaging with and understanding the world and our place in it), which perceives these stages as simultaneously experienced and as an ongoing process, intentional as well as unintentional, and not starting at any one particular location.

Exploring indigenous cosmologies and ways of knowing

This section provides a brief discussion and representation of ways of understanding participation and transformation from different indigenous perspectives. Although there is less focus on children and young people specifically, these representations expand how we can perceive and engage with theories and practices of participation, with additional discussion of how they can be perceived and experienced as transformative processes.

A resurgence of international indigenous social movements is linked to a broad array of issues such as education, land ownership, climate change and sustainability, involving children, young people and adults alike. The emerging legitimacy of indigenous ways of knowing is partly associated with the debate and recent adoption by some countries of the 2007 United Nations Declaration on the Rights of Indigenous Peoples as well as the increasing solidarity between different indigenous communities around the world.

An increasing literature describes 'indigenous knowledges' (or indigenous ways of knowing) and the threads of cosmological wholeness that link them together; *cosmology* meaning the ways we perceive the universe and our place in it (Battiste, 2000; Battiste and Henderson, 2002; Denzin et al., 2008; Semali and Kincheloe, 1999; Smith, 1999, 2003). Indigenous ways of knowing are fundamentally about interconnectedness; with the past, the present, the future, the land and the spirit. Mosha (2000) describes this interconnectedness as 'everything that is thought, said and done is done in the relationship to the whole of life and the world' (p. 5). Indigenous ways of knowing comprise all types of knowledge pertaining to a particular people and its territory (ecology) and can be better understood as a process (verb) rather than a thing (noun). The context is central and the history of knowing has been transmitted from generation to generation (Daes, 1993).

There are several accounts that describe indigenous processes of coming-to-know as inherently transformative. For example, Arbon (2008) helpfully describes indigenous knowledge as *being-knowing-doing*. These three terms are all portrayed as verbs (action) – *knowing* something means that it is part of *doing* (action) and is core to an overall way of *being* in the world, or the way of living one's life. This definition of knowledge is vastly different to a more commonly understood way of perceiving it as a noun, a 'thing' to be memorized. Peat (1994, p. 5–6) expands on this further, explaining that 'within the Indigenous world the act of coming to know something involves a personal transformation' (whereas in the 'Western' education system, we tend to think of knowledge as factual information that is structured and often passed on through books, lectures and programmed courses).

Bastien (2004) describes indigenous knowledge as linked with *Blackfoot* ways of knowing:

> Generally speaking, Indigenous knowledge is generated through an epistemology (or way of knowing) emphasizing dynamic transformation and a form of logic that transcends Eurocentred reason and rationality. It is found in ceremonial practice of tribal peoples ... knowing the 'self' in relationship to the alliances that form one's natural order ... premised on the goal of existing in harmony with the natural world. (p. 39)

Mosha's (2000) examination of indigenous *Chagga* culture in Tanzania illustrates how knowledge and wisdom reforms and transforms all members of the community through inter-generational transfers of knowledge. These knowledge transfers can happen purposively or spontaneously through ceremonies, cultural events or social movements of different types. There is a central importance of proverbs, myths, role-play and riddles. Mosha (2000) explains,

> Through stories we can marvel at our achievements and great capabilities, we can also see our folly, our mess, and our brokenness, and in the same context of the story, laugh at ourselves constructively. Personal and social transformation often takes place in these very moments. (p. 49)

In spite of the range of transformative learning processes that are core to indigenous ways of *being-knowing-doing*, there are deep structures of hierarchy within indigenous communities that enabled the sustainability of their cultural and community survival for thousands of years (prior to colonization, that is, in many parts of the world). In the Indian (South Asian) context part of the learning process is to generate a deep respect for Elders. This is similar in the *Maori* (New Zealand), *Aborigine* (Australia), *Quechua* (Peru), *Chagga* (Tanzania), *Blackfoot* (Canada) and *Navajo* (USA) contexts, as well as many other indigenous contexts across the world. For example, Fitzsimmons and Smith (2000) explain that the long-term survival of *Maori* language, knowledge and culture is bound to the survival of the *whanau* structure, which is constituted by hierarchical ordering of family relationships.

Certain inter-generational characteristics of indigenous communities can then be at odds with Freire's approach to questioning and changing hierarchical power structures. Yet this is not to say that children and young people are necessarily oppressed. In fact, children and young people often participate and are included within day-to-day indigenous societies that deeply challenge the ways in which non-indigenous communities include children and young people. The key point here is that we need to look beyond our own (often Eurocentric) worldviews to be able to discern and learn from other forms of participation we might not necessarily see as transformational at first hand.

Indigenous scholars such as Atkinson, Bastien, Battiste and Cajete have researched and written on school-aged children and young people, the destructive impacts of colonialism and the reclaiming of indigenous ways of knowing that can help to transform and heal their communities and others through emerging formal and informal cultural and educative contexts. Children and young people's engagement in communal storytelling, dance and song often occurs in non-formal and informal contexts of social and cultural events, particularly ceremony. These events inspire deeper learning and collective engagement that can build communality and deeper relationships. Indigenous ways of *being-knowing-doing* (Arbon, 2008) tend to value relationships as the primary way of learning – with each other and with all aspects of the world around us (human and non-human). Relationships and their transformative potential are also crucial within social movements, indigenous and non-indigenous alike.

Transformative processes and social movements

Social movements are often explicit in their intention to create autonomous and transformative spaces through the participation of young people and adults alike. What constitutes a social movement? New Social Movements were identified in the late 1970s as not just being focused on class but often on a single issue such as a particular environmental issue, women's issue and so on (Day, 2005). More recent social movements, as Day (2005) describes, have emerged since the mid-1990s with an overall aim of being autonomous of, or running in parallel to, government and corporate oversight. These social movements are usually organized around a variety of issues to do with social, ecological and/or historical injustices.

Social movements are often aimed at transforming (or eradicating) institutions. During the process of mobilizing and sustaining a social movement, a variety of transformative learning processes can occur, primarily through forming new relationships. Yet, the transformative power of social movements is often elusive (Day, 2005). This is for several reasons. First, the experiences of transformation tend to be complex and difficult to follow, particularly as a person is likely experiencing multiple forms of struggle and participation simultaneously (Smith, 2003). Yang (2000) attempts to explain how social movements transform participants' identities, whilst also acknowledging that 'there is no sustained explanation of the conditions that make movement participation an identity-transforming experience' (p. 380).

Scott (2003) explains that, although it is undeniable that social change and transformative learning often occur within social movements, these have not been systematically linked to the literature on transformative learning. Research on social movements has tended to examine 'what' happened, rather than 'why' or 'how'. Furthermore, the emotional side of the experience tends to be under-valued. Goodwin et al. (2001) argue that, since the 1960s, the study of emotions as part of political and social change processes has been marginalized, with 'no place in the rationalistic, structural and organizational models that dominate academic political analysis' (p. 1). Yet emotions are, as Robnett (1997) describes:

> the catalyst through which individual transformations emerge, new ideas are embraced and actions are undertaken that are against one's own self-interest, such as risking one's life for the movement. (p. 34)

Social movements can inspire deeper learning and collective engagement, which can build communality and deeper relationships. Relationships of any kind can be transformational – whether they emerge in our personal or professional lives as temporary or more permanent. Transformational experiences through participation in social movements are most often about relationships, harking back to the concept of 'communities of practice' described above.

Yang (2000) contends that the transformative power of social movements depends on their degree of liminality. A liminal condition suspends normal institutional constraints and can be seen as the inverse relationship of bureaucracy, which predominates within institutional structures. Liminality in other words is what Illich (1970) encourages all of us to do – to learn how to transcend the everyday constraints of institutions within our inner (personal) and outer (social) lives and levels of engagement, thus leading to experiences of transformation as Rahnema describes.

Social movements often are liminal phenomena that, as Yang explains, separate participants from pre-existing institutional and structural constraints, providing the opportunity to remold themselves and society. Yang explains that the ways in which normal social and cultural institutional structures are experienced as constraining can be challenged through the dimensions of: *freedom* (rejection of norms and rules); *egalitarianism* (weakening, unsettling or reversal of structural relations organized by caste, class, ranks or other institutionalized form); *communion* (rejection of alienation from generic bond of humanity – fostering emotions, helps to refashion self); and/or *creativity* (re-classification of reality).

The meanings and experiences of transformation associated with liminality can be paradoxical. Experiences of liminality, although offering potential spaces of autonomy, can also be culturally and socially alienating as indicated within Freire's notion of *transitive consciousness*. Yet, this liminallity encourages us (young people and adults alike) to transcend institutional boundaries, to immerse ourselves fully into inner and outer transformative processes, which as this chapter argued at the onset was one of the primary, initial purposes of participation.

Social movements are amorphous in how and where they mobilize, as well as their modes of communication, using a hybrid of communicative means, individuals and ideologies (Day 2005; Haider, 2011). Participation within social movements, especially for young people, is increasingly occurring virtually, through various modes of social media such as Facebook, YouTube and Twitter. Social media is an important mechanism for collective action, protests and social movements. With its widespread outreach, social media is widely perceived as contributing positively to government accountability, human rights activism, the development of civil society and practices citizenship (Haider, 2011). New forms of collective and critical consciousness can be attributed to the participatory infrastructure that social media can provide. These new methods of sharing and learning also create a greater diversity in who can be involved.

Drawing together and moving forward

The ideas and literature reviewed above provide many ways to understand the connections between participation and transformation. In particular we have discussed participation as transformation and the historical processes through which this has been co-opted through forms of participation that have been *instrumental, nominal* and *representative* (White, 1996), as well as *transitive* (rather than intransitive), *forced* (rather than free), and *manipulative* (rather than spontaneous) (Rahnema, 1992). We have provided examples of indigenous forms of knowledge, or *being-knowing-doing* (Arbon, 2008), as fundamentally transformative.

This chapter provides questions to ask of children and young people's participation. When and how are transformative forms of participation the actual aim? Transformative for whom? Are there different ways to understand transformational processes and, in particular, how they involve participation? Why does participation so often *not* translate into the transformative experience expected? A variety of resources has been provided and discussed to broaden potential meanings and practices of both participation and transformation.

Understanding *how participation can support and precipitate transformation* for individuals and communities is what this chapter has begun to explore, whilst acknowledging that how transformation happens and how we know whether it has happened remain under-explored. Furthermore, we consider how participating in deep learning experiences enables inner (personal) and outer (social) transformative processes. How is transformation a fundamental part of learning, not just in schools but in our daily lives?

This chapter also encourages us to recognize the often unanticipated consequences of transformation and participation. Greater transparency in our aims and objectives of engaging children is paramount, as is being clear about the theories and conceptual thinking behind our approach. We need to reflect deeply on how the dominant conceptual frameworks constrain what we research, learn and carry out in practice. The effect of children's participation being under-theorized and project-driven has presented significant challenges for the field (see Malone and Hartung, 2010).

This chapter incites us to consider how we can value and learn from various worldviews and experiences. Social movements, for example, can inspire deeper learning and collective engagement, which can build communality and deeper relationships. Future research has the potential to investigate the new contexts emerging with the increasing use of social media, particularly within current social movements that involve many young people. These offer avenues for understanding how transformative processes occur and are experienced, for individuals and communities. How can social movement theory and practice help us to better understand different forms and experiences of participation and their links with transformative processes?

The growing literature on indigenous ways of knowing, learning and being provides us with non-linear ways to understand participation and transformation, providing a deep relational connection for individuals to themselves (particularly in the emotional realm), to each other (particularly in an inter-generational sense) and the non-human world around them. The richness of this volume is in the concrete examples that illustrate this, provided from a range of worldviews and ways of knowing. These experiences demand greater reflection and research in the future.

Bibliography

Arbon, V. (2008) *Arlathirnda Ngurkarnda Ityirnda: Being-Knowing-Doing: Decolonising Indigenous Tertiary Education*, (New South Wales: Post Pressed).

Atkinson, J. (2002) *Trauma Trails: Recreating Song Lines, the Transgenerational Effects of Trauma in Indigenous Australia*, (Melbourne, Australia: Pinifex Press).

Au, W. (2007) 'Epistemology of the oppressed: The dialectics of Paulo Freire's theory of knowledge', *Journal of Critical Education Policy Studies*, 5(2), 175–196.

Bastien, B. (2004) *Blackfoot Ways of Knowing: The Worldview of the Siksikaitsitapi*, (Calgary: University of Calgary Press).

Battiste, M. (2002) 'Indigenous Knowledge and Pedagogy in First Nations Education: A Literature Review with Recommendations', Prepared for the National Working Group on Education and the Minister of Indian Affairs, Indian and Northern Affairs, Canada, Ottawa, ON, 31st October, 2002.

Battiste, M. and Henderson, J. (2000) *Protecting Indigenous Knowledge and Heritage: A Global Challenge*, (Saskatoon: Purich Press).

Boal, A. (1995) *The Rainbow of Desire: The Boal Method of Theatre and Therapy*, (London: Routledge).

Boal, A. (2000) *Theater of the Oppressed*, (London: Pluto Press).

Bowers, C. (2005) 'How Peter McLaren and Donna Houston and other "Green" Marxists contribute to the globalisation of the West's industrial culture', *Education Studies: A Journal of the American Educational Studies Association*, 37(2), 185–195.

Chambers, R. (1981) 'Rapid Rural Appraisal: rationale and repertoire', *Public Administration and Development*, 1(2), 95–106.

Chambers, R. (1983) *Rural development: putting the last first*, (Harlow: Prentic Hall).

Chouliaraki, L. and Fairclough, N. (1999) *Discourse in Late Modernity: Rethinking Critical Discourse Analysis*, (Edinburgh: Edinburgh University Press).

Clark, J. (1995) 'The State, Popular Participation, and the Voluntary Sector', *World Development*, 23(4), 593–601.

Cooke, B. and Kothari, U. (2001) *Participation: The New Tyranny?* (London: Zed Books).

Cornwall, A. (2008) 'Unpacking "participation": Models, meanings and practices', *Community Development Journal*, 43(3), 269–283.

Cornwall, A. and Brock, K. (2005a) 'What do buzzwords do for development policy? A critical look at "participation," "empowerment" and "poverty reduction"', *Third World Quarterly*, 26(7), 1043–1060.

Cornwall, A. and Brock, K. (2005b) 'Beyond Buzzwords', Programme Paper No. 10, http://www.unrisd.org/80256B3C005BCCF9/(httpAuxPages)/F25D3D6 D27E2A1ACC12570CB002FFA9A/$file/cornwall.pdf.

Cornwall, A. and Eade, D. (2010) *Deconstructing Development Discourse: Buzzwords and Fuzzwords*, (Rugby: Practical Action Publishing in association with Oxfam GB).

Daes, E. (1993) 'Study on the Protection of the Cultural and Intellectual Property Rights of Indigenous Peoples', Paper presented at the Sub-Commission on Prevention of Discrimination and Protection of Minorities, Commission on Human Rights, United Nations Economic and Social Council, 28 February 1993.

Day, R. (2005) *Gramsci is Dead: Anarchist Currents in the Newest Social Movements*, (Toronto: Between the Lines).

Denzin, N., Lincoln, Y. and Smith, L. (2008) *Handbook of Critical and Indigenous Methodologies*, (London: Sage).

Dirkx, J. M. (2000). 'After the burning bush: Transformative learning as imaginative engagement in everyday experience', Proceedings of *The Third International Transformative Learning Conference: Transformative Learning in Action*, (New York: Teachers College, Columbia University).

Edwards, M. and Hulme, D. (1996) 'Too close for comfort? The impact of official aid on nongovernmental organisations', *World Development*, 24(6), 961–973.

Esteva, G. (2010) 'Beyond education' from Meyer, L. and Alvarado, B. (2010) *New World of Indigenous Resistance: Noam Chomsky and Voices from North, South and Central America*, (San Francisco, CA: City Lights Books)

Esteva, G. (2012) Interview held with Gustavo Esteva, 28 November 2012, Universidad de la Tierra, Oaxaca, Mexico, in K. Teamey and U. Butler unpublished fieldwork notes.

Fairclough, N. (1989) *Language and Power*, (Harlow: Longman).

Fairclough, N. (2003) *Analysing Discourse: Textual Analysis for Social Research*, (London: Routledge).

Fitzsimmons, P. and Smith, G. (2000) 'Philosophy and indigenous cultural transformation', *Educational Philosophy and Theory*, 32(1), 25–41.

Freire, P. (1970) *Pedagogy of the Oppressed*, (New York: Continuum Books).

Freire, P. (1997) *Mentoring the Mentor: A Critical Dialogue with Paolo Freire*, (New York: P. Lang).

Freire, P. (1998) *Pedagogy of Freedom: Ethics, Democracy and Civic Courage*, (Lanham: Rowman and Littlefield).

Freire, A. and Macedo, D. (2001) *The Paulo Freire Reader*, (New York: Continuum).

Gaventa, J. (2004) 'Participatory Development or Participatory Democracy? Linking Participatory Approaches to Policy and Governance', *Participatory learning and action*, Theme Section 16, http://pubs.iied.org/pdfs/G02106.pdf.

Goodwin, J., Jasper, J. and Polletta, F. (2001) *Passionate Politics: Emotions and Social Movements*, (Chicago: University of Chicago Press).

Haider, H. (2011) 'Helpdesk Research Report: Social Media and Reform Networks, Protests, Social Movements and Coalitions', Governance and Social Development Resource Center (GSDRC) Research Report, (Birmingham: GSDRC), http://www.gsdrc.org/docs/open/HD764.pdf,

Hart, J. (2008) 'Children's Participation and International Development: Attending to the Political', *International Journal of Children's Rights*, 16(3), 407–418.

Hickey, S. and Mohan, G. (2004) 'Introduction', in S. Hickey and G. Mohan (eds) *Participation: From Tyranny to Transformation? Exploring New Approaches to Participation in Development*, (London: Zed Books).

Houston, S., Magill, T., McCollum, M. and Spratt, T. (2001) 'Developing Creative Solutions to the Problem of Children and their Families: Communicative Reason and the Use of Forum Theatre', *Child and Family Social Work*, 6(4), 285–294.

Ibrahim, S. and Alkire, S. (2007) 'Agency and Empowerment: a Proposal for Internationally Comparable Indicators', *Oxford Development Studies*, 35(4), 379–403.

Illich, I. (1970) *De-Schooling Society*, (New York: Harper & Row).

Jain, D. (2010) 'Review' in A. Cornwall and D. Eade *Deconstructing Development Discourse: Buzzwords and Fuzzwords*, (Rugby: Practical Action Publishing in association with Oxfam GB).

Johnson, V., Hill, J. and Ivan-Smith, E. (1995) *Listening to Smaller Voices: Children in an Environment of Change*, (London: ActionAid UK).

Lave, J. and Wenger, E. (1991) *Situated Learning: Legitimate Peripheral Participation*, (Cambridge: University of Cambridge Press).

Leal, P. A. (2010) 'Participation: The ascendancy of a buzzword in the neo-liberal era' in A. Cornwall and Eade, D. (eds) *Deconstructing Development Discourse: Buzzwords and Fuzzwords*, (Rugby: Practical Action Publishing in association with Oxfam GB).

Malone, K. and Hartung, C. (2010) 'A Handbook of Children and Young People's Participation', http://www.fairplayforchildren.org/pdf/1289572182.pdf.

Mosha, R. (2000) *The Heartbeat of Indigenous Africa: A Study of the Chagga Educational System*, (New York: Garland Publishing).

Narayan, D., Chambers, R., Shah, M. and Petesch, P. (2000) *Voices of the Poor: Crying out for Change*, (Washington DC: World Bank).

Needham, C. (2003) *Citizen-consumers: New Labour's Marketplace Democracy*, (London: The Catalyst Forum).

Norton, N. (2001) *A Rough Guide to Participatory Poverty Assessments*, (Washington DC: World Bank).

Orr, D. (1992) *Ecological Literacy: Education and the Transition to a Postmodern World*, (Albany, NY: State University of New York Press)

Peat, D. (1994) *Blackfoot Physics: A Journey into the Native American Universe*, (London: Fourth Estate).

Percy-Smith, B, and Thomas, N. (2010) (eds) *A Handbook of Children and Young People's Participation: Perspectives from Theory and Practice*, (London and New York: Routledge).

Prakash, M. and Esteva, G. (1998) *Escaping Education: Living as Learning within Grassroots Cultures*, (London: P. Lang),

Rahnema, M. (1992) 'Participation' in W. Sachs (ed.) *The Development Dictionary: A Guide to Knowledge as Power*, (London: Zed Books).

Robnett, B. (1997) *How Long? How Long? African-American Women in the Struggle for Civil Rights*, (New York: Oxford University Press).

Samman, E. and Santos, M. E. (2009) 'Agency and Empowerment: a Review of Concepts, Indicators and Empirical Evidence', http://www.ophi.org.uk/wp-content/uploads/OPHI-RP-10a.pdf.

Scott, S. M. (2003) 'The social Construction of Transformation', *Journal of Transformative Education*, 1(3), 264–284.

Semali, L. and Kincheloe, J. (1999) *What is Indigenous Knowledge? Voices from the Academy*, (New York: Falmer Press).

Smith, G. (2003) *Indigenous struggle for the transformation of education and schooling*, Keynote address to the Alaskan Federation of Natives Convention on Transforming Institutions: Reclaiming Education and Schooling for Indigenous Peoples, Anchorage Alaska.

Smith, L. (1999) *Decolonizing Methodologies: Research and Indigenous Peoples*, (London: Zed Books).

Vengroff, R. (1974) 'Popular Participation in Administration of Rural Development: the Case of Botswana', *Human Organization*, 33(3), 303–309.

White, S. (1996) 'Depoliticising Development: the Uses and Abuses of Participation', *Development in Practice*, 6(1), 6–15.

Yang, G. (2000) 'The Liminal Effects of Social Movements: Red Guards and the Transformation of Identity', *Sociological Forum*, 15(3), 379–406.

3
Decolonizing the Notion of Participation of Children and Young People

Savyasaachi and Udi Mandel Butler

What possibility is there for us to recognize and encourage children and young people's participation in our contemporary world, which is largely determined by adults? What role does listening have in this recognition and encouragement of participation and in nurturing particular forms of theorizing that are amenable to these? This chapter addresses these questions in relation to the power dynamics imbued in theories and practices surrounding children and young people's participation. In disentangling these relations (structures and histories of power) we make use of the notion of decolonizing, suggesting some avenues for how such decolonizing could be practiced and theorized with reference to children and young people's worlds.

A growing body of work has been produced across different disciplines in the last several decades that draw on some notion of decolonizing. Whether in the field of literature and language, in history or philosophy, in politics or social research, what draws these approaches together is a decolonizing aspiration to identify, analyze, critique and provide alternative possibilities to the ways of thinking, knowing, feeling, organizing and describing that have been imposed on numerous societies across the world through centuries of colonialism and imperialism (Arbon, 2008; Freire, 1970; Illich, 1970; Rahnema, 1992; Smith, 1999; Wiredu, 2010). Such fields tend to focus on the historical effects and present-day legacies of, most often, European expansion over the last five centuries and the consequences of this from the perspective of the cultures and peoples caught up in these traumatic processes. Decolonizing then is also the complex process of disentangling colonialism's consequences in the aftermath of national independence; even whilst the political governance of territories has been changed, colonialism has left deeply changed communities, particularly in their ways of speaking, knowing, relating and being in the world.

How does children and young people's participation relate to processes of colonialism (or post-colonialism) and decolonization? As described in Chapter 2, children and young people's participation has often been part of a broader field of international development. Over the last few decades a range of participation activities have been initiated by grassroots, national or international non-governmental organizations (NGOs) or government agencies across the world. Such projects have sought to encourage children and young people's involvement in the area of education, health, environment, sports, arts and media.

The most commonly mentioned spaces of children and young people's participation are documented in the report for UNICEF *The Participation Rights of Adolescents* (Rajani, 2001). The report includes a table on 'Common activities, roles and settings of young people's participation'. The 'institutional settings' column includes: family, school, workplace, the street, media, youth organizations, international agencies, cultural or religious organizations, internet chat rooms, amongst others. In the 'roles' column the activities that children and young people practice within these various settings, which can be considered as different forms of participating, are listed: discussing and deliberating, speaking, culture-making, representing, advocating, planning, reasoning, evaluating voting and so forth. Such practices and the acquisition of skills in mastering them are expected to help children and young people in the successful integration and participation in democratic societies. These skills and the spaces in which they are practiced have been structured by the ideals of 'development' of 'the good society' (Rajani, 2001, p. 14).

In contrast, the activities being pursued by street children, child soldiers, child workers, child-headed households, and children's membership of peer groups and gangs are not usually referred to as various forms of participation. Individuals in such circumstances can on many occasions be said to be making their way in adverse circumstances, learning a number of important skills in the process whilst also participating in diverse kinds of groups or practices that offer a sense of agency, control or solidarity (Boyden, 2003; Brett, 2003; Liebel, 2003; Myers, 1999; Rajani, 2000; Veale et al., 2000; Woodhead, 1999).

The exclusion of activities led by these often marginalized groups of children suggests that worldviews, values and histories embedded in the concept of participation potentially pre-empt forms of inquiry and theorizing from the 'ground up'. This means that listening to the experiences and meanings of children and young people themselves is either suppressed or ignored. What is deemed as necessary or appropriate is often entirely equated to what adults have dreamed up for children and young people's future.

Although the counter examples of children living on the streets, child-headed households, child soldiers, children involved in gangs, can be seen as 'extreme' examples, they nevertheless suggest that entire worlds in which children and young people participate are not receiving the attention nor access to the more formalized institutional spaces – such as schools, community projects, youth groups and so on that are in most cases organized and defined by adults.

This chapter seeks to investigate theories and practices of children and young people's participation and the extent to which they might be decolonized – that is disentangled from the historical and cultural meanings they have accumulated and the values and power relations they have tended to reproduce. Following this, we seek to make the concept and theory of participation work as a tool for creating new possibilities of relating to children and young people and the worlds they are engaged in.

To conceptually engage and learn, within a process of decolonization, requires a certain sensibility or orientation, a way of problematizing habitual ways of thinking and doing. This is similar to what philosopher, educator and activist Paulo Freire described as *conscientização* – the critical consciousness individuals and communities attain through a process of critical enquiry and action in relation to the oppressive structures and constrain their world (see also Chapter 2 for a fuller discussion of Freire). According to Wiredu (2010), writing from an African perspective, conceptual decolonization is:

> On the negative side, I mean avoiding or reversing through a critical conceptual self-awareness the unexamined assimilation in our thought (that is, in the thought of contemporary African philosophers) of the conceptual frameworks embedded in the foreign philosophical traditions that have had an impact on African life and thought. And, on the positive side, I mean exploiting as much as is judicious the resources of our own indigenous conceptual schemes in our philosophical meditations on even the most technical problems of contemporary philosophy. Try to think them through in your own African language. (p. 1)

The decolonization of children and young people's participation can be undertaken through four interconnected approaches, which we will examine in this chapter.

Firstly, we can seek to decolonize children and young people's participation by analyzing and becoming mindful of the historical origins and cultural specific baggage of 'participation' as commonly used in theories and practices within this field. This means becoming aware of the values and assumptions that inform such theories and practices. Secondly, by critiquing the dominant concept and practices of participation, we can analyze how it may be used and for whose benefit, highlighting the power relations perpetuated by theories and practices. Thirdly, by appreciating the pluralistic possibilities of participation through listening to stories, histories, values, practices and concepts at a local level, we can open up different spaces and forms of participation and give them greater visibility within the worlds of adults. Lastly, combining these three approaches can prepare the ground for listening to children and young people and for rejuvenating theories and practices of participation.

Historical origins and cultural roots of 'participation'

The concept and practices of participation that have become widespread in international agencies, NGOs and many national governments can be traced back to sixteenth century Europe. According to Henkel and Stirrat (2004), practices and ideas of participation originated from administrative principles of theology and liturgical practice during the Protestant Reformation when the discourse of Christianity shifted from Latin to local languages. The aspiration was that all individuals should be able to read the holy texts themselves. This shift, Henkel and Stirrat argue, was accompanied by decentralization:

> One central aspect of this reform was the so-called 'subsidiary principle', which states that all decisions that can be taken at a subsidiary level of the hierarchy should be taken at these levels, and that only those of overarching importance should be decided by the higher ranks. The Catholic Church, in contrast, championed, as it were, a strongly 'top-down' approach in its organization and minor and local issues were often decided in Rome. (2004, p. 173)

As such, in Protestant theology the relationships between believer and God are not mediated by the clerical hierarchy but are direct. The Reformation, the authors state:

> not only made the direct participation of the believer possible, but placed a moral imperative on participation. To be a good Christian

required participation: in reading the scriptures, in participating in the liturgy, in governing the Church. Salvation was to be attained through individuals actively participating in the duties of the community. (2004, p. 174)

This prepared the ground for 'participation' to become, according to Henkel and Stirrat (2004), the battle-cry of the emerging bourgeois claiming its share of the political and economic sphere in Europe in the eighteenth and nineteenth centuries. This civic involvement elicited participation in democratic decision-making processes in community life and polity (Henkel and Stirrat, 2004). Here 'to participate' is to begin to be part of deliberative forums and spaces of debate at various levels, and to have the right to vote for representatives.

A number of institutions, such as international development organizations and multilateral agencies, and various national and international rights instruments can be said to have a direct lineage from European religious, political and philosophical traditions of thought and social organization. Consequently, this model of participation that emerged during the Reformation has been propagated within various contexts without a consideration of local practices, concepts and values. Today the participation concept is no longer confined to political institutions and processes; it is now part of fields as diverse as education, community development, health, social science research, media production and consumption, product design, marketing and the world of business and management. That most of us are unaware of the rich histories, experiences and philosophies of participation that have existed, and some that continue to exist, across the world is a testament to the triumph of the dissemination of a particular story, set of ideas and practices of participation.

Power and participation

The second approach of decolonization is to critique and analyze power relations. This has been undertaken by a number of authors (see Chapter 2). Many authors have argued that 'participation' is often used to explain, justify and advocate many kinds of practices that are not progressive, emancipatory nor transformative of social relations and of institutions (Cooke and Kothari, 2004; Rahnema, 1992).

We do not have to look far to hear the call to 'participate' across a number of spheres in our daily lives, in running our schools or health services, in having more of a say in the products and services we buy.

Like in the field of international and community development, the depth of participation is not always authentic, meaningful nor transformative. As pointed out in Chapter 2, a number of the critiques leveled at participation in the domain of international and community development can also been applied to the worlds of children and young people's participation. As with adults, national, international and local institutions (governmental or non-governmental, or even grassroots) fall into patterns of tokenism and fail truly to be inclusive when involving children and young people. As Chapter 2 describes, another story of the practice and ideas of participation, as freeing individuals and communities from oppressive structures and political regimes, can also be traced. Originating in the liberation and anti-colonial movements of the 1960s, Chapter 2 points to how the transformative edge of participation was blunted by large organizations (World Bank, International Development Agencies, Governments) who high-jacked the language and tools of participation.

Appreciating the pluralistic possibilities of participation

Learning to listen to stories, histories, values and practices on the ground provides an opportunity to appreciate analogous notions of participation across different cultures and languages. This theme is also explored in Chapter 2 where Teamey and Hinton introduce the importance of considering 'Indigenous Knowledge' in accounts of participative transformation. By appreciating that the countless possibilities for children and young people to participate in playing a significant role in their communities, we can give them greater visibility within the worlds of adults.

A number of local concepts, akin to 'participation' in English, refer to collective organization and decision-making. For instance, *mutirão* (Brazil), *ubuntu* (South Africa) *bahgidari, joodna, sahbhagita, sharkat, seva and yogdan* (India) are some examples. These concepts are deeply embedded in other cosmo-visions: that is, ways of seeing and being in the world. Common features are the valuing of working together, collaboratively towards a common goal and with a spirit of reciprocity and celebration.

In Brazil, for instance, the term *mutirão* derives from the *Tupi Guarani* language and refers to forms of collective action, such as building a house, planting crops or harvesting. This term describes sharing of work that culminates in a celebration. Those who have been the primary beneficiaries of the activity organize this celebration. The term *mutirão* has been adopted more colloquially to describe cooperative collective practice or activity, shared amongst a group of people working towards a specific common goal.

Mutirão thus has a different history, meaning, feeling and form of organization from the concept of participation traced by Henkel and Stirrat (2004). It is reflexive, respectful of the moment. It is an ephemeral form of collective action, one that is de-centering at all moments and therefore can be started by anyone able to mobilize people towards an immediate goal. Its celebratory aspect comes from a sense of having the fruits of one's labor in the present rather than in a more distant or abstract future, as may be the case with the European notion of participation. Thus the pooling of labor itself is celebratory, as well as culminating in a celebration.

Another kindred category to participation in South Africa is *ubuntu*. It is said to be a pervasive ethic and philosophy found across different African societies and one that emphasizes individuals' interdependence as the basis of well-being for the individual and the community – 'I am what I am because of who we all are' (see Gade, 2012).

In India there are a variety of concepts that highlight different aspects of participation: *bahgidari* (to share and be included), *joodna* (to become part of), *sahbhagita* (to be co-partners), *sharkat* (to be present and be involved), *seva* (to be available), and *yogdan* (to gift work). In the semantic field of these vernacular Hindustani terms, recognizing a person's social being is itself a form of participation. These terms do not always necessarily include children and young people in the societal structure of people who use them. So the day-to-day language particular social groups use reveals something about the nature of who is included and excluded in such groups and in particular categories of persons.

These different terms and categories point to rich and complex cosmologies, histories and experiences analogous to participation. They also point to the possibility of attending to other practices, ideas and identities that are evident when people across different cultural contexts 'participate' in the reproduction of their day-to-day lives and their communities. Being more mindful of such experiences and cosmologies of participation in distinct settings also offers us other ways to understand how children and young people are part of their communities, how they organize themselves and how they relate to the world of adults.

An example of this can be seen in societies where children and young people form a demarcated age-set group with particular responsibilities to the community as a whole, whilst at the same time inhabiting a space with relative autonomy: that is to say, the adults largely do not impose the rules of social conduct. The *Koitors* are one such society. The *Koitors* are *adivasis* (literally those who were first to belong to a place: *adi*-the first; *vasi*-belong). They live in *Sringarbhum* in *Bastar, Chattisgarh* State of India. In their social structure the distinct institutional space for children and young people is called the *ghotul*. This space has been shrinking over the past two decades under the impact of patriarchal ideologies of 'Outsiders' – non-*adivasi* Indian culture, political, educational models and forms of production and consumption.

A brief description of *ghotul* is given here based on Savyasaachi's field work in 1980s when this institution was still prevalent. This case is presented here to give a sense of how children and young people have indeed had highly significant roles and status in societies across the world, participating in the day-to-day lives of communities in a way that is not usually acknowledged. Such traditions are less known and their legacies in the contemporary world are little understood. Their language and cosmologies are rarely heard in accounts of 'participation'.

Koitors are forest dwellers. *Sringarbhum* is the name of their living space. This term highlights the diversity in the forest as the ground for their way of life. Literally *Shringarbhum* means the beautifully decorated space. In their view, the presence of *Talurmutte* (the grand old mother) animates all elements of the forest. *Koitors* see the forest as the work of nature (personified as *Talurmutte*) over which they cannot have rights of ownership/disposal.

A *ghotul* is a hut constructed in the middle of a *Koitor* village. This space is blessed by the presence of *Talurmutte*. Here unmarried boys and girls come every night to play and dance. The rules and regulations that determine the life of a *ghotul* in fact define the social life of *Koitor* society. It is here that children grow into adults and acquire a sense of responsibility, of fair play, and of balance between individual interests and collective well-being.

As soon as children begin to understand household work they are sent to the *ghotul*. Here they are given a *ghotul* name that defines their membership to an age group and their socialization into the ways of living in society. A *ghotul* member acquires a sense of belonging, becoming part of the group/community.

A *ghotul* comes alive at the end of the day after the sun sets and households are asleep – boys and girls light a fire and gather to dance, sing songs and exchange conversations about the day. Without an active *ghotul*, life in a village is difficult, dull and sad. *Ghotul* members organize all festivals, prepare food for marriage, help out all families in a village in different stages of cultivation, participate in political discussions, and sing and dance to keep the cultural traditions alive.

The quality of social life in a village is judged by its *ghotul* life. An active *ghotul* indicates that the village has a good ratio of young boys and girls. This in turn is an indication of the festive mood in the village all through the year, for they sing and dance regularly, preparing a series of religious festivals. This also indicates that the village community is prepared to receive visitors and guests and extend appropriate hospitality.

The elders of the village interfere with the activities of the *ghotul* only when norms of social life are violated; then they intervene and the senior members are held responsible. Equally, the *ghotul* people can also intervene in the adult world when norms are violated.

The example of the *ghotul* brings us to the fourth approach of decolonization: namely, listening to children and young people in order to rejuvenate theories and practices of participation.

Listening to children and young people

Listening opens up the possibility of being surprised by the fact that young children can have better sense than adults. This creates a space for an inquiry into what 'being a part of' means for those considerably younger than ourselves. To be able to listen (not only to children), it is necessary to be quiet, to step back and listen to one's self first. For as long as an individual is preoccupied with himself or herself it is not possible to listen to anyone else. This is necessary in order to recognize the limits and possibilities of one's own being. In this recognition is embedded the most significant aspect of participation – being available to 'others' and leaving space and time for them. This constitutes the reflexivity of listening: that is, unlearning speaking as a mode of expressing the self and learning to be quiet.

Listening surprises us – we are surprised to learn that silences speak, that speaking is not necessarily about verbalizing and asserting. In speaking, the volume of voice and words takes away spaces, colonizing time. For instance, between children and young people, and adults, there may be few spaces and adults may have little (often no) time to listen to what children and young people have to say. The adult volume of voice and words often silences the voices of children and young people. This is the basis for the taken-for-granted notion of adulthood: namely, that adulthood is to give advice, direction and ensure transmission of traditions to a younger generation. The younger generations are

supposed to listen quietly – without an utterance. So here decolonization occurs through a different way of attending to children and young
people by just learning to listen.

Decolonization can open spaces and create time where children can
speak and be heard. This makes it possible to acknowledge the role children and young people play in social reproduction and innovation of
communities across the world. A number of such histories have already
been written: for instance, the role of children and young people in the
struggle against apartheid in South Africa (Reynolds, 1995), and in the
early part of the twentieth century in India (see for instance Ennew,
2000). As explained in Chapter 8, the public space young people carved
out for themselves in their struggle against apartheid was narrowed
down by the political establishment once the African National Congress
came into power. This suggests that there are certain historical moments
and social conditions in which children and young people are given or
take more space to organize. These may once again be closed off unless
a concerted effort is made to keep them open.

A significant question here is how the macro- and micro-politics
of day-to-day life are seen by children and young people themselves.
In a cross-country study on children and young people's perceptions
of citizenship in Australia, Brazil, New Zealand, Norway, Palestine
and South Africa, their understanding of the category of 'citizenship'
was based on children and young people's day-to-day realities (Butler
et al., 2009). Discussions on the meanings of citizenship, carried out
with different sectors of the population in Brazil, such as children
attending state and private schools and children who were living on
the streets, showed how specific socio-economic contexts elicited
quite different experiences and understandings of citizenship. For
instance, a young state school pupil narrated during a discussion
about citizenship: 'To walk into the mall wearing the [school] uni-
form is like you're naked. They look at you as if you've just got out
of jail' (quoted in Butler et al., 2009, p. 173). As such, the response
on the part of the researcher is one of surprise as a symbol or item
of clothing associated with state schooling, in itself an important
feature of citizenship, is experienced as a symbol of stigmatization in
the context of an unequal society. The authors go on to note in the
concluding chapter that 'citizenship talk', more often than not, is also
about the realization of how citizenship ideals remain elusive (Butler
et al., 2009). 'Citizenship' then comes to have particular associations
and evoke specific meanings and experiences for people according to
their circumstances.

A similar case can be made for 'participation' and research ought to be more attentive to how children and young people, in distinct social, economic, cultural and biographical contexts, experience participation. What are children and young people's own understandings of participative situations and contexts? Some of the case studies in this book explore aspects of such understandings in Brazil, India, South Africa and the UK.

Similarly Habashi (2008), in her research with Palestinian children, has recorded the words of a 12-year-old female participant from Nablus city:

> It [jihad] is resistance; the Palestinian jihad is not against Zionism but also to fight the people who are dropping out of school. They should get educated because when you grow up the only thing you could benefit from is education. When we resist, we are defending our homeland of Palestine. We do not give up or give in; this is jihad. (p. 275)

This child is not a passive listener to the talk of the adult world. She talks about subjects that are usually reserved for the adults. What difference would the inclusion of her views, and the views of other children and young people, make to how participation is conceived and theorized? What changes might the inclusion of children and young people's own experiences and views inspire, in their relationships amongst family and kin, communities and beyond?

Decolonizing theorizing itself

Following the four approaches to decolonizing participation addressed above, this section engages with decolonizing theory itself. Theorizing can be described as the act of thinking theoretically. But what does the act of thinking theoretically actually mean? And how/for whom does theorizing matter? The act of thinking theoretically brings in terms, categories and principles for making sense of the world. This is at the core of thinking. Every one of us is engaged in the process of making sense of the world in which we each live; this is not the monopoly of institutions or academic disciplines. All human beings use terms, categories and principles to give meaning to their experiences and make sense of the world. The act of thinking requires determination, which has a bearing on participation. The determination to think prepares the ground for participation to become a mode of determining one's place in the world.

The idea of determination has two interrelated meanings. First, it refers to the exercise of the will, volition and discretion. Second, it refers to the structure of historical circumstances, its limits and possibilities. History shows that there is a creative tussle between 'will' and 'circumstances'; the will is determined to transcend the determinations of circumstances and create new horizons. These intertwined meanings of determination draw out two aspects of participation: namely to be present and to have a presence. To be present refers to being there physically in any space. To have a presence refers to being there meaningfully, in relation to others and to the context. This meaningful relation comes from having intentions, will and interpretation vis-à-vis others. It is not possible to be present without having a presence and equally is it not possible to have a presence without being present.

This is important to a decolonizing mode of theorizing because its selection of terms, categories and principles to give meaning to experiences and to make sense of the world is grounded in the determination to listen. This mode is not concerned with making sense of the life of the 'other' (people who are present but their presence is mute), the often-marginalized across the world, but rather its orientation is to listen to them. The determination of marginalized people to speak up for themselves has contributed to the decolonization of theorizing and to prepare the ground for a different theorizing that now listens to the voices of marginalized people. Today, we could argue that the struggle is to be present and have a presence in decision-making processes at all levels of society – from international forums to everyday life. This struggle has opened up a discussion on the history of 'theory' and the creative potentials of the interdependence between theorizing and participation.

What are the links between theorizing, being present and presence? The act of thinking theoretically (described earlier) is the basis of theorizing. The child quoted earlier, who talked about jihad, is theorizing. In the act of theorizing a person begins to speak with determination, exercises the will and uses volition within the limits of the historically given circumstances. This is a mode of being present and having meaningful presence in relation to others and to the context.

When theorizing is determined by or in the interest of power structures of feudalism, capitalism and/or its key component 'capital', participation's creative potential is undermined. Such theorizing is part of a process of valorization – that is, theory becomes part of a larger network of forces and ideology that reproduces and legitimizes how a society is organized and how it sees the individual and the world. With regard to valorization under capitalism, Cleaver (1992) points out:

> 'Valorization' [*Verwertung*] designates the complex process through which capital is able not only to put people to work, but to do so in such a way that the process can be repeated on an ever greater scale. Technically, valorization involves all of the steps included in Marx's circuit of productive capital: the process of production, wherein people are put to work producing products which exceed their own requirements for living, the sale of those products at prices which permit the realization by the capitalist of surplus value, and finally the reinvestment of that surplus value such that people will, once more be put to work. To label this process 'valorization' is to emphasize the enormous transformation capital achieves by reducing the diversity of human productive activity to a unified mechanism of social control. (p. 8)

Valorization of theory and of participation becomes necessary in order to legitimize power structures. This leaves no time and space to listen to children and young people's voices.

To free theorizing from the clutches of capital and state power involves a 'stepping-back' or a series of re-orientations that we addressed above. This is a necessary for three reasons: first, to prevent theory from becoming hegemonic and colonizing spaces where participation is possible; second, to be able to listen to discourses that are part of decolonizing the hegemony of theory over practice; and, third, to prepare the ground for partnerships in the co-creation of knowledge.

For this, in addition to thinking through concepts about one's own language as suggested by Wiredu, it is equally important to listen to the voices of those who have been marginalized – children and young people, women, *dalits* in India, indigenous people across the world and so on. From such listening we learn that there are lethal words, generated by the capitalist valorization of theory.

Hinton (2002) suggests that these 'armaments of the mind' structure the dominant meta-narratives of modernity, legitimizing genocide, annihilating differences, rendering civilizations vulnerable and undermining the very basis of existence of the world we live in. In particular:

> Metanarratives of modernity supplied the terms by which the indigenous peoples were constructed as the inverted image of 'civilized' peoples. Discourse about these 'others' was frequently

structured by a series of value-laden binary oppositions: modernity-tradition; civilization-savagery; us-them; centre-margin; civilized-wild; humanity-barbarity; progress-degeneration; advanced-backward; developed-underdeveloped; adult-childlike; nurturing-dependent; normal-abnormal; subject-object; human-sub human; reason-passion; culture-nature; male-female; mind-body; objective-subjective; knowledge-ignorance; science- magic; truth-superstition; master-slave; good-evil; moral-sinful; believer-pagans; pure-impure; order-disorder; law-uncontrolled; justice-arbitrariness; active-passive; wealthy-poor; nation states-nonstate processes; strong-weak; dominant-subordinate; conqueror-conquered. (Hinton, 2002, p. 8)

In society, these binaries designate opposite ends of a social order and the terms of reference of social dynamics: the rich can become poor and poor rich; the conquered can become the conquerors; the undeveloped can become developed and so on. Underlying this is the fact that these opposites are valorized (by capital and state power) and are the anti-thesis of the other. These opposites are valorized by capital to determine the terms of reference of competition, the field and dynamics of participation. The categories introduce a whole new language and worldview, colonizing the linguistic and cosmological field of the places where they arrive.

Under these circumstances, theorizing 'stepping-back' raises a problem: namely, the possibility of decommissioning these terms. It becomes possible by bringing together theory and participation, and orienting these to listening to previously marginalized voices, to form the basis of a different mode of existence of living beings in the world. Here the concern is with grasping how speaking, listening and theorizing are aspects of theory as well as of participation and these are also embedded in the becoming and being of things in the world.

'Stepping back' creates time and space for the inner-most inspiration that shape the 'becoming' of things in the world, that dwells in 'listening/speaking', 'practice' and 'participation'. The theory that emerges becomes a part of a 'tree of knowledge' of the many ways of making sense of the world. A tree is a metaphor to look at the world and to grasp how people whose voices have been marginalized acquire a presence. The presence of a tree is generated from its 'grounded-ness' in earth. In a like manner, the presence of people on the margins is generated from their own earth-ground, their own language, culture, history, experience of being marginalized. The uprooting of trees in the course of deforestations has silenced the voices of these people. Consequently the process of being 'listened to' shapes a mode of theorizing as well as of participation – the one who is listening makes available time and space for someone to speak and for receiving what is being said on the one hand and the one who is speaking and being listened to comes to acquire a position and a presence in this time and space. The metaphor of the tree presents the possibility of participation under a canopy of shades and shadows. It is possible to step back in to the shade of the tree of knowledge, where there is time and space for theorizing modes of being present in the world. This becomes the basis of participation.

Questions to ponder

The four approaches to decolonization constitute for adults the praxis of stepping back, in order to create a milieu where children and young people may be able and willing to open up and speak. How can this step empower children and young people as well? Perhaps by accepting that there is a lot to learn from children and young people and that the learning process is reciprocal.

To listen to what children and young people say makes it possible to dialog with them. Can this be a mode of theorizing? This is part of a much larger question namely, whether philosophy is suitable for children. In this regards Murris (2000) says;

> Philosophers since as long ago as Plato have had plenty to say on the subject, most of it negative. The debate continues, but is often complicated by the confusion between 'doing' philosophy as a subject – that is, studying the ideas of the world's great thinkers since the Greeks – and 'philosophising', thinking about any question in a philosophical way. The debate is complicated further by disagreement over what the term 'philosophy' actually means. (p. 261)

Relating this question to children and young people's participation we can see a similar disregard for their life-worlds, their cultures and forms of social organization. How might these life-worlds, practices and forms of organization come to determine their day-to-day lives in a world ruled and defined by adults?

Bibliography

Arbon, V. (2008) *Arlathirnda Ngurkarnda Ityirnda: Being-Knowing-Doing: De-colonising Indigenous Tertiary Education*, (New South Wales: Post Pressed).

Boyden, J. (2003) 'Children under Fire: Challenging Assumptions about Children's Resilience', *Children, Youth and Environments*, 13(1), Spring 2003.

Brett, R. (2003) 'Adolescents Volunteering for Armed Conflict or Armed Groups', in Current Issues or Comments, *International Committee of the Red Cross*, 85(852).

Butler, U. M., Bjerke, H., Smith, A. B., Shipway, B., Fitzgerald, R., Graham, A. and Taylor, N. J. (2009) 'Children's Perspectives on Citizenship: Conclusions and Future Directions', in N. J. Taylor and A. B. Smith (eds) *Children as Citizens? International Voices*, (Dunedin: University of Otago Press).

Cleaver, H. (1992) 'The Inversion of Class Perspective in Marxian Theory: From Valorization to Self-Valorization' in W. Bonefeld, R. Gunn and K. Psychopedis (eds) *Essays on Open Marxism*, (London: Pluto Press).

Cooke, B. and Kothari, U. (2004) (eds) *Participation: The New Tyranny?* (Zed Books: London).

Ennew, J. (2000) 'The History of Children's Rights: Whose Story?', *Cultural Survival Quarterly*, 24(2), 44–48.

Freire, P. (1970) *Pedagogy of the Oppressed*, (New York: Continuum Books).

Gade, C. (2012) 'What is Ubuntu? Different Interpretations among South Africans of African Descent', *South African Journal of Philosophy*, 31(3), 484–503.

Habashi, J. (2008) 'Language of Political Socialization: Language of Resistance', *Children's Geographies*, 6(3), 269–280.

Henkel, H. and Stirrat, R. (2004) 'Participation as Spiritual Duty; Empowerment as Secular Subjection', in B. Cooke and U. Kothari (eds) *Participation: The New Tyranny?*, (London: Zed Books).

Hinton, A. L. (2002) *Annihilating Differences – The Anthropology of Genocide*, (Berkeley: University of California Press).

Illich, I. (1970) *De-Schooling Society*, (New York: Harper & Row).

Liebel, M. (2003) 'Working Children as Social Subjects: The Contribution of Working Children's Organizations to Social Transformations', *Childhood*, 10(3), 265–285.

Murris K. (2000) 'Can Children Do Philosophy', *Journal of Philosophy of Education*, 34(2), 261–278

Myers, W. (1999) 'Considering Child Labour: Changing Terms, Issues and Actors at the International Level', *Childhood*, 6(1), 27–49.

Rahnema, M. (1992) 'Participation' in W. Sachs (ed.) *The Development Dictionary: A Guide to Knowledge as Power*, (London: Zed Books).

Rajani, R. (2000) 'Introduction: Questioning How We Think About Children', *Cultural Survival Quarterly*, 24(2), Summer 2000.

Rajani, R. (2001) 'The Participation Rights of Adolescents: A Strategic Approach', *United Nations Children's Fund*, (New York: Working Paper Series Programme Division).

Reddy, N. (2000) 'The Right to Organize: The Working Children's Movement in India'. *Cultural Survival Quarterly*, 24(2), Summer 2000.

Reynolds, P. (1995) 'Youth and the Politics of Culture in South Africa', in S. Stephens (ed.) *Children and the Politics of Culture*, (Princeton: Princeton University Press).

Smith, L. (1999) *Decolonizing Methodologies: Research and Indigenous Peoples*, (London: Zed Books).

Veale, A., Taylor, M. and Linehan, C. (2000) 'Psychological Perspectives of "Abandonment" and "Abandoning" Street Children', in C. Panter-Brick and M. T. Smith (eds.) *Abandoned Children*, (Cambridge: Cambridge University Press).

Wiredu, K. (2010) in Kwasi 'The Need for Conceptual Decolonization', *African Philosophy*, http://www.galerie-inter.de/kimmerle/Kwasi.htm.

Woodhead, M. (1999) 'Combating Child Labour: Listen to What the Children Say', *Childhood*, 6(1), 27–49.

4
Children and Young People's Participation in Public Action in Brazil: Genealogies and Recent Innovations

Udi Mandel Butler and Marcelo Princeswal

Introduction

In this chapter we will give a historical overview of the changing dynamics of children and young people's participation in Brazil and point to emerging innovations in this field. We argue that particular historical moments impose specific challenges that are in turn faced through particular forms of participative organization and mobilization. As a result, there is not a 'participation in itself': that is, a category that is removed from the historical relations that produced it, nor even an ideal state of participation to be reached. Instead participation is made anew, influenced by the past but also re-emerging constantly to meet new challenges. In this chapter, we take a genealogical approach to investigate particular understandings of childhood that are found behind these policies and practices towards this group at different historical moments. Our focus here is on forums and institutions that make claims, deliberate, make decisions and regulate the worlds of childhood and young people within the state as well as the forms of public action that have mobilized children and young people around issues of rights and policies (see Butler and Princeswal, 2008, 2010; see also Chapter 2).

In 2011, Brazil became the sixth largest economy in the world. According to the census conducted by the Brazilian Institute of Geography and Statistics (IBGE), Brazil's population totaled approximately 191 million, in 2010 (IBGE, 2010). Of this total, 64 million were children and adolescents (0–17 years), corresponding to 33 percent of the population. The number of young people, considered in Brazil to be those aged 15 to 29 years, was 51 million (IBGE, 2010).

Taking into account the international poverty line, between 1990–2008 the number of Brazilians living below the poverty line decreased from 38.2 to 8.9 million (IPEA, 2010). Between 1997 and 2008, the percentage of the population between 0 and 17 years old below the poverty line fell from 43 percent to 36 percent. The reasons for the decline in poverty include economic expansion, increase in the purchasing power of the minimum wage and expanding income redistribution programs, such as the Family Grant, a cash transfer scheme handed to families through the school attendance of their children that currently covers 12.6 million people (Ministério de Desenvolvimento Social e Combate a Fome, 2011). Even with such improvements, in 2009, the proportion of children and adolescents (aged 0 to 17 years) in poverty in urban areas of Brazil was more than a third (34.6 percent).

Another contrasting scenario refers to schooling indicators. In recent decades school enrollment has increased between the ages of four and five years old, jumping from 54.1 percent to 77.4 percent between 1999 and 2009, and the percentage of 6 to 14 years of age enrolled has increased from 95.3 percent to 97.8 percent in the same period (IBGE, 2009, Centro Internacional de Estudos e Políticas sobrê a Infância (CIESPI), 2010). Despite these significant improvements, the education system has problems. The school dropout rate in Brazil, for example, is the largest among the countries that make up *Mercosur* (South America's free trade zone), reaching 3.2 percent. In Uruguay and Argentina the rates are 0.3 percent and 1 percent respectively. The problem gets worse during high school in Brazil, at 10 percent, whilst in Paraguay this is 2.3 percent and in Venezuela 1 percent (IBGE, 2009).

Another major problem facing the country is the high rates of homicide of children and young people. The increase in homicide rates of young people between 12 and 18 years old in Brazil has increased from 18.7 deaths per 100,000 in 1997 to 24.1 in 2007 (IBGE, 2009). International comparisons of homicides of young people show a large difference between countries in the northern and southern hemisphere. *Mapa da Violência – Os Jovens da América Latina* (2008) presents homicide rates in the range between 10 and 29 years as 51.6 per 100,000 in Brazil, 1.7 in Portugal and 12.9 in the United States. Like the data on poverty, youth homicide rates in Brazil vary greatly according to region, city and ethnicity, being higher for men than for women and higher for black and brown young people than for whites (Rizzini et al., 2010b).

The rest of this chapter is divided into three parts, each tackling a period in Brazil's history with its own social and political configuration: Part I looks at the period from the end of slavery in 1888 to the first decades of the twentieth century; Part II covers the period of the dictatorship from 1964 to 1985; and Part III addresses the post-dictatorship years and in particular the new laws for children and young people to have emerged in this period; that deepened the democratic processes within the state and their relationship to civil society.

Part I: Struggle and political repression, the difficult construction of democracy

Throughout Brazilian history, the spaces of decision-making and claiming resources from the state have always been restricted to a minority of the population (Sader, 2004; Skidmore, 1996). Unlike the popular struggles that shook Latin America in the nineteenth century, resulting in the proclamation of the republican model, Brazil witnessed a pact between elites, founding an imperial regime (Sader, 2004). In the process of drafting the first Brazilian Constitution, soon after independence in 1822, those who supported different ideals to the hegemonic class were exiled from the country. The Brazilian Constitution, inspired by the same ideals of liberty, equality and fraternity of the French Constitution, in practice retained slavery.

One of the first decrees on enrolling children in school, still in the Imperial period (which lasted from 1822 to 1889), depicts clearly the restriction of certain rights to only a portion of the population:

> Article 64. The parents, guardians, trustees or protectors who have in their company boys over 7 years without physical or moral impairments, and who do not give them at least primary education, will incur the penalty of 20$ to 100$, depending on the circumstances.
> Article 69. Admission will not be granted and they may not attend school:
> § 1. Boys who have communicable diseases.
> § 2. Those who are not vaccinated.
> § 3. Slaves.
> (Decree 1331-A/1854)

From Article 64 enrollment became compulsory for children over age 7 but already excluded girls and those with 'physical and moral impairments' (Decree 1331-A/1854). In Article 69, more exceptions are created for those who could not be registered or go to school. Considering that in 1854 many children were slaves and there were no extensive vaccination campaigns, schools were thus directed to a small group in society: male children of the wealthy. Moreover, the criterion of 'moral impairments' may exclude the poor according to the hegemonic view of the time, as there was a direct link established between poverty and immorality/vagabondage (Rizzini, 1997).

Before the time of Empire in Brazil, a series of repressive laws existed to control the poor, including children and young people. The presence of the latter in the streets (street children), for example, is recorded in the press and official reports from the late nineteenth century. The urchins and vagabonds – physically and morally abandoned children – are identified as the target of paternalistic policies, aimed at social control and containment, especially since the Republic's establishment, when the country was facing republican nation-building (Rizzini, 1997).

The Republic

The abolition of slavery in Brazil in 1888, the last American country to do so, had a high cost to the then Emperor Dom Pedro II, who was ousted from power the following year by an elite dissatisfied with the measure. A republic was proclaimed in 1889, with a new constitution (1890), but without significantly altering the position of the economically and politically privileged groups

In the period of the Republic at the end of the nineteenth century, there was a shift of focus towards addressing child poverty, referred to as 'scientific philanthropy' (Pilotti and Rizzini, 1995). Concern for abandoned children was not restricted to the salvation of their soul but also to the care of their bodies. Thereafter, abandonment became less tolerated and the category of the child began to be important to the decisions of society's builders (Pilotti and Rizzini, 1995). Children came to be regarded as the nation's future. As such, the actions directed to this population of poor children, especially, came to be seen as part of a moral and sanitizing mission. Gaining strength in this period were debates on the need for state intervention in order to build a nation free of 'ignorance' and 'backwardness' (Pilotti and Rizzini, 1995). The various instruments and institutional mechanisms designed to 'protect' children proved to be moralizing and disciplining. Decree number 145 of 1893 sought to 'isolate the vagrants, bums and *capoeiras*', authorizing the creation of a correctional colony, where people not subject to parental authority or without means of subsistence would be corrected by working, regardless of age and gender (Brasil, 1893 in Pilotti and Rizzini, 1995).

With the creation in 1923 of the Minor's Judge and in 1927 the Minor's Code, the first specific laws to regulate and normalize the situation of the childhood of the poor in Brazil, a legal division was established between the child and the minor. The differentiation between 'minor' and 'child' was coined at this time and started to have stigmatizing connotations towards those in poverty (Rizzini, 1993). Tracing the genesis of the term 'minor' in Brazil, Londoño suggests that before the nineteenth century 'minor' was used as synonymous with child, adolescent, or youth and used only to demarcate civil responsibility (Londoño, quoted in Faleiros, 1995, p. 209). However, from the end of the nineteenth century onwards the Brazilian judiciary,

> discovers the 'minor' in the poor children and adolescents of the cities, who by not being under the authority of their parents and tutors are considered abandoned by the jurists ... The minor was then not the son of 'a family' subject to paternal authority, or an orphan under tutelage but a child or adolescent materially or morally abandoned. [authors' own translation] (Londoño in Faleiros, 1995, p. 209)

More than simply a life stage in which a person was not legally recognized as a full member of society, the term minor came to mean, in legal, policy and popular discourses, the childhood of the poor who were in need of special attention by the state. This was often applied to children in an 'irregular situation' of abandonment. Behind such discourses there was often the belief that such a population, unless kept in check, might well come to pose a threat to the future social order (see Butler, 2008). It was not until the ratification of the Child and Adolescent Statute in 1990 that the category of minor in this discriminatory form ceases to be part of official policy towards children (see Part 3).

The Estado Novo

During the period of the *Estado Novo* (1930–1945), the National Conference on Child Protection (1933) was a landmark event because of its commitment to greater state intervention. Subsequently, in 1940, the National Department of Children was created, an agency of the Ministry of Education and Health, with a discourse driven by the motto: 'save the family, to protect the child' (Perez and Passone, 2010, p. 656). In the 1940s, an effective state policy of infant-maternal protection began:

> What was once viewed from a perspective 'technique', i.e. a medical problem of prevention and cure of disease, associated with an appropriate educational and moral training of children, for which mothers

should be properly prepared, came to be subordinated to a larger and more complex issue: the role of mother and child in the Brazilian family. (Pereira, 1994, p. 16)

However, state intervention became synonymous with the institution-alization of poor Brazilian children. In 1941, the Service of Assistance to Minors (SAM) was created, focusing on the internment of the 'minor', considered destitute and delinquent through the dangers they suppos-edly posed to society.

In 1937, one of the main actors to catalyze the participation of youth in the Brazilian political scene was formed: the National Union of Students – UNE. In the time between the two dictatorships (1945 to 1964), the UNE, in its speeches and practices, was concerned with the structural transformation of society. Adding its efforts to those of other social actors, the Student Movement becomes one of the key agents of mobilization and struggle for rights. *Reformas de Bases*, or Reforms from the Base, was a mass reform movement, which in the 1960s played a key role in the cultural and political scene in Brazil (Freire, 1993 [1970]). All the effervescence of these years in Brazil also related to youth and counter-culture movements occurring in differ-ent parts of the world, in Latin America, in North America as well as in Europe. The 1960s youth movements questioned the bourgeois values and ways of experiencing the world. Fighting for sexual liberation or against patriarchy, for instance, meant creating new meanings for existence, different from those until then esteemed by modernity (Reis Filho, 1988). In such cases the forms and spaces of participation were much broader than the more traditional forums and forms of political participation.

The military coup in Brazil from 1964 to 1985 harshly repressed many groups who were fighting for social transformation and pushed their activities underground. In these conditions, the dictatorship sponsored a hunt for the UNE leadership and all those who dared to challenge authoritarian rule. The dictatorship bound the unions to the State and repressed the various social movements. The UNE, for example, was dissolved in 1973.

Regarding children and young people from poor families, the mili-tary dictatorship instituted the Policy for the Well-being of Minors, implemented through the National Foundation for Welfare of Children (FUNABEM). The FUNABEM came to replace the SAM, which had been known in the late 1950s as a 'school of crime', a place of 'no love for the minor' and other such terms (Rizzini, 1993). However, FUNABEM created new internment centers with a capacity for hundreds of inmates (Rizzini, 1993).

Part II: The building of a democratic state and the key spaces of public action

The mid-1970s and early 1980s witnessed the strengthening of social movements. These challenged the military regime, and the conditions produced by the policies adopted by these governments, that had led many to poverty and the country's increasing foreign debt. At this time, several popular mobilizations emerged that later fostered the creation of the Workers' Party (PT) and the Workers' Central Union (CUT). In rural areas, land occupations come to form the Movement of Landless Workers (MST), among others (see Chapter 5).

A key actor in these movements and in the fight against the military regime was the Catholic Church, through the Ecclesiastical Base Communities (CEB) and their perspective of a Liberation Theology. Seeking to organize the workers in the fields and cities, the CEB increased their scope in the 1970s. The relevance of the CEBs in this period can be seen in the struggle against:

the expropriation of land and the exploitation of work. Migrants and oppressed, the members of these communities, if at other times sought in religion a sedative for their suffering, now find a space of critical reflection before a dominant ideology and a popular organization capable of resisting oppression. The national moment helped to reinforce the ecclesiastical base communities. In repressing the various channels of popular participation, the military regime made this same population seek another space to organize itself. This space was found in the Church. (Betto in Fernandes, 1999, p. 135)

In this way the CEBs represented a democratic space of meeting and reflection for the workers, emphasizing workers' role as historical subjects and politicizing them about the oppression they faced. Beyond this, it was possible to create strategies collectively for facing the challenges imposed by the military regime and the dominant elite. With this, one of the greatest achievements of the CEBs was the raised awareness amongst the working class of the need to organize and to struggle for change, as well as in aggregating different leaders who had been working independently in different political spheres.

Through the 1970s a left-wing Latin American mass social movement for Popular Education emerged, led by the Catholic Church and by civil society (Freire, 1993 [1970]). This movement sought reform of a whole series of oppressive practices, relations and institutions throughout the region. Liberation Theology was a non-conformist grassroots movement of members of the Catholic Church, who sought to reinterpret the scriptures through Marxism and other philosophical and sociological writings. Liberation Theology had a lasting impact on Brazilian society and catalyzed social movements (such as the MST) and political parties (such as the PT). Through its actions and the ideas of its proponents such as Paulo Freire (see Chapter 2), Liberation Theology generated forms of popular participatory education and notions of 'conscientization' that are still used by a number of non-governmental organizations in Brazil and elsewhere (De Castro, 1997; Freire, 1993 [1970]; Graciani, 1999; Pastoral do Menor, 1983).

During the 1970s and 1980s, the numbers of children living on the streets also multiplied. This showed the ineffectiveness of the policies previously established by the State, which were directed more toward controlling them than promoting their fundamental rights (De Castro, 1997; Graciani, 1999). The first alternative practices emerged for working with children and young people on the street. These practices were termed 'alternative community practices', based on the principles of Popular Education, which differed from the repressive state interventions seen until then. According to Graciani (1999), the guiding principle of Popular Education, as expressed by Freire and others, is that education is an emancipatory force, as a practice of freedom and a precondition for democratic life. As such, Popular Education is a political-pedagogical process in opposition to a colonial, or colonizing education, and it attempts to reverse the negative effects such an education has had on the popular classes over many decades (Graciani, 1999). Freire's most important contributions in this respect were two notions: that education is a political act; and that this act consists of an exchange between educator and educated carrying within it the potential for emancipation from a repressive order, narrowing the distinction between teacher and pupil.

Freire's analysis is evident in the Popular Education movements' critique of what came to be seen as the repressive system of internment and confinement of *menores* – the minors. This system came to be seen as discriminatory and inherently repressive and as such mimicking other repressive measures of the military regime and, more fundamentally, of other exclusionary aspects of Brazilian society (Freire, 1990 [1970]; Graciani, 1999; Pastoral do Menor, 1983). The political context of the early 1980s was also one of the experimentations with different forms of social action. Movements emerged of/for women, black Brazilians, for the environment. These movements became a reference for others that demanded not only traditional social rights (conditions essential for survival) but also social rights, seeking liberty and equality in race relations, gender and sexuality. One of the major movements in defense of childhood and young people in this period was the National Movement of Street Boys and Girls (MNMMR), created in 1985. This movement not only brought to public debate the situation of children and young people on the street but also other social problems involving children and young people, offering proposals for changes relating to the treatment to this population (Butler and Rizzini, 2001; MNMMR/IBASE/NEV-USP, 1991; Swift, 1991). According to Macedo and Brito (1998), the MNMMR was based on the principles of Popular Education, with its main line of action being:

> to inform and organize boys and girls on the street to debate the social condition of the excluded, to provide the acquisition of knowledge and awareness of rights and public services available and enable the development of solutions for their lives. (p. xx)

Linking up with other civil society initiatives, the movement played an important role in mobilizing sectors of society in the second half of the 1980s, calling for a new law where children and adolescents were seen as subjects of rights and not as in an 'irregular situation' (Macedo and Brito, 1998). Allied to these groups from civil society, the state sector and international organizations denounced and sought to change the official policy in the state orphanages and correctional institutions (Butler and Rizzini, 2001; MNMMR/IBASE/NEV-USP, 1991; Swift, 1991). With increased media visibility, there was growing interest to create and implement public policies rather than the more temporary actions and programs that were being carried out. All this mobilization marks an important break with the hegemonic view of the minor as being in an 'irregular situation' to another perspective where they are considered as subjects of rights.

Two campaigns in the 1980s are important examples of this mobilization. The first was the *Campanha Criança e Constituinte* – Child and the Constituent Campaign – proposed by the Ministry of Education in

1986 in order to 'aid the proposition that the Executive would make to the Constituent Assembly, focusing especially on proposals related to children aged 0 to 6 years' (EAD/FIOCRUZ, 2009, p. 37). Through this campaign meetings were held at the national and state level with civil society organizations to prepare a proposal to be debated by the Constituent Assembly, to ensure the rights of children and adolescents in the constitutional text.

At the same time, various civil society organizations throughout the country promoted an amendment to the new Federal Constitution entitled *Children a National Priority*. A mass petition ensued. It collected more than one million signatures, mostly of children and young people, to ensure the amendment's implementation (EAD, 2009, p. 38). This mobilization led to the Permanent National Forum of Non-Governmental Entities in Defence of the Child and Adolescent (Forúm DCA), which lobbied the Constituent Assembly for the cause of children and young people. In the end, Article 227 was included in the text of the Federal Constitution; it states:

> It is the duty of the family, society and the State to ensure children, adolescents and youth, with absolute priority, the right to life, health, food, education, leisure, professional training, culture, dignity, respect, freedom and family and community, and to keep them safe from all forms of neglect, discrimination, exploitation, violence, cruelty and oppression.

After this important goal was achieved, actions focused on policy changes at state and municipal levels, again relying on the experience and organization of the Forum. In parallel, a bill was prepared for Article 227 to become implemented more effectively (EAD/FIOCRUZ, 2009).

From intense mobilizations, studies, debates, lobbying, public hearings, the bill passed the Senate on April 25, 1990 and the House on June 28 of that year. The Child and Adolescent Statute (Law 8069/90) was enacted on July 13, 1990. It contained a set of laws for children and adolescents on the following fundamental rights: The Right to Life and Health; The Right to Freedom, Respect and Dignity; The Right to Family and Community Living; The Right to Education, Culture, Sports and Leisure; and The Right to Vocational Training and Protection at Work.

Part III: Deepening democratic participation

The Child and Adolescent Statute (ECA)

Until 1990, the country legally divided the population aged 0–17 years into two groups: children and minors. In theory this separation could be mandated by the judge based on the actions, history or family relationships of those defined as 'minor'. The function of the state was then compensatory and not structural: that is, it promoted palliative measures rather than going to the roots of the problem, leaving to the family responsibility for children and to the state the responsibility for the regulation and administration between the public and private duty to control children. The Child and Adolescent Statute (1990) breaks with the notion of the irregular situation set out in the Code of Minors from the 1930s. In its place the Statute states that children under 17 years of age are subjects of rights.

Thus, the dichotomy between child and minor, which lasted for over 60 years in Brazil, was extinguished in the initial articles of the Statute. The 'Doctrine of Integral Protection' is thus reaffirmed with the notion of legal-political-social protection and, with the new law, every child is guaranteed his or her fundamental rights as an absolute priority. According to the Federal Constitution, the Statute imposes a responsibility on the family, society and government to enforce children's rights and to safeguard them from any form of neglect, discrimination, exploitation, violence, cruelty and oppression. The consequence of this new Statute has been a large institutional reorganization of all state agencies working in the area of childhood, as well as an increased focus on their needs. The Statute affirms the family as the ideal place for a child to live and be raised. Children are only exceptionally to be placed in a foster family. The Statute provides that, in case of absence or lack of material resources, the child should be referred to assistance programs.

It is mainly in Article 16, concerning the right to freedom, that the Statute provides the right to participation of children and young people:

Article 16. The right to freedom includes the following:

I – coming and going, and remaining in public and community
     spaces, subject to legal restrictions;
II – opinion and expression;
III – belief and religious practice;

IV – play, sports and entertainment;
V – participation in family and community life, without discrimination;
VI – participation in political life, as provided by law;
VII – seeking refuge, help and guidance.

In the sections above, we find the guarantees of rights of children and adolescents to participation within the right to freedom. In this sense, the Statute is in line with the United Nations Convention on the Rights of the Child (UNCRC), reinforcing the importance of guaranteeing freedom of opinion and expression, to participate in family and community life, and in political life.

The associated Care Guidelines provide principles for the system of integrated protection of the rights of children and adolescents (Costa, 2011). Among its guidelines are (i) the municipalization of care and (ii) the establishment of children and young people's rights councils. Such councils operate in the three spheres of government (municipal, state and federal) and are composed of representatives of civil society and government. Rights Councils come to play a key role in the formulation, deliberation and monitoring of policies for children and young people. As we have seen, the Statute provides children and young people with the right to participate in political life surrounding matters of concern to them and the Councils are responsible for determining the policies aimed at them. It is worth asking whether these spaces have provided opportunities for the participation of children and adolescents and, if so, how it occurs.

The Human Rights Council and the participation of children and young people

Rights Councils are a democratic advance from the historical control of poor children and young people. The new powers of the municipality alongside the new care policies have meant a break with the vertical and centralized model of protection prior to the Statute of 1990. As such, these new ways of doing politics seek solutions within the community, connected to local realities and with the participation of the population.

The Rights Councils operate in the administrative spheres (municipal, state and federal) autonomously and independently from each other. However the Councils should be administratively linked to a specific organ of executive power, such as the various secretariats dealing with particular areas such as health, security, education and so on, which have the responsibility to provide the conditions for their operation. Just as these Rights Councils are not subject to each other's power, there is no hierarchical relationship between the municipal, state and federal levels either. In other words, the city council is not subject to the decisions of state and national councils. The National Council for the Rights of Children and Adolescents (CONANDA) provides policy guidelines at a national level, receiving input from state and municipal levels. The decisions taken by the Rights Councils are binding on the various levels of government. As such, their decisions must be implemented by municipalities, states and the federation. However, research (CIESPI, 2010) shows implementation is problematic, as governments can misunderstand or disrespect the roles of these councils. Every two years conferences are held on the Rights of the Child and Adolescent.

Brazilian youth

In Brazil, youth is a particular category, which includes those between the ages of 15 to 29 years. In relation to youth, great progress has been made in involving this population in decision-making processes.

Young people's participation has significantly changed over time, with less engagement in traditional forms of political organization. For many, this change is understood as the apathy of youth regarding politics and collective participation for social change (see Butler and Princeswal, 2010; Novaes and Vital, 2006). Young people of today according to this perspective are: consumerist (passive before a consumer society); individualist (involved in individual projects and not those of solidarity); conservative (and not progressive); alienated (and not engaged); and apathetic (not participative) (Novaes and Vital, 2006). But is such a perspective correct? In the case of Brazil, for example, young people participate in legislative assemblies, in unions, in political parties that are conservative as well as progressive, in student movements, amongst others (Butler and Princeswal, 2010). Young people have played significant roles in the Landless Movement, coming to take important leadership positions through this mass social movement (see Chapter 5). More young people are voting in elections in Brazil: according to the Superior Electoral Tribunal (Tribunal Superior Eleitoral, 2006), there was a growth of 39.9 percent amongst 16 and 17 year olds who were listed on their electoral register. In Brazil voting is compulsory after the age of 18 and voluntary from the age of 16. This increase shows that young people are far from disinterested in traditional political processes. 'Traditional' and 'innovative' forms of political engagement coexist in the public sphere. They are not mutually exclusive processes and it is not rare to find young people who participate in, for instance, relatively recent movements as well as political parties.

In the last decade, various sectors of society have sought to build public policies that guarantee the rights of this population. This is evident in the creation of the National Secretariat for Youth and the National Youth Council (CONJUVE) in 2005. CONJUVE consists of 60 members, 40 from civil society and 20 from the federal government. In order to encourage young people's participation in constructing policy, both agencies promoted the Youth Conference. The Youth Conference was organized in a decentralized manner in municipalities and states, mobilizing about 400 thousand young people across the country. This organization had preparatory steps, including pre-conferences, regional conferences at municipal and state levels, in addition to consultation with the peoples from traditional communities such as indigenous communities and *quilombolas* (historic runaway slave communities). The result of all this mobilization and debate came together for the National Conference, held in the capital Brasilia, in 2008. During this Conference 70 resolutions were passed, 22 of which were selected as priorities for the National Youth Policy.

Unlike the Conference on the Rights of the Child and Adolescent, this mobilization also permitted the holding of 'free conferences'. These were conferences organized by any group to formulate proposals to be taken to the municipal conferences. Thus, during a research project on young people entering the labor market of Rio de Janeiro held in five shanty-towns, our research team proposed a 'free conference' (Rizzini et al., 2010a). In line with the objective of this research project, the debates focused on the theme of work but allowing the dialog to move to other issues crucial to understanding this problem, such as education and media bias, among others. After briefly outlining the methodology of the 'free conference' we will present some of the challenges faced by youth in the current historical context and the importance of involving everyone in the democratic process of constructing public policies for this population.

This free conference was held in 2008, in downtown Rio de Janeiro, to facilitate access by participants. These were previously recruited by researchers with the help of community researchers, mostly young local residents who also worked in the research mentioned above. This conference was attended by approximately 40 young residents from four different low-income localities in Rio de Janeiro. Following from debates and deliberation in small groups, all young people jointly prepared proposals to be sent to the Municipal Conference. The group of young people selected seven challenges experienced by them and 21 solutions for tackling these. Below is a summary of these discussions outlining two of the priority challenges:

Challenge 1: Making state schools attractive to young people.
Solutions:

- Change in public school teaching model emphasizing the real needs of young people and respecting the local reality. To achieve this further training of teachers is needed.
- Implement and expand vocational and extracurricular activities, such as sports and leisure activities and courses after school. We suggest that theatres dedicate a percentage of places for public school students.
- Improvements to the physical conditions of the school to meet the needs of students and teachers.

Challenge 2: Prejudice towards low-income housing communities.
Solutions:

- Engage the media not to reinforce the stigma attached to the criminalization of poverty but to record and disseminate positive events held in low-income communities.
- Create and strengthen community media to highlight the qualities of the inhabitants of these localities and demystify the relationship between poverty/crime.
- Create projects that habituate young people to the routines, attitudes and behaviors in the workplace.

This space for debate favored the exchange of experiences between young people and the difficulties faced in each location, as well as thinking of solutions together to fight for them. The challenges and solutions voiced by the young participants and their attempt to prioritize each of these generated a rich debate, demanding a respect of the different realities experienced by everyone present. The dialogs were enthusiastic and critical about the current programs and policies and aroused a great interest in expanding their participation in forums, conferences and other spaces for discussion. Such forums have been occurring all over the country and at different levels encouraging participative processes of deliberation that are now enshrined in Brazil's legislation. The Child and Adolescent Statute, the Rights Councils and the National Youth Council demonstrate a deepening of participative processes at the heart of the country's political system.

Conclusion

In this chapter we have focused primarily on spaces, forums and institutions that govern, make claims, deliberate and make decisions concerning the lives of children and young people. The chapter emphasizes how changing views of childhood, and of the childhood of the poor, have been behind different policies and practices enacted by the state towards this age group. As we noted here, policy and institutional practices, as well as various forms of public action that seek to modify these, take place in particular social, economic and political contexts that have changed over time.

In the case of Brazil, a country marked by a turbulent colonial history and the legacy of slavery, deep inequalities and prejudice shaped the discourse, policies and practices associated with the category of the minor, some of which can still be seen in the present day. These discourses, policies and practices are no longer institutionalized in the country's legislation as it once was and, since the 1970s and 1980s, the country has experienced novel ways of thinking about and engaging with children and young people, culminating in the Child and Adolescent Statute in 1990. In the post-dictatorship period, the processes of deliberation and policy-making around the areas of childhood and youth have also been democratized, aligning themselves with broader trends of decentralization and participation in political decision-making in the country. The independent Rights Councils operating at municipal, state and national level have been set up with the power to draft and ratify specific policies in the area of childhood. Similarly, over the last decade the National Secretariat for Youth has been set up with the participation of civil society members and with the capacity to make and ratify policies for this population. The capacity to make laws with civil society's participation, within the apparatus of the state, is an important achievement in the deepening of democracy.

At the same time, the deep social inequalities and the vestiges of prejudice that have marked the country's history continue to affect the lives of countless children and young people, especially in relation to housing, health, education, employment and violence. The challenges of providing adequate resources for the poorest sectors of this age group are added to the challenge of ensuring that the ratified legislation at the various levels of government is in fact implemented. These are the battle-fronts that these participatory movements are now fighting. How to ensure that legislation is applied and that the resources are available? As recent experiences emerging from these experiments with deeper forms of democracy have shown, a close knowledge of the workings of the state is required as well as the elaboration of innovative ways of keeping it in check through different forms of citizen pressure.

Bibliography

Brasil Constitution (1988) *Constituição Da República Federativa Do Brasil*, (Brasília: Senado).

Butler, U.M. (2008) 'Children's Participation in Brazil – a brief genealogy and recent developments', *International Journal on Children's Rights*, 16(3): 301–312.

Butler, U. M. and Princeswal, M. (2008) 'Cultures of Participation: Young People's Engagement in the Public Sphere in Brazil', (London: NGPA Working Papers Series, London School of Economics).

Butler, U. M. and Princeswal, M. (2010) 'Cultures of Participation, Young People and Public Action in Brazil', Special issue on 'Learning from Latin America', *Community Development Journal*, 45(3), 335–345.

Butler, U. M. and Rizzini, I. (2001) 'Young People Living and Working on the Streets of Rio: Revisiting the Literature', *International Journal of Educational Policy, Research and Practice*, 2(4), Winter.

Centro Internacional de Estudos e Políticas sobre a Infância (CIESPI) (2010) 'Os Processos de Construção e Implementação de Políticas Públicas para Crianças e Adolescentes em Situação de Rua', www.ciespi.org.br.

Conselho Nacional dos Direitos da Criança e do Adolescente (CONANDA) (2006) 'Resolução Nº. 116. Altera Dispositivos Das Resoluções Nº. 105/2005 E 106/2006, Que Dispõe Sobre os Parâmetros para Criação e Funcionamento dos Conselhos dos Direitos da Criança e do Adolescente e dá Outras Providências', http://portal.mj.gov.br/sedh/ct/conanda/resolu%C3%A7%C3%B5es/resolucoes.htm.

Conselho Nacional dos Direitos da Criança e do Adolescente (CONANDA) (2006) 'Plano Decenal dos Direitos Humanos de Crianças e Adolescentes', http://www.sdh.gov.br/sobre/participacao-social/conselho-nacional-dos-direitos-da-crianca-e-do-adolescente-conanda.

Costa, A. C. G. (2011) 'A Política de Atendimento, Promenino Fundação Telefônica', http://www.promenino.org.br/Ferramentas/Conteudo/tabid/77/ConteudoId/7e182eb6-075b-4064-9550-d7c08701a19f/Default.aspx date accessed 20 October 2011.

De Castro, M. R. (1997) *Retóricas da Rua: Educador, Criança e Diálogos*, (Rio de Janeiro: Universidade Santa Ursula).

EAD/FIOCRUZ (2009) *Curso Teoria e Prática dos Conselhos Tutelares e de Direitos das Crianças e Adolescentes*, (Rio de Janeiro: Fiocruz).

Faleiros, V. P. (1995) 'Infância e Processo Político no Brasil' in F. Pilotti and I. Rizzini (eds) *A Arte de Governar as Crianças: A História das Políticas Sociais, da Legislação e da Assistência á Infância no Brasil*, (Rio de Janeiro: Santa Ursula/CESPI).

Freire, P. (1993 [1970]) *Pedagogy of the Oppressed*, (London: Penguin Press).

Fernandes, B. M. (1999) MST: Movimento dos Trabalhadores Rurais Sem Terra – Formação e Territorialização em São Paulo, (São Paulo: Hucitec).

Graciani, M. S. (1999) *Pedagogia Social de Rua*, (São Paulo: Cortez).

Instituto Brasileiro de Geografia e Estatística (IBGE) (2009) *Pesquisa Nacional por Amostra de Domicílios*, (Rio de Janeiro: PNAD).

Instituto Brasileiro de Geografia e Estatística (IBGE) (2010) 'Censo demográfico: resultados preliminaries', http://www.ibge.gov.br/home/presidencia/noticias/noticia_visualiza.php?id_noticia=1722&id_pagina=1.

Instituto Brasileiro de Geografia e Estatística (IBGE) (2011) *Pesquisa Nacional por Amostra de Domicílios*, (Rio de Janeiro: PNAD).

Instituto de Pesquisa Econômica Aplicada (IPEA) (2010) *Objetivos de Desenvolvimento do Milênio. Relatório Nacional de Acompanhamento*, (Brasília: IPEA).

Macedo, M. J. and Brito, S. M. D. O. (1998) 'A luta pela cidadania dos meninos do Movimento Nacional de Meninos e Meninas de Rua: uma ideologia reconstrutora', *Psicologia Reflexão e Critica*, 11(3), 511–522.

Ministério de Desenvolvimento Social e Combate a Fome (2011) 'Bolsa Família: 12,9 milhões de famílias recebem R$ 1,4 bilhão em maio', http://www.mds.gov.br/saladeimprensa/noticias/2011/maio/bolsa-familia-transfere-r-1-4-bilhao-para-12-9-milhoes-de-familias-em-maio.

MNMMR/IBASE/NEV-USP (1991) *Vidas em Risco: Assassinatos de Criancas e Adolescentes no Brasil*, (Rio de Janeiro: MNMMR/IBASE/NEV-USP).

Novaes, R. and Vital, C. (2006) 'A Juventude De Hoje: (Re)Invenções Da Participação Social' in A. A. Thompson (ed.) *Associando-se à Juventude para Construir o Futuro*, (São Paulo: Peilópolis).

Pastoral do Menor (1983) *Educador Social de Rua*, (São Paulo: Arquidiocese de São Paulo).

Pereira, André Ricardo. 1994. Criança X Menor: a origem de dois mitos da política brasileira. In: Rollemberg, Denise (org.). *Que História é essa?* (Rio de Janeiro: Relume Dumará).

Perez, R. and Passone, E. (2010) 'Políticas sociais de atendimento às crianças e aos adolescentes no Brasil', http://www.scielo.br/pdf/cp/v40n140/a1740140.pdf date accessed February 6th, 2014.

Pilotti, F. and Rizzini, I. (eds.) (1995) *A Arte de Governar as Crianças: A História das Politicas Sociais, da Legislação e da Assistência á Infância no Brasil*, (Rio de Janeiro: Santa Ursula/CESPI).

Reis Filho, D. A. (1988) *1968: A Paixão De Uma Utopia*, (Rio de Janeiro: Espaço e Tempo).

Rizzini, I. (1993) *Assistência À Infância No Brasil: Uma Análise De Sua Construção*, (Rio de Janeiro: Universitária Santa Úrsula).

Rizzini, I. (1997) *O Século Perdido – Raízes Históricas Das Políticas Públicas Para A Infância No Brasil*, (Rio De Janeiro: EDUSU / MAIS).

Rizzini, I.; Bush, M. and Soares, A. (eds) (2010a) *Juventude e Elos com o Mundo do Trabalho, Retratos e Desafios*, (São Paulo: Cortez).

Rizzini, I., Caldeira, P., Ribeiro, R. and e Carvalho, L. M. (2010b) *Crianças e adolescentes com direitos violados. Série Os processos de construção e implementação de políticas públicas para crianças e adolescentes em situação de rua, Caderno de Pesquisa 2*, (Rio de Janeiro: CIESPI em convênio com a PUC-Rio).

Sader, E. (2004) *A Vingança Da História*, (São Paulo: Bomtempo).

Skidmore, T. (1996) 'Racial Ideas and Social Policy in Brazil, 1870–1949' in G. Richard (ed.) *The Idea of Race in Latin America*, (Austin: University of Texas Press).

Swift, A. (1991) *Brazil: The fight for childhood in the city*, (Florence: UNICEF).

Tribunal Superior Eleitoral (2006). 'Relatório de gestão eleições 2006', http://www.tse.jus.br/arquivos/relatorio-de-gestao-eleicoes-2006/view. Date of access 6 February 2014.

5
Brazil's Landless Movement and Children and Young People's Participation

Marcelo Princeswal and Udi Mandel Butler

Introduction

This chapter analyzes children and young people's participation in one of the country's (and indeed, for some, the world's) key contemporary social movements: the *Movimento Nacional dos Trabalhadores Rurais Sem Terra* – MST (the Movement of Landless Workers). According to Carter 'the MST has 1,14 million of members, more than 2,000 camps, 1,800 schools, a national school for higher education, a number of media out-lets, 161 cooperatives and 140 agro-industries' (2009, p. 38).

The MST places a great weight on education and lifelong learning for social transformation. In the MST around 160 thousand children attend elementary level classes at the 1,800 state schools inside camps and settlements. The education sector of the movement works with infant education (newborns to six-year-olds); it has a literacy program with close to 30,000 adolescents and adults; and 750 active members are studying in universities. The Movement has also created its own higher education institution, the *Escola Nacional Florestan Fernandes* (Florestan Fernandes National School), in the state of São Paulo with a variety of courses. This institution links with faculty and universities across the country.

In the MST, education goes beyond schooling. With a focus on politi-cal formation of the subject, the MST perceives at least three aims for education: as a broader process of human development; as training for particular societal role; and as training for working on social struggles roles in our society and for the work of social struggles as a whole. The MST has constructed its own pedagogy to address these aims (Princeswal, 2007).

Figure 5.1 A tour around the campus: shown around the *Escola Nacional Florestan Fernandes*, the main higher education institution of the MST, by two children who lived there with their parents
Photographer: Udi Mandel Butler, 2012.

Just as education became a crucial concern of the MST, so has creating democratic processes as its way of organizing. These combine with the broader project of forming subjects and of human development, for adults, children and young people. This chapter seeks to show the links between these processes of education, organization and the formation of subjects within the MST, especially as they apply to and are experienced by children and young people. This is evident in the statement from a young activist who we interviewed. This young man had been part of the MST for a number of years and at the time of the interview he was one of the key organizers of the Communication Sector of the Movement based in Rio de Janeiro. He compares his first encounter with the MST with the sighting of a UFO (Unidentified Flying Object).

> It was such a shock that I could not talk right and then I saw those people under the canvas, some making food, others talking, children playing, some happy, then, all that was very moving for me. ... Because I did not know the camp, it was like another world, you live in a society, see the whole issue of social exclusion, the question that

society puts forward that 'for you to be you have to have' the ideological domination is huge, the cultural issue that they seek to impose on people, the question of individualism which is often very great, and you arrive in another reality, another social structure, which is different from what it is out there, it's as if you were in another environment from one minute to the next. (24 years old activist)

The MST shows that effective agrarian reform is not reducible to its economic dimension, i.e. the distribution of land for those who want or need it to work. As such it differs from other social movements that, in the 1980s, had possession of land as their only goal. In the analysis of Prado Junior (1979), the agrarian question in Brazil should be seen as not just a technical issue but also as a way of humanizing the countryside. An effective agrarian reform, for him, should encompass a discussion of the political and the economic, as well as the dimensions of social and human development that surround the issue of the land. These different forms of organizing work and education are observed by the young participant quoted above.

This chapter has three sources. First, it utilizes a long-running study of the MST, which includes visits to its camps, regional offices and its new institute of higher education. Second, the chapter uses findings from research carried out in Rio de Janeiro on young people's participation in public action; MST was one of the organizations and social movements included (Butler and Princeswal, 2010). Throughout these two research studies, a number of conversations took place with participants in and supporters of the movement, including children and young people. Third, the chapter incorporates the now extensive literature on the MST, including writings produced by the movement itself.

Below, a sketch is provided of the MST's historical development, to ground the subsequent discussion of children and young people's involvement in the MST.

The development of the MST

As Stédile and Mançano (1999) argue, the MST is the product of previous struggles against the expropriation and expulsion from the land in Brazil, where runaway slave colonies and peasant insurgencies were violently suppressed. Learning also comes from trying to answer current social, cultural and political challenges and define the format these take in the present historical context. But even with the MST and other social movements achieving several advances, the situation for families who live and work on the land is still frequently bleak due to the power of large agribusiness led by groups linked to international finance capital and encouraged by the Brazilian state.

The military coup in Brazil in 1964 subjected millions of peasants to brutal land expropriation. The coup halted a process of organizing amongst the peasantry that had been ongoing since the 1940s. In rural areas, living conditions worsened for much of the population, due to increased land concentration resulting from the military's policy. This was further aggravated by the replacement of manual labor by mechanized agriculture. There was a transition from some large unproductive properties to large capitalist enterprises, favoring the foreign market and driving out small farmers who did not have the same resources. These developments intensified the rural exodus, long underway, bringing serious consequences for both rural and urban areas.

With the intensification of popular struggles generally, various movements arose in the countryside and the city, and conflicts about land increased. More specifically in the southern regions, different occupations and land struggles by peasants challenged the established order, contributing to the organization of a movement for those who were dispossessed or expelled from the land for capitalist expansion. Several authors (for example, Carter, 2009; Lerrer, 2008) point out this moment as the gestation of the MST, reinserting the discussion of land reform in the Brazilian political agenda. In 1984, a national mass movement was formed, under the slogan 'land to those who work it' (Bonamigo, 2002).

The MST went through a second phase of development during the years of 1986–1987 in response to new challenges that it faced (Caldart, 2004). According to Caldart (2004) two decisions are responsible for this second phase of development. First, those MST members who were newly settled on land forged an alliance with those who were still fighting for their right of access to land. This attitude of the settlers strengthened the fight under one single banner, avoiding fragmentation. Second, the MST's settlements were set up as alternative social organizations to capitalist ones. The *Cooperação Agrícola* (Agricultural Cooperation) followed this direction, seeking to develop the Settlers' Cooperative System and creating local and regional cooperatives.

The Agricultural Cooperation is encouraged and developed mainly from the process of land regularization and when forming a settlement. The main idea is to prevent settlers from producing in isolation, as this leads to greater difficulties in obtaining credit and materials. According to the MST, Agricultural Cooperation is not limited to the economic field of production and circulation of goods:

> In addition to the improvement of the housing, with easy access to basic infrastructure such as roads, water and electricity, agricultural cooperation facilitates the education of children and adults, accelerating the conquest and the construction of this important social tool. Also, access to public transportation and health care are built through cooperation. Cooperation leads to the settled members of the movement to participate in specific struggles (linked to their immediate needs) as well as the general struggles of society as a whole. In a system of cooperation, farmers see themselves as a force that, in addition to the other categories, can contribute to building a new society. (MST, 2011)

The camps, where activists have not been granted the right to land, and settlements, where participants of the movement are eventually settled, are divided into small groups of about ten families who come together by affinity, forming the so-called core base – *núcleos de base*. Each of the core bases elects one man and one woman as coordinators for, amongst other responsibilities, coordinating meetings, raising any problems and collectively debating proposals to solve them (MST, 2005). In this space, matters of daily life are discussed, such as gender issues, the actions proposed by the MST, planting crops and health. Following these discussions, the positions of each core base are taken to the Assemblies where they are discussed again with all members of the camp/settlement. If no consensus is reached, an open vote takes place. The Assembly is the highest decision-making in a camp or settlement of the MST. In this space other matters of daily life or the demands from the Coordination Committee at National, State or Regional level are raised so they can be discussed in the *núcleos de base*, feeding back to this system of decentralized participation.

Asked what was different about the organization and dynamics within an MST camp from the way of life in the city, a participant of the movement replied:

> This issue of cooperation, the issue of work, the camp has an organizational structure that beyond the *núcleos de base* – the core bases – which is a space for discussion ... you have the Assemblies, the coordinators and for any type of activity, any type of work that

arises within the camp, the families discuss these issues and draw up proposals to move forward with that work. So that's a different thing. You will do a job, but not only in order to work in the same way, but in building together how to develop this work. And this is also something that glorifies us. And if we go deeper into the question of work, this is what builds man in the sense that work has a major role in construction of the consciousness of the individual and within the camp of the Landless Movement. We work not only to perform manual labor and for an economic return, but also in the work of reflection. It is reflection and the action of work, this then raises the awareness of the individual and then you will begin to build awareness. (24 years old activist)

These procedures and practices allow widespread participation, based on the right of equal voice and vote. Challenges, however, persist. One of these relates to the heterogeneous nature of the movement itself. Differences in participation in each camp or settlement can be noticed, as some activists have occupied the land for decades, whilst others only for a few weeks or months. Those who have gained the right to land through settlements, for example, have been part of the Movement for longer, experiencing its participatory structure and its training courses or else have their children in schools with the MST's own pedagogy. In the more recent camps, there has only been a brief(er) experience of collective living.

All these structures, from the camps to the National Coordination, are formed by sectors (for instance the education sector, the housing sector, the culture sector, etc.) that have the function to discuss, plan and drive forward the objectives of each specific sector in the settlements and camps. These are divided into the Sector for Mass Mobilization (responsible for mobilizing new land occupations among other things), as well as into sectors for production, education, training, health, gender, cooperation and environment, culture and communication, finance, projects and human rights.

Children and young people in the MST

From the above outline of the MST's genesis, and its political and organizational structure, we now focus on the movement in relation to children and young people. First, the *Sem-Terrinha* – Landless Children – was created within the movement for the identity and activities of children who are sons and daughters of activist families.

Figure 5.2 Ciranda Infantil Saci Pererê: A pre-school education space for the Sem Terrinha – the 'Little Landless People' – at the *Escola Nacional Florestan Fernandes*, the main higher education institution of the MST
Photographer: Udi Mandel Butler, 2012.

Education of its members is a top priority for the Movement: as soon as a farm is occupied the first barracks to be built is the one responsible for education. Caldart (2001), based on the reflections and experiences of the Movement, points to several interrelated pedagogies. Two are most relevant here, in relation to children and young people's participation: first, the pedagogy of struggle; and, second, collective organizing.

First, the everyday participation in the struggle waged by the Movement is an educational process. Experience within this movement produces a new 'social subject who is active in class struggle with its identity and its own name: the Landless' (Caldart, 2001, p. 130). In this sense, the author differentiates the term land-less (lowercase, with a hyphen) to the term Landless (no hyphen, uppercase and invariant). The first is the social category of workers who are land-less; the second is broader with the understanding that:

> it is a name that reveals the identity, a heritage that has been received and can be left to his descendants, and that has to do with historical memory, and a culture of social contestation. (Caldart, 2001, p. 130)

For example, the social struggle has a formative character on the subject, as a story of an activist living in a camp illustrates. According to this activist, at a meeting held in a settlement, a scheduled trip for the children had been cancelled. This decision was not accepted by those most interested – the children. This caused a great revolt and the children decided to join together to elect their representative to negotiate with the adults. The actions taken by this collective of Landless Children mirrored similar actions by their parents: to occupy the cooperative, which was located within the settlement. The designated representatives to negotiate an end to the standoff were father and son. The adult representative addressed the Landless Children representative calling him 'my son'; the young representative promptly replied that kinship ties did not matter at that time, as he was a representative of a collective. After much discussion, the children were able to re-schedule the date for their trip. From this example, we can see how the training process occurs from accumulated experiences of being in a camp and settlement.

The second aspect of the MST's pedagogy identified by Caldart, collective organization, refers to the educational dimension of members discovering themselves as collective subjects. Thus, organizing for the division of labor, cooperating in production and other such activities are also educational processes, deconstructing intimate and individualistic values in society. Cooperation is a central idea. By rethinking the social relations established by capitalist logic, a new mode of production can be constructed, with a new way of being in the world. In this sense, 'when the school functions as a learning cooperative, where the collective takes co-responsibility to educate the public, it becomes a learning space not only of forms of cooperation, but also primarily of a worldview' (MST 2005, p. 202). The collective activities developed by the MST with children and young people are not only about schooling but about community development. Working in the gardens of the school or camps, in the meetings of the Landless Children and in the marches, there is always a process of collective organization and cooperation.

An important area that includes the active participation of children and young people is the meetings of the Landless Children. Generally conducted in October, corresponding to National 'Children's Week', these events are held in Brazilian states where the MST is active. Hundreds and sometimes thousands of children participate. On average, the meetings last three days and include various cultural activities, studying, playing, building toys, flags, and making music collectively. In the evening, cultural activities composed by the children and young people themselves and supported by educators are performed. At each meeting the coordination at the Regional or State levels elects together with children a theme that will be the main focus of the meeting. These themes have included such topics as 'For school, Earth and no Poison in our Food', 'For school, Earth and Dignity', 'Seeds as patrimony of humanity', and 'Land Reform, a struggle of all, including the Landless children'.

Besides the activities mentioned, during these meetings a political act is often taken (most often associated with action for better schools and education). The Landless Children prior to the meeting begin drafting a document with some claims that will be discussed, finalized and put to a vote during the event. Then the children and young people march to a particular government agency responsible for meeting the demands, pleading for a meeting with the competent authority for the formal handover of the document. The same document is distributed to other people during the trip and later released to other sectors of society, seeking to raise awareness for the cause in question. For instance, in August 2011, a committee of Landless Children was received by the Minister of Education to protest the closure of more than 24,000 schools in rural areas. The children and young people described to the Minister the difficulties they face as schools moved to the cities. They asked the government to prevent school closures and to construct new units in the rural areas.

The collective structures of camps or settlements are replicated during the meetings of the Landless Children. Rossetto (2009) describes that, in the first day of the meeting, the children are divided into *núcleos de base*. Each chooses three coordinators: always one girl and one boy and one educator. All coordinators elected from these nuclei come together to form the overall coordination of the meeting, to help 'in the conduct of the meeting, organizing activities, assembly and resolution of infrastructure problems that may occur throughout the meeting' (Rossetto, 2009, p. 53).

However, this organizational experience of the children of the MST also carries some contradictions in their relationship with adults. According to Rossetto:

> The marks of contradictions appear in the education of adults at times when they seem not to believe in the ability of self-organization of children, and sometimes try to command them and control

them, preventing them from fulfilling their potential to perform tasks which are as important as those of adults. (2009, p. 53)

Thus the process children and young people's participation put in motion by the MST cannot be idealized. At the same time, it is no easy task to implement a pedagogy and methodology based on collective values, given that a capitalist model gives primacy and value to extreme individualism.

In the same way that the MST has been seeking strategies to encourage the participation of children and young people, the movement sought to encourage the participation of youth in rural and urban areas. In a number of publications, the Movement stresses the need to mobilize rural youths towards the struggle for agrarian reform, for more opportunities in education, work, health and culture in the countryside. This has led to the emergence of the Youth Collective within the MST, in several states and nationally (Castro, 2009). Among the objectives of this Youth Collective is 'the task of giving visibility to the questions involving young people, organize them in camps and settlements and to promote political, cultural and economic activities' (MST, 2011). Several topics of interest to this group are gaining greater prominence in the MST such as education, work, culture, sexuality and abortion, among others.

Young people are seen as a resource for the struggle:

It is young people who have been stepping forward, interested in the struggle. It is much harder for an older man, a peasant who has children, who is already of a certain age to be available to travel, to organize the camp, to go to a course. It is much harder than for the young man who is unmarried and is still young, and has time available. (24 years old activist)

Traveling, meeting new people and places and having new experiences are reported by young people as transformative. For example, a young activist reports the impact of being able to travel and get to know another state and attend a training course by the MST in one of the most important Brazilian universities:

I never imagined going to another state or tour around or anything along those lines, then suddenly I am faced with an opportunity to go to São Paulo, and also step into a university and take a course in political training. It had a very big impact on my life. (24 years old activist)

But young people are not always sufficiently involved, as one young activist criticizes:

> A very large portion of youth (in the field) is not inserted in anything at all, and is working in the settlements and the tendency of youth with these characteristics is to want to know many things. The MST has to take that potential, take advantage of this desire to want to go out and experience new worlds and strengthen it with political education, to be a social activist in society. We found also that the fact of wanting to know lots of things also creates an unstable situation in the camp, as youths want to go out visiting cities, other states, which is part of being a youth. In MST the young can have this opportunity of knowing the world in a more organized way. (22 years old activist)

The slow process of construction of the Youth Collective resulted from an initial mistrust of adult leaders, as we were told by one respondent. However in several events, lectures, demonstrations and courses organized by the MST in Brazil it is clear that young people are present in large numbers and often assume a coordinating role in several instances (at National, State, Regional levels, across different sectors and in the core bases). What seems most important is that, despite tensions, this has not prevented the MST from seeking to create mechanisms to overcome these challenges. This is slow work, which presents contradictions, given that it emerges in opposition to individualistic values and to the pervasive relationship between adults and children/young people in society as a whole. But what we can see is that this mass movement does not shrink from questioning these values.

Conclusion

From the MST's concern for educating their children and young people, creating their own schools in settlements and camps with their own methods, investing in staff training that will strengthen the organization, the MST has created a new way of doing politics. Participation permeates the core ethos of the MST in how it organizes itself as a movement and how it strives to reproduce this through its educational activities. In doing so the movement seeks to form different kinds of subjects, relations and a different kind of democracy. The Movement seeks through political and organizational practices to create a different ethics and set of moral values based on fellowship, solidarity, of belonging to a community that breaks with the individualism prevalent today. This path, however, also has its contradictions, its challenges and its uncertainties within a broader context that increasingly (re) produces poverty, unemployment and social fragmentation. As such the struggle for deeper forms of participation is constantly faced with challenges, pulled by various social, economic, political and cultural forces which disrupt the formation of different ways of organizing, living and relating.

Bibliography

Bonamigo, C. (2002) *Pra Mim foi uma Escola: o princípio educativo do trabalho cooperativo*, (Passo Fundo: UFP).

Butler, U. and Princeswal, M. (2010) 'Cultures of Participation, Young People and Public Action in Brazil', *Community Development Journal*, 45(3), 335–345.

Caldart. R. (2001) 'O MST e a formação dos Sem Terra. O Movimento social como princípio educativo' in P. Gentili, and G. Frigotto, (eds) *A Cidadania negada: políticas de exclusão na educação e no trabalho*, (São Paulo: Cortez).

Caldart. R. (2004) *A Pedagogia do Movimento Sem Terra*, (São Paulo: Expressão Popular).

Carter, M. (2009) 'Introdução' in M. Carter (ed.) *Combatendo a Desigualdade Social: o MST e a reforma agrária no Brasil*, (São Paulo: Editora Unesp/Nead).

Castro, E. (2009) 'Juventude rural no Brasil: processos de exclusão e a construção de um ator político', *Rev.latinoam.cienc.soc.niñez*, 7(1), 179–208.

Lerrer, D. F. (2008) *Trajetória de militants sulistas: tradição e modernidade do MST*, PhD Thesis (Rio de Janeiro: Universidade Federal Rural do Rio de Janeiro).

Movimento Nacional dos Trabalhadores Rurais Sem Terra (MST) (2005) 'Escola Trabalho e Cooperação' *Boletim de Educação no. 4, Dossiê MST Escola* (São Paulo: Editora Expressão Popular).

Movimento Nacional dos Trabalhadores Rurais Sem Terra (MST) (2011) *Levanta Juventude: juventude e pra lutar!* www.mst.org.br/jornada.../Levanta-juventude-juventude-e-pra-lutar.

Prado Junior, C. (1979) *A Questão Agrária no Brasil*, (São Paulo: Brasiliense).

Princeswal, M. (2007) 'MST e a proposta de formação humana da Escola Nacional Florestan Fernandes: uma síntese histórica', Unpublished MA dissertation (Rio de Janeiro: Faculdade de Educação da Universidade Estadual do Rio de Janeiro).

Rossetto, E. (2009) '"Essa criança não é só minha, é de todos nós" a educação das crianças Sem Terrinhas do MST', Unpublished MA dissertation (Sao Paulo: Faculdade de Educação da Universidade Estadual de Campinas).

Stédile, J. and Mançano, F. (1999) *Brava Gente: a trajetória do MST e a luta pela terra no Brasil*, (São Paulo: Fundação Perseu Abramo).

6
Children and Young People's Participation in India: Framing Law, Policy and the Media

Saima Saeed

Introduction

India is home to the largest child population in the world, with 448 million children and young people aged 0 to 18 in 2011 (see Chapter 1). Since Independence, the Constitution and policy more generally illustrate in principle the State's willingness to fulfill its human rights' obligations towards India's children. The reality presents a different story. Six intractable problems continue: abject poverty, food insecurity and malnutrition, illiteracy, child labor, child marriage and discrimination against the girl child. The State's adoption of neo-liberal policies in 1991 has created a discourse for privatization, leading to a shrinking of the already poor provisioning and access to resources. This has been further complicated by increases in forced economic migration, trafficking across borders and child labor.

Such urgent and persistent welfare concerns have dominated development. The role of participation to meaningful development policymaking and to catalyzing positive social change has been poorly understood. Participation is not looked upon as a right and, if given attention at all, is assigned a secondary status to the intractable problems that the State has claimed to address but has steadfastly failed to deliver upon. In this catastrophic cleavage between policy and practice, children and young people are relegated to being mute spectators, never acting but always only acted upon.

This chapter is divided into three parts. Part I approaches children and young people's participation in India from a social and cultural lens. Children and young people are expected to be subservient, docile and obedient to the elders in a society steeped in child exploitation and oppression. India's dismal performance on key social indicators for children and young people suggests that children's rights are far from met. Having set this context, Part II examines the legal and policy frameworks of children and young people's participation, bringing out the sharp contrast between the traditional conservative norms of the subservient child vis-à-vis the constitutional mandate and the policy foci that entitle children and young people to a host of rights and freedoms. In the final part, more substantive programs, available modes and platforms for children and young people's participation in India are discussed. It is further argued that the media need to be involved in a big way if participation in India is to become a reality.

Part I: An ancient Indian perspective to understanding the limited mode of social participation for children

The Indian Civilization, one of the oldest in the world, has a deeply traditional and ritualistic understanding of the position, status and role of children and young people in its social structure and this is extended to their level and degree of participation as well. So there are rites and ceremonies that are meant to facilitate and indoctrinate children even before they are born, from the time mothers are pregnant through to the growing-up years. The Indian traditional extended family system – although now withering away and giving way to nuclear family set-ups, particularly in urban areas – has been long hailed as a warm and loving environment ideal for early child development. Most of these institutions, especially the private sphere of the family, tend to initiate children into the social, cultural and religious fold. That children will grow up to participate in the public life of the world's largest democracy is more often than not an after-thought, consigned to college and university life.

Patriarchal and hierarchical societies like India have traditionally construed and constructed children and young people as listeners and not speakers, as family members to be seen but not heard. Popular local wisdom across communities in India is that a child should be taught to take a structurally dependent and subordinate social relationship to elders. This is encapsulated in the proverbial *kam bolo* (in Hindi meaning 'speak less') 'rule'.

In the folk and religious literature children and young people have been largely expected to obey their elders, particularly parents and teachers, without question. They should be dutiful students within the *guru-shishya parampara* (the ancient Indian teacher-taught tradition in which the teacher was usually a saint or religious instructor). These expectations are exemplified by two famous sources.

First, the legend of Eklavya centers on a young boy (Eklavya), who is a *shudra* (in Hindi signifying the lowest caste, many of which were considered untouchables). He zealously wants to learn archery from the renowned guru of the kingdom, Dronacharya. Dronacharya denies admission due to Eklavya's lower caste. Dronacharya is very fond of his disciple, the prince Arjuna, whom Dronacharya has vowed to make the greatest archer on Earth. Unwilling to give up on his passion both for archery and Dronacharya, Eklavya installs a clay statue of Dronacharya and practices archery to perfection, until the day when Arjuna and Dronacharya chance upon this extraordinary archer. Dronacharya is quick to foresee that very soon Eklavya will beat Arjuna and therefore devises a clever plan to eliminate the competition. He expresses his willingness to accept Eklavya as his disciple but on the condition that Eklavya give him *guru-dakshina* (the price or the gift that a student gave to his guru in the *guru-shishya* tradition). Rejoicing on being accepted by Dronacharya, Eklavya agrees to give him *guru-dakshina*. Much to everyone's dismay, Dronacharya asks Eklavya to 'gift' his right thumb to him. Without any protest or a sense of grief or even anxiety, Eklavya cuts his right thumb and places it at the feet of his teacher. Obviously, losing the right thumb meant that he could never practice archery again!

Second, this famous couplet by the great fifteenth century Indian poet-saint Kabir Das points to the teacher's greatness:

गुरु गोविन्द दोनों खड़े, काके लागूून पाए
बलिहारी गुरु आपकी जिन गोविन्द दियो बताये

The couplet addresses whose feet must be touched if both the teacher and Lord-God were standing side by side. The answer is to fall first at the feet of the teacher (who is great) because he is the one who has made us aware of the presence of God.

As exemplified by these traditional narratives, cultural and religious traditions leave limited autonomy and agency for children and young people and revere their unquestioning compliance with authority. This is worsened by acute social and economic backwardness and a burgeoning population, leaving a permanent state of crisis and insecurity for the country's children and young people.

The state of the world's largest child population in the world's biggest democracy

Demographically speaking, India accounts for 2.4 percent of the world area, making it the seventh largest country in the world. India supports just over 16 percent of the world's population. By 2007, the population crossed the billion mark making it second only to China in being the most populous country in the world (Population Foundation of India and the Population Reference Bureau, 2007). As of March 2011, the population of India stood at 1,210,193,422 (Census of India, 2011). With 41 percent of the country's population below the age of 18 years, India is home to the world's largest child and youth population (Census of India, 2011).

India's child and youth population continues to be excluded through their limited opportunities of survival, protection, growth and development. For instance, the approach paper to the Twelfth Five-year plan of the Government of India recognizes that some of the poorest sections of the population in terms of income/consumption are women – and child-headed households (Planning Commission, 2011). Some of the most pressing problems faced by children and young people can be mapped within the following key concerns:

Abject poverty, health and food insecurity

India reported a high infant mortality rate of 47 per thousand lives as of 2011 (World Bank, 2013). According to a World Bank discussion paper (Gragnolati et al., 2005), approximately 60 million children are underweight in India. The prevalence of underweight children in India is 'among the highest in the world, nearly double that of Sub-Saharan Africa, with dire consequences for morbidity, mortality, productivity and economic growth' (Gragnolati et al., 2005, p. 5). This is despite the government's Integrated Child Development Services (ICDS),[1] which is the one of the largest such programs in the world and has operated for the last 35 years. It offers a wide range of health, nutrition and pre-school education services to children under six, pregnant and lactating women. However, the mismatch between policy goals and actual outcomes is evident from the fact that the ICDS program reaches just over one-third of its target child population (Sinha, 2006). On 17 July 2013 more than 20 children died in Chhapra in Bihar after consuming the free midday meal served to them. Forensic reports revealed traces of pesticides used in agriculture.[2] The news shocked the nation and resulted in villagers setting ablaze four police vehicles.[3] The food scheme serves more than 120 million children in India and represents a considerable budgetary expenditure. For 1999–2000, the program's budget was over 8,557 million rupees and more than US$400 million have been allocated under India's Tenth Five-Year Plan, 2002–2007 (Gragnolati et al., 2005). Yet these programs have not ensured all children have their basic needs met.

Illiteracy and low school attendance

The provisional data of the 2011 Census shows that the literacy rate in India is 74.0 percent, which is almost 10 percent below the world average literacy rate of 84 percent (Census of India, 2011).[4] Between the ages of 6 and 14 years, all children and young people should attend school. However, the Census 2001 reveals that only 68.7 percent of children in this age group were attending school. Of this total, 72 percent were males and 65 percent were females. It is a telling failure of past legislation that the right to education, covered by India's Constitution at the time of its commencement in 1949, was within Part 4 where rights are not enforceable. It was only after the incorporation of the Constitution (Eighty-sixth Amendment) Act 2002, that the new Article 21-A made education an enforceable right: 'The State shall provide free and compulsory education to all children of the age of six to fourteen years in such manner as the State may by the law, determine.' Following this Article, the Right of Children to Free and Compulsory Education (RTE) Act 2009 establishes that every child has a right to elementary education of equitable quality in a formal school. Article 21-A and the RTE Act came into effect on 1 April 2010.

Child labor

A problem directly emanating from conditions of poverty is child labor. India is said to have the highest number of child laborers under 14 years of age in the world.[5] No reliable data exist on its exact figure so as to enable planned action to control it, with all major agencies providing different sets of figures. According to the Census 2001, 5.2 percent of children and young people – that is 12.5 million children and young people aged 5 to 14 – are working in hazardous occupations. The 2006 UNICEF report held that 14 percent of children and young people, that is 25 million, were child laborers. Legislation to curb child labor has been sluggishly enacted, despite the existence of National Child Labor Policy since 1988. Only in a 2012 amendment to the Child Labor (Prohibition and Regulation) Act 1986 did it become an offence to employ children not only in factories or industries but also in homes as domestic help.

Gender discrimination

The gang rape of a 23 year-old girl in a moving bus in the heart of the capital on 16 December 2012 shocked and horrified the nation. It sparked a national debate on Violence Against Women (VAW) in India, a country where a woman is raped every 22 minutes. Statistics like these stirred the nation's conscience as rampant street protests, candle light vigils and silent marches forced the government to respond.

In the Indian society, gender-based discrimination starts even before a child's birth. Males continue to make up a higher proportion of the population than females and this differential has only increased over time. The 1901 National Census recorded a female-male ratio of 972 females to 1,000 males, for all ages (IACR, 2004). In 1981, the ratio for children aged zero to six years was 962 girls to 1000 boys; in 1991, this decreased to 945 girls to 1000 boys and, in 2001, to 927 girls to 1000 boys (Census of India, 2001). Sex-selective abortion, or what is called female foeticide, is seen as the reason. This practice continues despite the Pre-Conception and Pre-Natal Diagnostic Techniques (Prohibition of Sex Selection) Act 1994. Age-old customs like child marriage are also still prevalent. This is despite a law dating back to 1929, the Child Marriage Restraint Act (CMRA), popularly known as the *Sharda* Act, which sets 14 years as the earliest age girls could marry. As reported by UNICEF (2009), 'More than half of all 20 to 24 years old women in the world who were married or in union by age 18 live in South Asia, and more than one in three women in the world who were married as children are from India' (UNICEF, 2009, p. 26).

Moreover, child sexual abuse, rape, child prostitution and trafficking remain to be tackled. Prostitution in India is a Rs. 40,000 *crore* annual business (a common unit of measurement in Indian numbering system; one *crore* is equivalent to ten million). It has been estimated that 30 percent of the sex workers are children, earning approximately Rs.11,000 *crore*. Poverty and deprivation, coupled with a low status of girls in society, are seen as primary factors leading to child prostitution (Saravanan, 2000).

This account of extreme rights violations is only a part of the complex problem in which India's children are deeply entrenched. Child policy therefore has to be specifically geared to tackle these issues in a sustained and systemic manner.

Part II: Children's rights in India: a legal and policy perspective

This section provides a critical analysis of the legal and policy frameworks that have been operational in the six and half decades of the Indian Republic. It examines the slippages between policy, practice and outcomes, which in turn reflect the State's failure to provide the four basic rights of the child – the right to survival, development, protection and participation.

When India changed from a colony under the British Raj to a 'Sovereign Socialist, Secular, Democratic Republic', the task of 'development' ahead was mammoth. Amongst the many difficulties the new democratic nation faced were: high levels of illiteracy; deep-rooted religious-, caste- and language-based discrimination; and a traditionally rural setting that made providing education, healthcare and immunization challenging. The Constitution's provisions for children were contained within a welfare-state development framework, rather than a rights-based legal framework guaranteeing every citizen their fundamental rights. Thus the subsequent *Nehruvian* Socialism chased core development goals under a modernization paradigm, that was highly statist and interventionist, and over reliant on economic measures instead of addressing deep-rooted social problems.

Given this background, the macro-social and the cultural composition created neither spaces nor a discourse for children and young people's participation. In India, no legislation expressly supports children and young people's participation, although the Constitution confers freedom of expression and does not exclude children or young people from this (UNICEF, 2004). Several constitutional provisions protect children and young people in India: the right of the State to make special provision for women and children (Article 15); the ban on employment of children below the age of 14 years (Article 24); Article 39 (f) requires children to be given opportunities and facilities to develop in a healthy manner and in conditions of freedom and dignity. Additionally, Article 45 of the Directive Principles of State Policy provides for free and compulsory education for all children up to the age of 14 which has been substituted by the Constitution (Eighty sixth Amendment) Act 2002 making elementary education a fundamental right under Article 21-A. Therefore, it now falls within the purview of the Right to Freedom of the Part 3 of the Constitution which pertains to the basic human rights of all the citizens of India. As noted in the earlier account, the policy direction much like the legal safeguards has been struggling to move from a welfarist to a rights-based perspective. The movement has been rather slow and tenuous, partly because the burgeoning population has historically made tremendous demands on the limited food, educational and healthcare provisioning that the country has struggled to meet.

The Five-Year Plans and early policies on child welfare

The State has focused on child welfare schemes to provide access to basic minimum services for children right from the First Five-year plan (1951–1956) following the setting up of the Planning Commission in

March 1950, up to the Fifth Five-Year Plan (1974–1979). The adoption of the National Policy for Children in 1974 was a landmark as it signaled the shift from welfare to a development approach and the adoption of integration and co-ordination of services under the flagship and novel program, the ICDS.

Human development was the catch phrase of the Eighth Five-Year Plan (1992–1997), which emphasized a reorientation of development paradigms towards advocacy and community empowerment. It aimed to generate employment and control population growth and to improve literacy, education, health, drinking water and provision of adequate food and basic infrastructure. It was only in the Ninth Five-Year Plan (1997–2002) that the Government of India declared its commitment to 'Growth with Social Justice and Equity', spelling out a policy shift from a welfare to an empowerment stance. Further, it clearly stated that, as children have neither a voice nor a political constituency, special safeguards were required to ensure their welfare, protection and development as laid out by the Constitution. Participation though did not find any mention here.

It was in the Tenth Five-Year Plan (2002–2007) that an integrated rights-based approach was adopted to ensure the survival, development, protection and participation of children. It provisioned for a National Policy and Charter for Children, a National Commission for Children to ensure protection of their rights and a National Nutrition Mission, as well as setting empirical targets for improving key social indicators, like family welfare and health for women and children.

The Eleventh Five-Year Plan (2007–2012) emphatically stated that a 'successful integration of survival, development, protection, and participation is closely linked to all aspects of a child's wellbeing' (p. 208). Notably the Plan was entrenched in a rights framework that viewed women and children as agents, not recipients. The Plan included a separate section on 'Children's rights' in the chapter 'Towards women's agency and children's rights', emphasizing the need for a protective environment ensuring every child's right to survival, participation and development. It recognized the importance of a holistic approach, focusing on child development outcomes and indicators as well as macro-perspective trends and governance issues. It recommended the need to undertake a children's rights review of all existing developmental policies and plans, to assess their impact on children to prevent their further marginalization. In order to address the lack of adequate budgetary allocations to children, it went on to create a Budget for

Children (BFC) as a percentage of the Union Budget with sectoral allocation and expenditure under the headings of health, development, education and protection.

BFC has in recent times garnered a lot of attention. For instance, the HAQ: Centre for Children's Rights, a civil society organization based in Delhi, has been publishing a decadal analysis of the Union Budget and States' budget allocation for children from a children's rights perspective. Their analysis of the Union Budget 2000–2001 to 2008–2009 showed that a mere 3.75 percent of the Union Budget was allocated for children (HAQ, 2010). The HAQ center critiques this small percentage, given the vast array of plans and policies to do with children and young people. The center cites this as a concrete example of the difference between governmental promises and its actual commitments.

The Twelfth Five-Year Plan had been pushing to 'make children an urgent priority' (p. 89) but children's right to participation does not find any mention in the approach document. The draft approach paper lays out the overall framework, strategy and goals that serve as a template and inform the preparation of the prospective Five-year plan.

In addition to the Five-Year Plans, four key policy documents – the National Policy on Education 1968 and 1986, the National Policy for Children 1974 and the National Plan of Action 1992 – can be read as concrete manifestation of the State's attempts to better the lot of its children and young people. They also narrate the growing policy attention to children and young people as a particular constituency.

National Policy on Education 1968 and 1986

In the mid-1960s the need to spread educational access came to the fore, particularly in the Kothari Commission report in 1964–1966 that recommended establishing a Common School System for all children irrespective of their class, caste or religious categories. The following National Policy on Education of 1968 was a significant step in that direction. However, it looked at education not as a specific right of the child but as a tool for nurturing citizenship attributes and strengthening social cohesion, thereby making it an instrument of the State's agenda. A little less than two decades later, the National Policy on Education 1986 focused on social inclusion. It called for the provision of equal educational opportunities for women, scheduled tribes and schedule caste communities, recognizing that women's empowerment was a crucial pre-condition for the participation of girls and women in the educational process.

National Policy for Children 1974

The first big policy impetus on children's development more generally came with the adoption of the National Policy for Children 1974. Emanating from India's commitment to the UN Declaration on the Rights of the Child 1959, this policy reaffirmed the constitutional provisions:

> that it shall be the policy of the State to provide adequate services to children, both before and after birth and through the period of growth to ensure their full physical, mental and social development.[6]

It is the first government policy document that uses the language of children's rights and directly addresses children's specific needs, especially implementing the First National Policy on Education in 1968.

National Plan of Action for Children

In the 1990s, as India formally adopted globalization and liberalization as State policy, civil society began to exert itself more strongly amidst fear of shrinking social welfare provisioning and a concomitant slimming of the State. This occurred as transnational discourses began to shape national debates and policy foci. In the light of such shifts in polity, politics and policymaking, following the World Summit on Children in 1990, India for the first time articulated a set of quantifiably deliverable and time-bound goals for children through a National Plan of Action (NPA) for Children in 1992. The 1992 NPA concentrated on the areas of child health, maternal health, nutrition, water and sanitation and education for children in especially difficult circumstances.

On February 9, 2004, the Government adopted the National Charter for Children, which was a statement of intent embodying its agenda for children. The document emphasized the State's commitment to: children's rights to survival, health and nutrition, standard of living, leisure, early childhood care, education, protection of the girl child, equality, life and liberty, name and nationality, freedom of expression, freedom of association and peaceful assembly, the right to a family and the right to be protected from economic exploitation and all forms of abuse.

The following year, the 2005 NPA held that in

all actions concerning children, whether undertaken by public or private institutions, courts of law, quasi-judicial bodies, executive or legislative bodies, the best interests of the child shall be a primary consideration .... besides looking upon this population below the age of 18 as constituting a significant national asset. (p. 2)

The 2005 NPA committed itself to providing the following four rights to every child – child survival, child development, child protection and child participation. It further stated that its guiding principle was to 'regard the child as an asset and a person with human rights' and to accord utmost priority to the most disadvantaged, poorest of the poor and least served children in all policy and programmatic interventions (NPA, 2005, p. 3). Child participation and choice in matters and decisions affecting their lives was one of the 12 key areas identified by the NPA 2005, making it one of the first documents to address directly children's right to participation.

Besides the policies discussed in the preceding account, there has been a slew of legislative action on children's rights especially in the last ten years, including those of Protection of Children's Rights Act 2005 and the setting up of the National Commissions for Protection of Children's Rights (NCPCR) Act 2006.

Part III: The state of children and young people's participation in India

The previous section shows that children and young people's participation in formal policy has not gained any serious policy and legislative interest in the last decade or so. Little wonder that a suitable model or even practice for children and young people's participation has yet to emerge. This becomes all the more pressing given that two-fifths of the population in our society are composed of children and young people and yet this vast population has fewer spaces than others to let their opinions be known or factored in on issues that concern them. Interestingly, while the initial push for children's right to participation resulted from developments outside of India, the first concrete experiments and mobilizations can be credited to local non-governmental organization (NGOs) rather than their international counterparts. Figure 6.1 shows the different actors (State and non-State) and the opportunities they have made available for children and young people's participation in India.

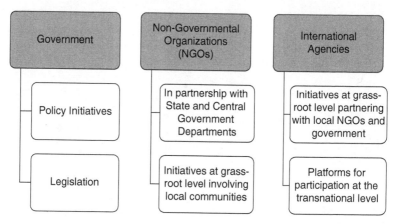

Figure 6.1 Formal and non-formal actors working on children and young people's participation in India

Government policies and initiatives to promote children and young people's participation

National policies are frequently framed within the 'best interests of the child', echoing Article 3 of the United Nations Convention on the Rights of the Child (UNCRC). More recently, the right to participation has gained attention as well. The NPA 2005 is guided by the philosophy to empower all children and young people as citizens and to facilitate their participation. It aims to build children and young people's competencies in decision-making and communication in all matters concerning and affecting them. To this end, all stakeholders should contribute including family, community, schools and institutions, as well as judicial and administrative bodies, to promote children and young people's participation. The mechanisms to achieve these rights can be divided into three strands.

First, awareness on children's rights, laws and policies should be promoted, especially amongst children and young people belonging to marginalized classes, so that they internalize them. Using multimedia to do so is particularly mentioned. Second, families and program planners, administrators in government and NGOs and other civil society organizations should respect the views of children and young people and integrate opportunities for their participation. Third, strategic partnerships should be developed with families and local communities, administrative and social structures including school management, village councils, local governance committees and so on to address the traditional constraints to children and young people's participation. Together, the strands aim to create enabling environments and spaces for participation in the daily lives of children and young people. These include establishing children's groups, councils, associations and forums and strengthening NGOs' capacity to facilitate participation. The NPA recommends research to document best practices of participation.

The National Commission for the Protection of Children's Rights

Headway in securing children's rights in general and that of participation in particular was made in March 2007, when the Government set up the NCPCR. The NCPCR was set up to protect, promote and defend children's rights in India. It is entrusted with a supervisory task of ensuring that law and policymaking are in keeping with the framework upheld by the UNCRC (especially Article 12) as well as the Constitution of India.

The NCPCR maintains that meaningful children's participation is integral to addressing children's rights in the 'best interests of the child'.[7] It facilitates participation to enable children and young people to access their rights and entitlements. The Rules of the Commission for Protection of Child Rights Act 2005 require the Commission's work to be informed by children and young people's views, so the work reflects their priorities and perspectives. To this end, NCPCR has ensured that it listens to children and young people, child advocates and voices from the ground, responding to direct complaints and taking *suo moto* (an act of authority or a judge, taken without formal prompting from another party) cognizance of violations of children's rights. Some mechanisms for this include: forming thematic working groups; consultations through seminars, public hearings, workshops and conferences; and highlighting issues relating to children and young people so that the judicial and other administrative systems address gaps in recognizing children and young people's entitlements.

The NCPCR undertakes State visits to assess children and young people's lives in local areas through *gram panchayats* (meaning grassroots institutions of governance at the village level, discussed in detail below). Most importantly, the NCPCR has been organizing hearings in which children and young people's grievances are publicly heard in the presence of the NCPCR and senior government officials. For instance, its public hearings in cotton seed farming revealed the ordeals of India's child laborers, when a delegation visited Banaskantha and Sabarkantha districts to investigate allegations of child labor being used in Bt cotton fields (Shah, 2011). In another part of the country, the testimonies of children and young people affected and infected with HIV and AIDS in the public hearings in Manipur revealed their stigmatization and the lack of health services available to them (NCPCR, 2010). NCPCR's public hearings in the Maoist conflict-ridden, South Bastar region of

Chhattisgarh in India showed tribal children and young people's fears and vulnerabilities, and the denial of their basic rights to education and health care facilities (NCPCR, 2007).

Organizations facilitating children and young people's participation at the national level

Besides these major steps by the state, over the years there has been a steady growth in the number of *Bal Panchayats*, Child Assemblies/ Parliaments and *Bal Manchas* attempting to promote children and young people's participation. At the national level, organizations like *Nehru Yuva Kendra Sangathan* (NYKS), *Bal Bhawan* Society (which organizes sports and recreational activities for children) and the *Bharat* Scouts and Guide (with its history dating back to the colonial India and primarily given to activities to ensure full physical, intellectual and spiritual development of children and youth) have been initiating various programs and activities to encourage participation of children and young people in India. The *Nehru Yuva Kendra Sangathan* (NYKS) was set up in 1987–1988 as an autonomous organization under the Government of India, Ministry of Youth Affairs and Sports to channel the power of youth along the principles of voluntarism, self-help and community participation. Over the years, NYKS has been forming Youth Clubs, which are village level voluntary action groups of youth at the grassroots level to involve them in nation-building activities.[8]

Children's participation at the local government level: *Bal Panchayats* in India

Increasingly, children and young people seem to be better organized and tend to participate more successfully having negotiated formal recognition by local government officials. They have done so by establishing their own *Bal Panchayats* (children's assemblies), which are recognized by their adult equivalent. The *Panchayat*, a grassroots locally based institution, is structurally a feasible forum for children's participation enabling them to build a close relationship with elected adult representatives. These *Bal Panchayats*, promoted by a combination of the State and non-profit organizations across India (for example see case study Chapter 7), have been functional for over a decade now and have brought a turnaround in children and young people's participation – especially in rural India. Typically they are meant to work with the *Gram Panchayat* (in Hindi meaning a village level 'Assembly of Five'), the local self-government at the village level in India, and have been central to fostering grassroots democracy.

Pioneering in this regard has been the State of Karnataka, which has incorporated children and young people's participation for over 15 years. As early as 1995 The Concerned for Working Children (CWC) organization introduced *Makkala Panchayats* (Children's Councils) in rural Karnataka. The organization runs forums for, by and of children by creating spaces for children within the *Panchayati Raj* Institutions. What started out as an experiment in 1995 with five *Makkala Panchayats* today has over 50 active forums. Eventually this experiment was institutionalized. In 2006 the Rural Development and *Panchayati Raj* Department of Karnataka issued an order to make it mandatory for all *Panchayats* in the state to provide a platform for children and young people to voice their concerns before the elected representatives at special children and young people's *Gram Sabhas* annual meetings. In terms of the organizational structure, *Makkala Panchayats* are composed of representatives elected by all children and young people between 6 and 18 years in the *Gram Panchayat* area, as well as a proportional representation system with leaders from across interest groups. A tripartite task force, consisting of *Makkala* and *Gram Panchayat* representatives, government officials, elected representatives and community-based organizations, is set up to link the *Makkala Panchayats* with the *Gram Panchayats*. The *Makkala Panchayats* funding come from the Ministry of Rural Development and Decentralization, Karnataka.

The urban corollary of *Makkala Panchayats* can be seen in the formation of *Bhima Sangha* and *Namma Sabha* in the state's capital city, Bangalore, the renowned IT hub of the country. In Bangalore where there is no *Makkala Panchayat* and Task Force, children and young people have devised innovative ways of getting the Municipal Corporation to accede to their demands, including mass rallies, demonstrations, using mainstream media and publishing enquiry committee reports, exposing the exploitation of children working in urban occupations (Reddy and Ratna, 2002).

Violence, abuse, harassment by police and shelter are the main concerns of *Bhima Sangha* in rural areas. Expansion of job opportunities, issues of migration and hazardous employment in urban areas are priorities for *Makkala Panchayats*. Children and young people have taken up issues of adults, like banning of arrack (alcohol) and asking for the prevention of child marriages. The result is 'a humanization of the adults of the community and the entry of a new ethic with regard to governance and all dealings' (Reddy and Ratna, 2002, p. 27). Furthermore, Karnataka has nurtured 'child friendly legislators', willing to raise children's issues in State Assemblies. A 'children's manifesto' drafted by children and young people themselves was prepared in advance of the Assembly Elections of Kerala and Karnataka in 2006 and 2008 respectively.

Other State governments like Maharashtra, Goa and Bihar have set up children's parliaments, suggesting such forums are gaining formal recognition with the political class. In Bihar, they are commonly called the *Bal Sansad* (in Hindi meaning children's parliament) and they operate in most elementary schools.

Similarly, in the desert state of Rajasthan, the positive interventions by the Social Work Research Centre (SWRC) in Tilonia have resulted in setting up of *Bal Panchayats*, which actively serve to sensitize children and young people about their rights. The SWRC community work includes night schools, which cater to the needs of rural working children and young people. The SWRC eventually supported them to set up their own *Bal Sansad* in the early 1990s to teach children and young people about democratic systems, the electoral process and the functioning of a government (O'Kane, 2003).

The 'NGOization' of children and young people's participation

As stated above, local NGOs took the lead in promoting children and young people's participation, especially in regards to the rights of street and working children. They helped children and young people form their own unions and initiate programs to empower marginalized children and young people (UNICEF, 2004). A clutch of NGOs, like the Delhi-based *Bachpan Bachao Andolan* (BBA), Community Aid and Sponsorship Program (CASP) and *Bal Utasav* among others, has also facilitated *Bal Panchayats*. In metros and in Delhi, highly networked and large NGOs like Child Rights and You (CRY), through its *Bal Panchayat*, take up children's rights at the national level using media across platforms including the internet. One innovative variation of a children's collective is modeled by another Delhi-based NGO, *Chetanalaya*. 'Neighborhood Children Parliaments' (NCPs) allow children and young people to voice local concerns and play an active role in finding their own solutions, with the help of elders and local authorities. NCPs are organized at the level of each *gali* (street) or village such that nearly 30 children from neighboring houses gather together and form one Children's Parliament. Every NCP elects its own Prime Minister and

Council of Ministers including portfolios like health, education, sports, law, social justice, etc. NCPs are organized at local, block, district, state and national level and even congregate into a world parliament.

O'Kane (2003) discussed how Young India Project (YIP) has a long history of supporting the formation and development of agricultural wage laborers unions in Southern Andhra Pradesh and has worked with children and young people since 1999. So far, YIP has effectively promoted the formation of Child Clubs in 40 villages and is working towards forming *Sanghas* in at least ten of them. Under *Bal Sanghas* (Children's Unions), children and young people have organized rallies and other activities against sexual abuse and harassment, re-enrollment of dropouts in school, developed wall-slogans and dramas on HIV/AIDS and planted trees (O'Kane, 2003)

Another NGO based in Delhi, Butterflies, has been organizing the Butterflies Program of Street and Working Children (for more see Panicker, 1996). It is informed by a democratic, participatory, rights-based and non-institutional approach to children's rights.[9] Their strategy is to organize street and working children and young people through street educators, at contact points in places where the children and young people congregate. The apex body of Butterflies is the *Bal Sabha* (Children's Council) where children and young people meet fortnightly to discuss issues that concern them, ranging from education, police harassment and wages. Since 1991, Butterflies has also initiated a Child Workers Union (*Bal Mazdoor* Union). Its other collectives for children and young people include the use of media platforms like print, radio and theatre through programs like, the *Bal Mazdoor kee Awaaz* (Child Workers' Voice), Butterflies *Bal Rang Manch* (theatre group), Butterflies Broadcasting Children, and a Children's Development Bank called *Bal Vikas* Bank.

International agencies addressing children and young people's participation in India

International agencies have played a key role in introducing to India a participatory approach to strengthen children's rights. They have made available pedagogical roadmaps for local NGOs and provided financial assistance and technical support to develop an understanding of children's rights, extending the notion of citizenship to children and young people. The efforts of UNICEF and Save the Children have been seminal in this regard.

UNICEF's work is more at the policymaking level, using its international reputation to lobby governments on the need for children and young people's participation at regional and international levels

(UNICEF, 2004). A second approach used by UNICEF has been to link up with local NGOs as well as state actors. One such program, the Child Reporters Initiative, uses the media effectively to give children and young people the means to express their views publicly. In Orissa, the UNICEF spearheaded the initiative called 'Child Reporters Reporting on Children's Issues'. The children and young people produced a bimonthly newspaper called *Ankurodgama* (in Hindi translated as 'the sprouting of a seed').[10] Under this, children and young people reported on a host of issues ranging from the paucity of safe water, child marriages, poor educational opportunities and food insecurity. Four years on, the program involves more than 1,800 children, aged 10 to 14 years, from over 150 schools within Koraput. Lalatendu (2010) discusses how the reporters have acted as 'agents of change' in Koraput.

In Maharashtra, another leading international NGO working on children's rights, Save the Children Canada, partnered with a local NGO *Paryay*, to form *Bal Panchayats* in Tuljapur Block of Osmanabad district in 2002 to facilitate children and young people's participation in community development programs. This project has expanded to 15 villages with a special emphasis on working children who were out of school (O'Kane, 2003). Also, in the Himalayan region of Ladakh and Kashmir, Save the Children UK has supported children and young people since 1997 to form their own Children's Committees for Village Development (CCVDs). Through these, children and young people have sought reforms in the education system and have demanded better roads and health facilities. In Kargil, the CCVDs came together and organized a march in the Kargil town, forcing district education authorities' attention to children and young people's plight in receiving a proper school education and limited opportunities available to them. Overall the children and young people sought a review of the overall system.[11]

Children and young people's participation and the enabling role of media

Apart from the triple levels of the state, NGOs at local and national levels and large international agencies, the media have a special role to play in spreading awareness about children's rights in general and children and young people's participation in particular. News media raise children and young people's issues in the public domain and build a critical public sphere that recognizes children and young people as citizens with rights. News stories can ensure that any violations of children's rights are heavily reported and such stories cross the classification of 'soft human-interest stories', as they are called in the newsroom parlance, and acquire the status of 'national stories'. For instance, media coverage has raised public attention to the numerous responses and complaints made to the NCPCR on corporal punishment, child malnutrition, poor educational infrastructure, child labor and trafficking, and child abuse. The Commission categorically states on its website that its *suo moto* cases were brought to its attention by print and electronic media. It acknowledges the media's role at all levels – local, state and national – in reporting cases of violations and also generating public debate.

Conclusion

So while India has ratified the UNCRC, more effective implementation would address the disjuncture between policies and practice, theoretical assumptions and concrete outcomes. Bridging these could take a long time. Even though steps have been taken in the last decade, the spaces and structures available for children and young people's participation are not enough to do justice to the vast population in the country. Many programs are geared less to building a critical consciousness about children's right to participation and more to fulfilling the requirements of the sponsoring agencies.

So even if children and young people's participation in India is growing, the fear of its colonization by a handful of NGOs cannot be dismissed entirely. The problem with this is that it does not necessarily create a culture of children and young people's participation in society at large; instead, the State shifts the onus of responsibility (that it has towards its citizens) to the arena of non-state actors and organizations. The very sustainability of these NGOs is heavily dependent on foreign funding, making the entire exercise ad hoc and incapable of creating a lasting impact. The shift to NGOs might amount to either the State's withdrawal from such welfare programs or even the undermining of its authority. At a more systemic level, real changes have to be brought about to impact positively on key development indices, especially in education, food and health sectors, in order for children and young people to be able to participate fully in their communities. A shift in attitude and perceptions from looking upon children and young people as objects of pity that the State must provide for to citizens with social and political entitlements will go a long way in preparing society to accept children and young people in more participatory and not dependent roles. Therefore, there is a need to create enabling spaces for children and young people's participation on the one hand, and an environment that is supportive of and respects children on the other. Both children-centric and children-sensitive production of media content can help them to understand their own issues better and enable them to participate and articulate the same in public. Further, news producers need to be made aware of the UNCRC literature and primed to a child-rights discourse perspective in order to add value and right orientation to the kind of reportage that children and young people have so far attracted in India. Such critical reportage can play the role of a whistleblower and the footage can be used as evidence to address the violations of children's rights. There is an urgent need to prepare adults, children and young people for such a marked shift. Moreover, the media can play a critical role in the kind of cultural and representational rights that it accords to children and young people both in their portrayal and in providing access to the communicative architecture in order to instill them with the confidence to participate and ultimately to prepare them as future citizenry based on dialogical and democratic exchange.

The concept of children and young people's participation is still to be internalized by society at large. Three steps are required: first, rights programming and on-ground intervention, evaluation and monitoring to see if targets have been met; second, legislation and policymaking that addresses the right to participation; and, finally, a proactive media as a sentinel for children's rights to ensure that a critical mass of information and public knowledge about children's rights and, more importantly, about the right to participation is made available in the public sphere. This production and dissemination of rights information through media should not be kneejerk or event-based as is usually the case; instead it should be issue-based with a sustained coverage over a long period of time, in order for it to be entrenched in public consciousness so that we as a society learn to listen to children and young people.

Notes

1. For details on ICDS see http://wcd.nic.in/icds.htm.
2. See media reports like http://www.ndtv.com/article/india/bihar-s-mid-day-meal-disaster-forensic-report-confirms-presence-of-pesticide-in-food-394958.
3. See *The Hindu* news report at http://www.thehindu.com/news/national/other-states/chapra-on-the-boil-after-midday-meal-disaster/article4925001.ece.
4. See literacy rate in the provisional population totals in the Census of India, 2011 at http://www.censusindia.gov.in/2011-prov-results/indiaatglance.html.

5. See UNICEF country report's India section at http://www.unicef.org/infoby country/india_background.html.
6. The policy document is available at http://wcd.nic.in/national_policy_for_children_1974.pdf.
7. See webpage of NCPCR available at http://ncpcr.gov.in/.
8. For details on NYKS activities visit its homepage at: http://www.nyks.org/.
9. See the website at: http://www.butterflieschildrights.org/strategy.php.
10. For more information refer to the webpage: http://www.unicef.org/infoby country/india_50846.html, date accessed 27 March, 2013.
11. Refer to the newspaper article archived at: http://www.jammu-kashmir.com/archives/archives2002/kashmir20020402d.html.

Bibliography

Census of India (2001) *Census Data Online*, http://censusindia.gov.in/2011-common/censusdataonline.html.
Census of India (2011) *Provisional Population Totals of 2011*, http://www.census india.gov.in/2011-prov-results/PPT_2.html.
Eleventh Five-Year Plan (2008) *Volume II: Social Sector*, (New Delhi: Oxford University Press).
Gragnolati, M., Shekar, M., Das Gupta, M., Bredenkamp, C. and Lee, Y. (2005) *India's Undernourished Children: A Call for Reform and Action: Health, Nutrition and Population (HNP)*, (Washington DC: World Bank).
HAQ: Centre for Child Rights (2010) *Budget for Children: A Summary Report 2004–2005 to 2008–2009*, (New Delhi: HAQ: Centre for Child Rights).
India Alliance for Children's rights (IACR), review note submitted on the September 17, 2004, Day of Discussion of the UN Committee on the Rights of the Child on the issue 'Implementing Children's rights in Early Childhood', CRC review note #1: 'India's Girl Child: Crisis of "Early Disposal" (Declining Juvenile Sex Ratio – 0–6 years)'.
Kabeer, N. (2001) 'Deprivation, discrimination and delivery: Competing explanations for child labor and educational failure in South Asia', IDS Working Paper No. 135, (Brighton: Institute of Development Studies).
Lalatendu, A. (2010) 'Child Reporters as agents of change' in B. Percy-Smith and N. Thomas (eds) *A Handbook of Children and Young People's Participation: Perspectives from Theory and Practice*, (London and New York: Routledge).
National Commission for Protection of Child Rights (NCPCR) (2007) *Visit to Dantewada (Chhattisgarh) & Khamman (Andhra Pradesh): To Investigate Status of Health and Education of Children affected by Civil Unrest*, (New Delhi: NCPCR).
National Commission for Protection of Child Rights (NCPCR) (2010) *Rights and Entitlements of Children Affected and Infected by HIV/AIDS 2010–2011*, (New Delhi: NCPCR).
National Commission for Protection of Child Rights (NCPCR) (2013) *Media and Child Rights*, http://www.ncpcr.gov.in/childparticipationtv.htm, date accessed 15 September, 2013
National Plan of Action for Children (1992) *Department of Women and Child Development and Ministry of Human Resource Development*, http://wcd.nic.in/npac.htm.

National Plan of Action for Children (2005) *Ministry of Human Resource Development and Department of Women and Child Development*, http://wcd.nic.in/napaug16a.pdf.

O'Kane, C. (2003) *Children and Young People as Citizens: Partners for Social Change*, (Kathmandu: Save the Children, South and Central Asia).

Panicker, R. (1996) *History of Butterflies Programme of Street and Working Children: Our Experience in Empowering Children*, (Delhi: Butterflies Programme of Street and Working Children).

Planning Commission (2011) *Faster Sustainable and More Inclusive Growth: An Approach to the Twelfth Five Year Plan (2012–2017)*, (New Delhi: Government of India).

Population Foundation of India and the Population Reference Bureau (2007) *The Future Population of India: A Long-range Demographic View*, (Delhi: Ajanta Offset and Packagings Ltd.).

Reddy, N. and Ratna, K. (2002) *A Journey in Children's Participation*, (Bangalore: Concerned for Working Children).

Saravanan, S. (2000) *Violence against Women in India: A Literature Review*, (New Delhi: Institute of Social Studies Trust (ISST)).

Shah, R. (2011) *Bt cotton fostering illegal child labor?*, Times of India, September 2, 2011.

Sinha, D. (2006) 'Rethinking ICDS: A Rights Based Perspective', *Economic and Political Weekly*, 41(34), 3689–3694.

UNICEF (2004) *Wheel of Change: Children and Young People's Participation in South Asia*, (Kathmandu: United Nations Children's Fund, Regional Office for South Asia: Kathmandu).

UNICEF (2009) *Progress for Children: A Report Card on Child Protection, Number 8* (New York: UNICEF).

World Bank (2013) UNICEF (2009) *Progress for Children: A Report Card on Child Protection, number 8* (New York: UNICEF). *World Bank Development Indicators*, http://data.worldbank.org/indicator/SP.DYN.IMRT.IN, date accessed 7 July, 2013.

7
Transformative Participation: Experiences of a Children's *Sangam* in Tamil Nadu (South India)

Carine Le Borgne

Introduction

Arunodhaya (Centre for Street and Working Children) is a non-profit children's rights organization, founded in 1992 in Chennai. The organization's vision is to create 'a just society in which every child enjoys childhood assured of its rights with dignity and happiness'. In the past decade, *Arunodhaya* has delivered integrated programs to remove children and young people from the labor force and mainstream them into formal education. Their motto is 'say no to child labor and yes to education'. It has adopted a community-centered approach by involving different stakeholders of the community, including children and young people, parents, a women's self-help group,[1] employers,[2] community leaders and schools. In 2000–2001, they introduced children's rights and children and young people's participation rights through children's clubs. Later on, these were named children's *sangam*.

This case study considers, firstly, *Arunodhaya's* experience of implementing children and young people's participation and, secondly, the path of three former members of the children's *sangam* to draw attention to the transformative potential of children and young people's participation. Whilst acknowledging the many challenges in implementing children and young people's participation in meaningful ways, the goal here is to highlight that participation can transform both individuals and society at large.

The case study is partly based on the work that I carried out in 2008 when *Arunodhaya* asked its funding agency, *Asmae-Association Soeur Emmanuelle*,[3] to do an impact evaluation of the children's *sangam*. At the time, I documented the children's *sangam* model and undertook surveys (with children and young people, parents and local leaders),

114 *Children and Young People's Participation*

discussion groups (with children and young people, parents and staff) and interviews (with four former members between 19 and 22 years). This case study is also based on interviews that I conducted in 2013 for my PhD, with the director, a former staff member, a board member, three former members of children's *sangam* (now 22 to 24 years old) and an academic from a local university in order to gain a better understanding of the wider context of children's participation in Tamil Nadu. In this work, ethical considerations have been a high priority, including consent and anonymity for workers, children and young people. It was agreed from the start that the organization would be named.

Background

Arunodhaya (Centre for Street and Working Children) is located in Chennai, the capital and the largest city of the state of Tamil Nadu in the South East of India. With a population of 72.14 million people, Tamil Nadu is one of the most populous states in India (Census of India, 2011). The majority of Tamil Nadu's population (88 percent) is Hindus (Census of India, 2001).[4]

According to the Human Development Index, Tamil Nadu ranks sixth amongst the 28 Indian states (Suryanarayana et al., 2011). Tamil Nadu is one of the most prosperous states with the second largest per capita income in India. Life expectancy in the state was 66.2 years in the early 2000s – just above the India average of 63.5 years (Suryanarayana et al., 2011). In 2004–2005, the mean years of schooling of the adult population (those aged 25 and above) was 4.79 years. This is just above the national average of 4.10 years but well below the goalpost for the Human Development Index of 20.6 years of schooling (Suryanarayana et al., 2011). In an effort to close this gap, the Government of India has enacted the Right of Children to Free and Compulsory Education (RTE) Act 2009. This provides free and compulsory education to all children in the age group of 6 to 14 years. As noted in the previous Chapter, the RTE came into effect nationally on April 1, 2010. It took, however, another 17 months to be implemented by the Tamil Nadu government.[5]

Arunodhaya origins

Arunodhaya first opened separate child laborer centers for boys and girls, as transitional settings before they joined formal schooling. In 1996, evening centers were established to assist children and young people with their studies and help them remain in school. Later on, in 2000, fortnightly sessions were organized by *Arunodhaya* staff at the evening centers to address special issues including value education sessions, moral values and an introduction to children's rights.

Arunodhaya has been developing children and young people's participation since 2001, as part of its overall aim to include former child workers in mainstream schools. The organization seeks to work with children and young people to give them an understanding of their rights and their ability to contribute to the society.

As participants become more aware of their rights and keen to take actions, *Arunodhaya* established ten children's clubs in May 2001. These clubs aimed to provide spaces where children and young people could come together to discuss issues that were important to them, to set up campaigns and to learn about their rights. As these groups became more established, *Arunodhaya* organized a three-day leadership and motivation residential camp to gather leaders from each children's club to draw up a list of actions they wanted from *Arunodhaya*. This list included an expectation that *Arunodhaya* would organize fortnightly meetings after school and conduct an annual survey on children and young people's education status. Children and young people also wanted the organization to do more to eradicate child labor in the community.

In 2004, during a residential camp, children and young people decided to change the group's name from children's club to children's *sangam*, as the latter means a platform where people can express their views. They felt this was an important change as they wanted others to recognize the collective as a group of children and young people 'acting' rather than simply 'playing'. In later years, members prepared their own definition of children and young people's participation, as follows:

Children's participation refers to children expressing themselves, taking decisions, planning, implementing and evaluating their activities with guidance of the adults in matters concerning children.

This definition largely evolved from children and young people's experiences in the children's *sangam*. *Arunodhaya* adopted this definition and later included it on its child participation policy as a tool to mainstream participation through the organization. It is important to note, however, that the inclusion of 'guidance of adults' came from the staff rather than from children and young people, indicating the central role of (adult) members of staff in facilitating this participation process. The role of (adult) members of staff within the children's *sangam* is a point to which I shall return to later on in the chapter.

The children's sangam model

In 2013, there are 75 children's *sangams* in Chennai, with a total membership of 1,697 underprivileged children and young people aged between 10 and 18 years old. Both girls and boys who live in slum areas are involved in the activities.

There are three levels of participation in the children's *sangam*. The first level is the community. Children and young people meet twice a month after school to review and plan activities of the children's *sangam*. Decisions are reached through informal votes and leaders (president, secretary and treasurer) are elected every six months. Meetings are led by the members with the support of *Arunodhaya* staff.

Second, at the zonal level, representatives from the community level meet every three months to discuss events and programs for the zone. A zonal executive committee is elected and reviews community reports are submitted by representatives. They also serve as a go-between for the community level and the confederation level network.

Third, at the confederation network level, representatives from the zonal levels and the confederation executive committee[6] meet every three months to discuss common issues to all areas. This provides a forum for members to share their experiences, evaluate activities, discuss overarching issues such as a Convention topic[7] and develop a strategic plan.

Activities of the children's sangam

The children's *sangam* organizes a number of activities for and with children and young people, with the aim of supporting them to claim their rights. Those activities are as follows.

Capacity building

Capacity building is a major part of the children's *sangam* activities. For *Arunodhaya*'s director, 'capacity building is essential as children and young people need to be very well informed'. The members have the opportunity to participate in different residential training addressing:

Figure 7.1 Former member introducing the Children's *Sangam* newsletter to the members
Photographer: Carine Le Borgne, 2013.

Figure 7.2 Young facilitators capacity building
Photographer: Carine Le Borgne, 2008.

young facilitators, leadership, journalism,[8] and cultural activities. These activities usually take place in May during the summer holiday to facilitate children and young people's attendance. Capacity building aims to empower children and young people through enhancing their abilities and knowledge.

Actions on children's rights violations

In the children's *sangam*, children and young people can advocate and lobby, to defend their rights and to improve their situations. The struggle against child labor is one of the main concerns of this children's organization. Every year, on the 12 June, children and young people organize awareness-raising activities to eradicate child labor. Around the same time, the members also conduct a survey on the education status of children and young people (they go house to house in their area and ask parents whether their children are attending school or not).

Issues arise from the children's *sangam* themselves. For example, Prem[9] (a member of the children's *sangam*) has campaigned to address the lack of privacy in male and female toilets in his school. After learning of an incident at his school, Prem worked with *Arunodhaya* staff to gather evidence about the lack of privacy in the school toilets. He then wrote a report to the Education Commission Office to demand a resolution. As a direct result of Prem's report, a wall was built to separate the boys' from the girls' toilets.

Generally, after identifying issues in the community, members of the children's *sangam* write petitions to adult decision-makers such as local leaders and municipal councilors. Then *Arunodhaya* staff arrange a meeting with such decision-makers to present the petitions. Time to obtain what the petition asks for varies considerably: sometimes three or four months to have street lights fixed or areas cleaned; sometimes one to three years to repair roads and improve transport facilities. Children and young people reach out to the community by organizing national celebrations in their community.

Ensuring children and young people's participation in family

Parents' meetings were established in 2005. Children and young people wanted to build up a relationship with their parents, to orient them to the children's *sangam* and to involve their parents in their activities. Further, the meetings sought to change parents' views about children and young people and help increase children and young people's participation within their families. Most of the mothers who participate in the parents' meetings are involved in the Self Help Group (SHG) or in the Domestic

Workers group in the *Arunodhaya* projects. This is an advantage for the children's *sangam* activities as mothers come to trust the staff and then encourage their children to participate in the activities.

It is, however, mainly mothers who are involved in the meetings. Fathers are still difficult to reach. *Arunodhaya's* director is hopeful that the present generation of boys involved in the children's *sangam* will lead to more paternal involvement in the future. She also hopes that, as members of the children's *sangam* grow up, they will be a strong force against the violation of children's rights and strongly advocate for children and young people.

Transformative 'potential' of the children's *sangam* and challenges

To illustrate how participation in the children's *sangam* can be transformative, the stories of three former members of children's *sangam* (Sadish, Devna and Mani) aged from 22 to 24 years old are presented. For these young people, taking part of the children's *sangam* activities has transformed their lives. Their testimonies indicate that their participation also has the potential to transform society. Nevertheless, as further explained later, there are still many challenges in making transformative participation an integral part of life in Tamil Nadu.

Three former members' stories

Sadish

From the ages of five to eight years, Sadish worked in a steel factory with his father and two older brothers. When *Arunodhaya* intervened in this factory, Sadish was taken away by *Arunodhaya* with the agreement of his parents. He joined the *Arunodhaya's* child laborer center (transit school run by *Arunodhaya*) before enrolling in a formal school. At the age of ten, he was one of the first to join the children's *sangam* and he remained a member for eight years. Sadish was the president of the children's *sangam* for one year.

Sadish continues to volunteer with *Arunodhaya* despite his other commitments; he is now undertaking his third College degree, has different part-time jobs and has recently become a father. According to Sadish, he is motivated to continue volunteering because:

> Today whatever I have is because of this *sangam*. Without them, I would have definitely been just a daily wage laborer or a coolie. I should not forget that it is only because of them that I have achieved all this.

For Sadish, participation in the children's *sangam* has changed his life and he is now committed to make children's rights a reality for others. When I asked him what job he was planning to do, he told me with determination, 'I want to become a politician.' This idea arises from his childhood experiences: 'Because I was a child laborer when I was young, I do not want the other children to suffer like me.' His first political priority is to stop child labor. His second priority is to assist women for, he says, 'It's not safe for women here.' I asked Sadish why he wanted to become a politician and not work for a non-governmental organization (NGO) lobbying for such improvements, as political corruption is a major issue in India. His answer was clear: NGOs submit demands to politicians but he does not want to be the one who makes the demands; he wants to be the one who receives them. He added that, 'Even though the corruption scares me, the reform will come from inside.'

By becoming a politician, Sadish hopes that he will be able to effectuate wider changes to the way in which children, young people and women are viewed in society.

Mani

Mani was involved in *Arunodhaya*'s tuition classes, and then joined his children's *sangam* when he was ten years old. He attended a few capacity building events and started to express himself during these sessions. Children, young people and staff encouraged him to continue to speak up. Through the capacity building events he attended, he discovered hidden talents such as drawing, writing, singing and team management and learnt the *parai* (a traditional music instrument).

When he was president of the *Confederation of Arunodhaya Children's Sangam*, his relationship with his mother changed. Previously, his mother had been very strict. For instance, he had to return home by 6 pm every day. One day, when Mani went back home, his mother was crying as she was just watching him on TV, shaking hands with a politician. She understood that he was doing something good and started asking him questions about the children's *sangam* activities and allowed him to come back home late.

After leaving the children's *sangam* at the age of 18 years, he joined the central committee[10] with Sadish and Devna to keep connected with *Arunodhaya*. He went on a two-year course in film technology multimedia. During his second year, he questioned what he wanted to do with his life:

I was selfish, thinking about my own personal life to grow, I sat on the road and saw children in the street without proper guidance. I took some time to think about who I am.

He decided 'to become a director of a NGO and do something different, not copy other NGOs.' He wanted to work with children and young people to help them recognize and develop their 'hidden talents'. He discussed his project with some friends from the children's *sangam* and they agreed to work together. Mani sought to learn how a NGO functions by being part of the staff of *Arunodhaya*. From his experience, Mani has learnt so far that 'if you work with passion, you find more positive things in your life.' He is also transferring what he had expected from the staff when he was a member, such as being friendly and giving new information and knowledge to others in a dynamic way.

Devna

Devna joined the children's *sangam* as she was taking tuition classes with *Arunodhaya*. As the family did not have enough money to pay her school fees, her father decided to send her to work as a domestic worker. Devna used to work before and after school. Meanwhile, she continued to be involved in the children's *sangam* as the employer allowed her to attend the fortnightly meetings.

Devna also had the opportunity to attend capacity building events with the children's *sangam* at the local and international levels with Child Workers in Asia (CWA) in Sri Lanka and Thailand. As part of the young facilitator team, she used to train members of the children's *sangam*, as well as *Arunodhaya*'s and other NGOs staff on children's rights and participation.

Due to her involvement in the children's *sangam*, she gained a part-time job to co-ordinate/organize the domestic workers' project in her area. Since that time, Devna continues to work with *Arunodhaya* and is now in charge of four projects, including the children's *sangam* in her area. In her work she makes use of her skills developed in the children's *sangam*, such as planning, writing and facilitator skills. Being part of the children's *sangam*, she is able to share her experience with current members.

Apart from her work, Devna continues to study; she has enrolled for a distance-learning Master degree in Sociology. She is still in contact with former *sangam* members and is part of the aforementioned project helping children and young people to discover their hidden talents. She added, 'Wherever I am, whether there is an organization or not, I will take it upon myself to organize children into groups and work with them.'

The experience of the three former members illustrates how, by supporting the development of individual skills, such as communication, planning and leadership skills, the children's *sangams* have transformed the lives of these young people. These activities have fostered their enthusiasm to contribute to society. Indeed, all of them wish to be an actor of change through being involved in politics, part of *Arunodhaya* staff or in creating their own NGO. Friendships that they have gained with members of the children's *sangam* during their childhood make them stronger as young adults and able to continue to develop projects together. Their involvement in the children's *sangam* allowed them to overcome difficulties in their childhoods and gave them new aspirations. They are the first generation in their families to go to college. Their processes of individual transformation therefore have the potential of having a wider societal impact.

From these three case studies, it would seem that the alchemy of transformative participation takes time. All three young people were involved with *Arunodhaya* for at least eight years, volunteering in the organization and/or being part of the staff. They had the opportunity to gain knowledge on children's rights and children and young people's participation, and to practice it during their childhood in the children's *sangam*, in their families and communities.

To conclude this section, *Arunodhaya* aims to change the status of children and young people in society through its activities and projects and by fostering new relationships between children, young people and adults. By participating in the children's *sangam*, a generation of young adults is now committed to implementing, defending and promoting children and young people's participation. They are the future workforce that is mature, confident, articulate and has the capacity for critical thinking. They are becoming parents of the next generation of children that will, potentially, be more aware of their rights and able to participate.

Challenges faced by children's sangam for transformative participation

The following part will consider challenges in implementing children and young people's participation, from the viewpoints of the adult interviewees.

According to the director, a key challenge is staff perception of children and young people's capacity to form their own opinions: 'Staff will give answers to the children as they think that they are helping them.' As this quote illustrates, and my own observations corroborate, staff will often 'speak for children' rather than assist children to speak for themselves. This view of children and young people as lacking the capacity to speak for themselves is hardly surprising since, as argued in the previous chapter, children and young people have limited autonomy and agency within traditional Indian culture. Children and young people are expected to obey their elders and do as they are told, as a mark of respect. As Sadish observed, the generational hierarchy prevalent in Tamil Nadu prevents children and young people to participate:

> When you take it from the perspective of adults, when they look at children, they immediately think, 'You are too young to know about these things so I am not going to ask you for your opinion.' They actually control their children and they say, 'Go sit down in a corner because you don't know how to think about these things.' That's why they are not asked for their opinions.

The greatest barrier to listening to children is therefore adults' own perceptions about children and their willingness to hear what they have to say (McLeod, 2007). Thus, as Lansdown (2010, p.12) argues, for children to be able to express their views freely there needs to be a cultural change where all 'adults begin to recognize the importance of listening to and respecting children.' One way to start this 'cultural change' could be by supporting *Arunodhaya* staff to develop further their understandings of children's rights and children and young people's capacity for participation. This first step could, potentially, have a 'ripple effect' whereby staff will promote children's rights within their own communities and encourage others to listen to children and young people and respect their views.

However, as a former staff member (Raaj[11]) observed, it is difficult for staff to take part in further training and development as no courses in Tamil Nadu teach about children and young people's participation. Additionally, despite there being a multitude of documents and guides on how to put 'participation into practice', only a few of these are in the local language. Furthermore, as Raaj emphasized:

> Children's participation needs to be interpreted in an Indian context otherwise it will be like Valentine's day, Christmas or mother and father's days. We will try to promote this concept called participation without understanding it really.

Raaj compares the importing of foreign holidays, that have little connections with the Indian context, with the concept of children and young people's participation. Thus, as his comment implies, it does not suffice to translate international policy documents and guides on children and young people's participation into the local language. The concept of participation also needs to be made meaningful in local realities. Furthermore, children and young people's participation have to be meaningful to them and society at large. So far, children and young people's participation tends to be limited to issues that are traditionally related to the childhood years (such as schools, play parks and so on). As Palani, a lecturer at the local university, noted:

> The government doesn't follow the children's rights and children's participation approach. They say that they will do it but they don't. They might ask opinions of children on certain schemes for children but they will not encourage the empowerment of children like the NGOs are doing it as children and young people will question the government.

Children and young people's participation is therefore still limited in its scope and impact. As mentioned by Lansdown: 'The last 20 years have been a period of both advocacy to promote and legitimate the concept of participation, and exploration of strategies for translating into practice' (2010, p. 34). Indeed, many have argued that despite children and young people's participation in decision-making becoming more prolific, this has resulted in few real changes affecting their position in society and there is little evidence of long-term changes in children's life conditions (Hart, 2008; Hill et al., 2004; Tisdall et al., 2008, p. 348). According to the director, one way in which to increase the scope and impact of children and young people's participation is by having those NGOs that are already implementing children and young people's participation working more closely together with the government, schools and civil society to enhance their understandings of, and willingness to support, children and young people's participation. By working together these organizations can enhance children and young people's status in society and widen their participation.

Another significant challenge within the Indian social context is involving girls in activities. According to the director, 'Parents are afraid to send girls for meetings or residential programmes resulting in girls being excluded from, or underrepresented in, the NGO's activities'. My own observations indicate that parents are reluctant to allow their daughters to mix with unrelated boys, particularly during puberty. Girls, on attaining puberty, are seen by the parents primarily as brides in waiting and potential child bearers. Care is taken to ensure that girls' reputations are never tarnished, for their good reputations are vital in securing the best offer for arranged marriages. Thus, parents tend to restrict girls' movements and access to opportunities outside the home.

In contrast, in the children's *sangam*, equality between boys and girls to participate is considered essential. This can create some difficulties. For example Rama[12] was studying in an all-girls' school and did not have the opportunity to interact with boys. During one leadership training, which involved both boys and girls, she was left speechless when required to talk to a boy during a game. The staff encouraged her to talk to the boys for the next exercise and she was eventually able to overcome her shyness and talk to the boys. She even made male friends in the children's *sangam*. However, the new confidence girls may gain to talk to boys can cause some problems later as the community and parents can disapprove of girls having non-related male friends. The traditional view of the society in Tamil Nadu is then a barrier to involving girls, alongside boys, in participation activities and will have an impact on the extent to which girls might be able to utilize the skills they gained at the children's *sangam* in their communities.

Lessons learnt from the children's *sangam*

What can be learnt from the children's *sangam*, after 12 years of practicing children and young people's participation? The director identified four key lessons learnt. Firstly, that the role of staff is:

> Not to take over what children do but be always there when they are taking issues in the community or meeting a local authority, especially when children and young people struggle against the violation of their rights.

Thus, staff should support children and young people in having their voices heard, rather than to speak on their behalf.

Secondly, that organizations promoting and practicing children and young people's participation should not only facilitate and support the process of engagement with adults but also offer their protection when make demands of adults. As the director says, 'Children should be in contact with us because some actions might have some negative impacts for them'. As an example she described a particular incident where children from the children's *sangam* went to meet with the Chief Education Officer of the Corporation of Chennai without informing their parents or *Arunodhaya*. They had a petition, asking for a teacher to be appointed to a school as they were concerned about the lack of teaching staff. The Chief Education Officer was very angry and threatened not to allow the children to complete their exams. The children informed *Arunodhaya* about this incident. The organization spoke with their parents, and then sent a letter to the Officer to explain that the children had gone to the Corporation with parents' approval. The problem was solved and the children were able to sit their exams and get a teacher. While successful in this way, the example underlines how children and young people may require the support and protection of adults and organizations to have their demands heard.

Thirdly, engaging with parents is necessary to children and young people's participation. The parents' meetings, and communication between children's *sangam* and parents more generally, have helped parents know about children and young people's activities and increase trust between staff and parents.

Fourthly, more needs to be done to engage more children and young people. The director sees the city children's council as having the potential to involve more children and young people from the community. The city children's council has been established by *Arunodhaya*. Children and young people from the *sangam*, as well as non-members, have been elected in ten wards in Chennai in December 2012. Children and young people meet with the decision-makers in the ward four times a year to discuss the needs related to children's issues in the communities. At long term, *Arunodhaya*'s goal is to have children's council model introduced in legislation.

From my own observations a fifth lesson of these 12 years of *Arunodaya*'s work is the key role of leadership in putting children and young people's participation into practice. Since the organization's start, the director was sensitized to children's rights and children and young people's participation through reading documents, working with the United Nations International Children's Emergency Fund (UNICEF) in Chennai on child labor issues, and by being part of different networks such as CWA. She encouraged other staff members to acquaint themselves with this agenda. As Raaj explained, 'It is difficult to internalize the concept of participation in the Indian context but it was easy for me because I had the support of the director.' The director's ongoing support for children and young people's participation has been crucial.

Conclusion

This case study points to the transformative potential of participation – both at the personal and community levels. The experience of the children's *sangam* indicates that adults are critical to the successful implementation of children and young people's participation. Adults can either hinder or assist children and young people to express their views, ask questions and act; they can listen and take account of children and young people's views, or they can sideline and silence them. Whether adults hinder or assist children and young people's participation is closely linked with their views of the child, which are in turn based on cultural values that privilege adult views. Key adults, like the director, can help make systemic change – within her own organization and also, potentially, the wider community. The interviews with the three young adults show how their experience of participation in the children's *sangam* transformed their lives. They gained in confidence, developed new skills and discovered hidden talents. These young people benefited from their participation in the children's *sangam* and they now want others to have access to these same opportunities. They want to engage in, and bring about, societal change by becoming leaders within their communities and by practicing these values within their own families. Thus, this generation of children and young people, who have experienced participation, may well be able to introduce such participation within their future families and communities as adults. This will challenge the status quo whereby children and young people are expected to obey their parents silently. This indicates the transformative potential of participation.

The case study also shows the importance of time to effect change. *Arunodhaya* has been able to develop and continue its work for over 12 years. It has had continuity of leadership over this time and networks established and renewed with community decision-makers, parents and other adults. While personal change can be traced over the short term, the 'cultural change' required takes considerably longer.

Acknowledgments

Thanks to the Director of *Arunodhaya*, Virgil D'Sami, for sharing her experience and other participants for their contributions to this case study. Thanks to the *Asmae-Association Soeur Emmanuelle* who funded the evaluation in 2008.

Notes

1. Self Help Group is an area-based financial intermediary usually composed of between 10 to 15 local women. In *Arunodhaya*, they also support any activities of children's *sangam* and contribute to identify child labor in their community.

2. From the beginning *Arunodhaya* has been contacting employers, especially in metal factories, where children were employed in large numbers. *Arunodhava* organizes small meetings, awareness programmes and exhibitions with the employers. Even if it has been very difficult to get their cooperation, *Arunodhava* has succeeded in developing a model employer who took an oath not to employ children and young people in its factory. This employer then spread the message to other employers.

3. *Asmae-Association Soeur Emmanuelle* is a French non-profit organization working towards the improvement of the situation of deprived children. It has projects in nine countries and works in partnership with local NGOs. For further information see their website www.asmae.fr

4. These are the most recent figure available.

5. Further information can be found at: http://righttoeducation.in/sites/default/files/tamilnadu_rte-rules_2011.pdf, date accessed 27 January, 2014.

6. The executive committee is composed of nine members and the advisor (former president of the Confederation Executive Committee). The role is to monitor the activities of children's *sangam*.

7. Events gather children and young people from children's *sangam*, civil society and policy makers to express their views on issues related to children and young people's rights violations.

8. Children's *sangam* has produced a newsletter since 2003. The newsletter is released three times a year to express the children and young people's right of free expression and exchange experiences between children's collectives. Children and young people are part of the editorial board.

9. Prem was interviewed in 2008 for the purpose of the impact evaluation of the children's sangam.

10. Members of the children's *sangam* aged 18 or over have the opportunity to be part of *Arunodhaya's* central Committee. The goal is to strengthen the meetings at the area level, share their own experience, organize training for members and staff and supervise events organized by members of the children's *sangam*. Currently, the Committee is not in operation.

11. Pseudonyms have been used throughout the case study.

12. Rama was interviewed in 2008 for the purpose of the impact evaluation of the children's *sangam*.

Bibliography

Arunodhaya report submitted to Asmae-Association Soeur Emmanuelle for the period April 2012–March 2013.

Census of India (2001) *Census Data Online*, http://censusindia.gov.in/2011-common/censusdataonline.html.

Census of India (2011) *Chapter 3: Size, Growth Rate and Distribution of Population*, http://censusindia.gov.in/2011-prov-results/data_files/india/Final_PPT_2011_chapter3.pdf.

UN Committee on the Rights of the Child (2009) *General Comment No. 12: The right of children to be heard*, http://www2.ohchr.org/english/bodies/crc/docs/AdvanceVersions/CRC-C-GC-12.doc.

Hart, J. (2008) 'Children's Participation and International Development: Attending to the Political', *International Journal of Children's Rights*, 16(3), 407–418.

Hill, M., Davis, J., Prout, A. and Tisdall, K. (2004) 'Moving the Participation Agenda Forward', *Children and Society*, 18(2), 77–96.

Lansdown, G. (2005) *The Evolving Capacities of the Child*, (Florence: UNICEF).

Lansdown, G. (2010) 'The Realisation of Children's Participation Rights: Critical Reflections', in B. Percy-Smith and N. Thomas (eds) *A Handbook of Children and Young People's Participation: Perspectives from Theory and Practice*, (London and New York: Routledge).

McLeod, A. (2007) 'Whose Agenda? Issues of Power and Relationship When Listening to Looked after Young People', *Child Family and Social Work*, 12(3), 278–286.

Suryanarayana, M. H., Agrawal, A. and Prabhu, K. S. (2011) *Inequality-adjusted Human Development Index for India's States*, (New Delhi: UNDP).

Tisdall, K., Davis, J. M. and Gallagher, M. (2008) 'Reflecting upon Children and Young People's Participation in the UK', *International Journal of Children's Rights*, 16(3), 419–429.

8

Unsettling Notions of Participation: A View from South Africa

Shirley Pendlebury, Patricia Henderson and Lucy Jamieson

Introduction

On the day of his release from prison in 1990, Nelson Mandela read Ingrid Jonker's poem *The child who was shot dead by soldiers in Nyanga* to the crowds who welcomed him in Cape Town. In the poem, the child becomes a symbol of freedom and defies death through living on in others in the quest for freedom, a quest whose message travels without restriction throughout the world. It is a poem that demonstrates how children are part of all aspects of social life, a reality sometimes ignored in circumscribing the 'proper' place of children.

In this chapter, we trace children and young people's claims to public space through the last years of apartheid and into the formation of the democratic state, where children's rights have become enshrined in the Constitution of South Africa (1996) and in legislation pertaining to children. Shifts in the political landscape since the end of apartheid have, at a formal level, opened spaces for children and young people to influence decision-making and to shape social change. Yet – despite South Africa's strong commitment to public participation in its early years of democracy, a supportive legislative framework and the pervasive influence of international conventions such as the UN Convention on the Rights of the Child (UNCRC) – the environment for children and young people's public participation is constrained (Bray and Moses, 2011). Also, although equality is both a founding value of the Constitution and first among the rights it recognizes, within formally regulated political spaces, people under the age of 18 years do not have 'participatory parity' (Fraser, 2009) with adult citizens.

The chapter examines discrepancies between the principles of participatory democracy in the Constitution and *de facto* ways in which respect, power and participatory efficacy are linked to age and position in everyday life and in formally regulated public spaces. It is within the context of children and young people's political and creative practice rooted in history, and specific changes taking place in the institutional architecture of the state, that we begin to unsettle and expand notions of children and young people's participation and to explore possibilities for transformative participation.

'Participation' and 'transformation', like other buzzwords in the 'lexicon of development', are at once commodious and drained of meaning – consensual hurrah-words meant to convey obvious goods but host to competing political and funding purposes (Cornwall, 2011; Leal, 2010; see Chapter 2). What, then, do we mean by transformative participation? If we resist the broad sweep of slogan-like concepts, what is understood by the terms 'children and young people's participation' is historically and culturally situated, varying over time and between social spaces. Children and young people, collectively and individually, contribute to the unfolding of everyday life in multiple ways, many of which are inadequately described or ignored within adult society (Bray et al., 2009). The ways in which children and young people are called to participate, often through brief commentary in governance and policy formulation, may be formulaic and may miss the manner in which they engage in the minutiae of local politics in their lived environments, as well as the terms they bring to bear on these processes.

Theoretically, the notion of participation within a neoliberal global order re-inscribes the idea of the sovereign individual as bearer of particular rights (Arneil, 2002; Jenks, 1996). The individual as an abstraction is presumed to give voice to desires and demands in uncomplicated ways and equally presumed to be heard in good faith. Yet, within particular historical horizons, individuals are shaped by and give shape to relations threaded through with the effects of gender, age, race, class and cultural practices. While there are many contexts in which the reception of what children articulate may be limited, in others the challenging voices of children and young people may emerge, sometimes during moments of conflict that dislodge taken-for-granted certainties (Das, 2007). It is these moments of dislodgement that typify transformative participation.

Two themes run through the chapter: one is the relationship between transgression and transformation, in and through participatory practices; the other is the entwinement of respect, responsibility and power in shaping the nature of children's participation in social dialog. The chapter illustrates some South African particularities of our assertion that participation is historically, politically and culturally situated. We begin by sketching children and young people's involvement in social change from 1976 onwards during the latter half of the apartheid regime (1948–1994). In the second part, against the backdrop of South Africa's Constitution and establishment of children's legal rights, we chart a discursive counter-current of 'normalizing' childhood that gained prominence in the emergent democratic state, partly in reaction to extensive lobbying for children's rights to be included in the Constitution. The third part outlines aspects of the current socio-economic context of children and young people in South Africa and describes some cultural practices that shape participatory possibilities in everyday life. Entwined practices of power, respect and responsibility affect who is heard and taken seriously, not only within everyday life but also – as Part IV illustrates – within formally defined public arenas. Finally, through a sketch of protest and performance, we consider prospects for transformative participation in children and young people's assertion of their claims to public space and social commentary.

Part I: Political action and social transformation

In opposing apartheid, children and young people in South Africa became visible in the public domain in challenging ways. Previously living within the circumscribed space of home and school – institutions in which hierarchical forms of power between adults and children were taken for granted – a substantial group of young activists became politically effective within the public domain. In doing so, they blurred the demarcation between private and public, and often transgressed and overturned pre-existing forms of authority. Here the binary construction of child and adult as distinct kinds of persons with differing claims to authority began to disintegrate, thus bringing about transformations within the public sphere and, arguably, for a time also to some extent within domestic environments where young people played a leading role in opposing the apartheid regime.

The legislative landscape during apartheid meant that the majority of people were denied spaces to participate legally in public life in relation to state governance. Possibilities for social dialog within officially recognized domains of public life were severely constrained or altogether foreclosed for the majority, children and adults alike. Dimensions of public life in which children and young people's shaping of societal change became more overt began with the student uprisings in Soweto in Johannesburg and beyond in 1976, triggered by large-scale protests against – among other things – the state's insistence that school education for Africans be conducted in Afrikaans. Five hundred children and young people were killed between June and August of the first year of the uprisings (see, for example, Ngomane and Flanagan, 2003). Children and young people instituted school, rent and consumer boycotts and set up people's courts in which individuals accused of collaboration with the state were 'tried'; some joined the armed wings of liberation movements in exile. At the forefront of resistance, 'the young called down the wrath of an armed state on their heads' (Reynolds, 2008, p. 153), as the police and army routinely rounded them up, subjecting them to brutal treatment and indefinite detention without trial.

The degree to which even very young children were shot, beaten and taken into detention is an indictment of a racialized society in which the childhoods of a white minority were deemed worthy of protection and those of the African majority were regarded as occupying a place of exception, where acceptable standards of conduct could be abandoned. Such practices instantiate Agamben's (1998) notion of how sovereignty is threaded through with violence that reaches beyond the bounds of its own legitimation. During the height of the struggle against apartheid (from 1985–1989), between 26 and 45 percent of people incarcerated were under the age of 18 years – exact numbers cannot be established (Dawes, 2008).

Set up shortly after the first democratic elections in 1994, the Truth and Reconciliation Commission (TRC) sought to provide a record of gross violations of individuals and of deaths and disappearances during the apartheid regime. In many respects, it failed to document adequately the often protracted and responsible involvement of children and young people in transforming the socio-political order.

In ethnographic studies conducted in Zwelethemba (a suburb of Worcester, a farming town in the Western Cape), Reynolds (2012) and Ross (2003) show how young men and women, respectively, opposed the regime in multiple ways, including in some cases leaving the country to join liberation movements and to receive military training. They portray young people's involvement in the transformation of their country in ways that transcend narrow conceptions of child soldiers as passive victims of forced recruitment into armies. Reynolds (2012) found that a number of the young men began their political involvement at a very young age, drawing inspiration from older relatives or neighbors, and had sustained their commitments for long periods, in some instances for as long as 15 years. In their political practices, they revealed, in some cases, a political and ethical maturation well above the levels of development typically portrayed in some liberal and neo-liberal understandings of the child. Among their many preoccupations were how to take up responsible mediation between the state and one's own community and how to reconstitute community life within a small town where it was not unusual to encounter people who had tortured or betrayed one. The work of Reynolds (2012) and Ross (2003) stands out in tracing lines of political involvement through time for individuals who when very young had to face the might of a brutal state and were transformed in the process in often extremely painful ways, but ways that demonstrated wisdom and forbearance.

More broadly across South Africa, concerted action by children and young people not only helped to transform a brutal society but was personally transformative for many, as is evident in much of the other writing on children and young people's engagement in political struggle (see, for example, Hyslop, 1988; Marks, 2001; Seekings, 1993; Straker, 1992). Largely hidden from these various accounts of young activists are what Seekings calls 'the parameters of normality in conflict-ridden townships' (2006, p. 3). Although a lot is known about who participated in political protest and why they did so, Seekings points out that little is known about who did not participate and why – a matter of concern for any thoroughgoing attempt at theorizing public participation. In the period to which Seekings refers, silence and anonymity were necessities of safety and survival for some.

Understanding who does not participate and why, or how and why particular kinds of talk are renounced, curbed or forbidden in different social domains, are as much a part of theorizing participation as is understanding who can and does participate, how and with what consequences. An implicit promise of constitutional democracy in South Africa was to vouchsafe a diverse and open public in which ordinary people could speak their minds and reveal their affiliations without fear of reprisal. What the standing of children was to be within such a reconstituted public was a subject of contention in the formation of a democratic state.

Part II: Reconstituting 'childhoods'; constituting rights

In the early years of the emergent democratic state, campaigns for the recognition of children's rights ran against a discursive counter-current of 'normalcy' that sought to diminish participatory spaces for children and young people. Late in 1990, the mass media began to emphasize the importance of reconstituting 'normal' childhood, a return to a cordoned space of innocence. Ndebele (1995), a renowned thinker in South Africa, was among those who stressed the importance of a protected space for childhood. Beneath the call lay a discomfort at the extent of children and young people's active involvement in social transformation and of the violence to which they had been exposed and in which they had sometimes taken part. Perhaps discomfort lay, too, in a recognition of how the apartheid state had separated out the governance of children with some deemed worthy and 'nestled' in 'layers of care and protection' and others, identified as 'nonwhite', left 'vulnerable before the forces of the state' (Reynolds, 2012, p. 14). Whatever the sources of discomfort, calls for normalcy focused attention on children and young people themselves, rather than on the treatment they had received under the former regime. Young people were pathologized as a problem for the new society and labeled 'the lost generation' (see Seekings, 1996, for a critical account of this labeling). Some had sacrificed their education in order to bring about social change and it was widely thought that their exposure to violence would lead to their own perpetuation of violence.

For a time, appeals for restoring normalcy threatened to diminish the social space in which children and young people could publicly make a contribution to the issues of the day. Quintessentially, normalcy meant a reinsertion of 'appropriate' social hierarchies in which men, women and children resumed their 'accepted' places and, in particular, with the return of children to a space of 'safety' which emphasized their dependency on adults (for example, Ndebele, 1995). Prior to the 1994 elections, it was briefly mooted that young people of 14 years and upward be entitled to vote in acknowledgment of their contribution to social transformation. It was an idea quickly quashed to align the new nation state with international definitions of childhood correlated to age. Such age-tethered notions of childhood as a cordoned space of innocence fail to recognize the power of children in shaping the world through their transgressions (Jenks, 1996) and the critique of dominant society they may provide.

Calls for a 'return' to normal childhoods occurred in parallel with the development of a Constitution that places participation at the center of political transformation. All parties to the negotiations approved the inclusion of a section in the Constitution that explicitly recognizes children's rights (Du Plessis and Corder, 1994; Sloth-Nielsen, 1996). An extensive campaign led by South Africa's National Committee on the Rights of Children (NCRC) helped to ensure that children's rights in the Constitution mirrored those in the UNCRC (Skelton and Proudlock,

2011). Children, too, participated in this campaign. At the International Summit on the Rights of Children held in 1992, over 200 children between the ages of 12 and 16 years drafted and adopted a Children's Charter of South Africa (Woodhouse, 1999). One of their demands was for a children's council of representatives in any future government of the country.

While the Constitution of South Africa does not name participation rights for children, it requires the Bill of Rights to be interpreted in reference to international law and on these grounds can be interpreted as granting participation rights to children and young people. Two international instruments are critical for interpreting children's constitutional rights: the UNCRC and the African Charter on the Rights and Welfare of the Child (ACRWC). The principle of the child's best interests in the UNCRC requires consultation with children on matters that concern them (UN Committee on the Rights of the Child, 2009). Following international convention, South Africa's Constitution defines children as persons under the age of 18 years and as political minors without the right to vote. Nonetheless, people under the age of 18 years share with adults many civil and political rights: the rights to freedom of expression, to be part of political campaigns, to protest and to participate in the development of laws and policies (Jamieson, 2011).

In keeping with Constitutional values, several laws recognize children and young people's participatory rights in particular domains. The South African Schools Act (1996) was one of the first post-apartheid laws to allow for children and young people's participation in institutional governance. It requires secondary schools to establish Learner Representative Councils and make provision for the election of learner representatives to School Governing Boards (SGBs). Much longer and more contentious in the making than the Schools Act was the Children's Act (2005), the legislation that is the most explicit in establishing children and young people's participatory rights (as well as their rights to protection). The rights established in the Children's Act supplement those in the Bill of Rights; also, all legislation pertaining to children must comply with the general principles of the Children's Act. The Act specifies the general principle on participatory rights:

> Every child that is of such an age, maturity and stage of development as to be able to participate in any matter concerning that child has the right to participate in an appropriate way and views expressed by the child must be given due consideration. (Section 10)

Progressive though the Children's Act is, its slow and contested passage marks a fundamental tension in South African society. During the parliamentary hearings on Children's Bill, advocates for children's rights clashed with a conservative lobby appealing to various 'traditional' approaches to children and young people. Children's rights organizations convinced Parliament to recognize the evolving capacities of children and give them the power to consent to an HIV test at any age, on condition that the child has the capacity to understand the risk and benefits of taking the test (Budlender et al., 2008). Concurrently, a strong lobby against the abolition of corporal punishment drew fuel from popular beliefs about children and young people's incompetence to assess what is best for them, from moral panics about the social consequences of relinquishing a traditional approach that keeps children and young people in their place, and a widespread view that poor discipline and unruly behavior in schools had resulted from the abolition of corporal punishment provision in the Schools Act. Ultimately, the abolition of corporal punishment provision was removed from the Children's Amendment Bill of 2007 because of a technicality related to the drafting procedure. However, both Parliament and the Department of Social Development have committed to inserting the ban as an amendment in the future (Hansard, 2012; Portfolio Committee on Social Development, 2007).

South Africa's Constitutional allegiance to a rights-based participatory democracy, coupled with an enabling legislative framework, in principle allows for more open and expanded spaces for civic participation. Law, however, is not seamlessly translated into the ways lives are lived nor into the often unconscious ways in which people's senses of self are invested in various situated and enacted forms of difference (Bray et al., 2009).

Opportunities for participatory agency are differently constituted within different social and relational spaces and within different cultural practices, as we show in the next two sections. Socio-economic factors, diverse understandings of childhood and social status in South Africa, as well as popular opinion about children and young people's 'place' and capacities all circumscribe the environment for their participation – in families and communities, as well as in the more structured spaces for participation in governance.

Part III: Context matters

People under the age of 18 years make up 37 percent of South Africa's population, with a total of 18.5 million children in 2011 (Hall, 2013).

Two thirds of children are living in four of South Africa's nine provinces – in urban Gauteng and in three largely rural provinces that incorporate several of the former apartheid homelands (Meintjes and Hall, 2011). Whereas the distribution of children is concentrated in large rural provinces, only 27 percent of the adult population live in rural areas (Hall and Wright, 2011; Meintjes and Hall, 2011). Age-related population distribution reflects the durability of apartheid spatial planning and consequent patterns of migration among adults in search of work. About 24 percent of children do not live with either of their biological parents and 39 percent live with their mothers but not with their fathers (Hall, 2013). Contrary to popular opinion, orphaning is not the primary reason for children living apart from their parents, as 78 percent of children who are not co-resident with their parents have at least one parent living elsewhere (Meintjes and Hall, 2011). Child poverty is especially prevalent in two of the country's rural provinces – Limpopo and the Eastern Cape – where, in 2011, almost 76 percent of children were living in households whose income fell below the poverty line (Hall, 2013).

In a society still 'rife with inequalities', chronic poverty and a burgeoning HIV epidemic, together with their associated multiple deprivations, impinge on the effective exercise of agency among adults and children alike (Bray and Moses, 2011). Also, in rural areas especially, a culture of respect characteristically leaves little leeway for children to express their needs or make themselves heard among adults, except through traditional repertoires of interaction within the household and community (Meintjes, 2011).

Families and local communities are the everyday contexts in which childhood is understood and experienced, and where patterns of intergenerational dialog are promoted, cordoned into special spheres, or altogether proscribed. For example, as Henderson (2009) observes, a culture of respect permeates most southern African cultural domains. Approximate generations treat one another with a degree of avoidance, and closeness is expressed between peers and with some members of a third ascendant generation. Children in these domains are socialized into obeying older people and into practices that underscore repertoires of respect: in bodily comportment, forms of address, in naming and in the muted volubility of enquiries. In contrast to contemporary 'western' models of 'normal' childhood in which, ironically, protection and empowerment are conjoined, more local forms of childhood assume obedience to older people alongside greater degrees of responsibility and independence amongst peers (Henderson, 2011b). In the next chapter, Meintjes depicts the relationship between respect and responsibility in the fabric of everyday life in a remote rural community in KwaZulu Natal. A family study conducted by Bozalek (2004) paints a somewhat bleaker picture of the interplay of respect and power. Bozalek collected data from university students about perceptions and practices regarding children within their own families. Rural African family profiles drawn from the study illustrate how power differentials, resulting from a culture of respect for older people, may inhibit participatory possibilities for children and young people. Using an analytical framework derived in part from Fraser's (2009) trivalent conception of social justice, Bozalek (2011) concludes that, in families of this kind, children and young people do not have participatory parity with adults. Fraser (2009) specifies three jointly necessary conditions for participatory parity: redistribution of resources for fair and equal entitlement and access by all participants, recognition of the value of each member of the polity (or, in this case, the family), and representivity – the requirement that each participant's voice be heard as legitimate. None of these conditions appears to have been met for children and young people in Bozalek's study. Family profiles depict a situation of hierarchically ordered practices of respect, in which children had the lowest status, were accorded little respect and were cast as supplicants in relation to their elders. In these families, age and gender regulated who may do what and when, determined the distribution of family resources, and constrained who may comment upon discrepancies in access to resources.

Intricately woven cultural practices may limit the manner and scope of children and young people's participation, especially in rural African communities. Yet within circumstances of chronic poverty, children and young people take on critical responsibilities in sustaining communities by caring for sick relatives, maintaining links between scattered family, gathering wood and water and assisting with farming (Bray and Brandt, 2007; Bray 2010, 2011; Henderson, 2006).

Local practices of respect and their assumption of obedience to older people run alongside the institutional structures of South Africa's constitutional democracy and are among the factors that may hinder children's and young people's uptake of opportunities for, and efficacy within, formally defined public participation.

Part IV: Inclusion and exclusion in formal participation

Since the advent of democracy in 1994, changes in the institutional architecture of the state have expanded the spaces for participatory democracy. There are now opportunities for citizens to present their views in parliamentary hearings at national and provincial levels, as well as through local governance structures and in the institutional governance of schools and care facilities. Realization of this democratic intent has been sporadic. Even when formal participatory spaces are opened to children and young people, exclusionary practices by those who claim authority within the space may impede participation.

To borrow a distinction from Young (2002), children and young people may be externally included (brought into a predefined public space to which they previous had no access) but internally excluded (silenced or disempowered through predominant discursive practices within the space or through the persistence of everyday social and power relations). Within formally constituted spaces of public deliberation, there is an intricate interplay of inclusionary and exclusionary moves and of deliberative uptake and deliberative refusal – as we illustrate in the following examples of participation within the formally constituted spaces of Parliament, local government and SGBs.

During the third democratic Parliament (2004–2009), the legislatures considered several major laws affecting children and young people. This provided an impetus for civil society groups to support children and young people's participation in Parliament's consultations with the public on legislation. While some civil society campaigners have argued, on the grounds of children's vulnerability, that it is in the best interests of children and young people to have adults representing their views (Jamieson, 2010), a growing number of campaigners have brought children and young people into the chambers to engage directly with decision-makers (Ehlers and Frank, 2008; Mniki and Rosa, 2007). Notable instances of self-advocacy occurred when children and young people came of their own accord to parliamentary consultations on the Children's Amendment Bill held in public venues in eight rural communities.

Parliamentary settings encourage the equal assertion of citizenship rights but remain an arena in which power relations and everyday practices infuse deliberative interchanges. From direct observation, Jamieson (2008) sketches a vignette of the interplay of power and participatory uptake. She describes how at a Parliamentary Select Committee on Social Services hearing on the Children's Amendment Bill in October 2005, Inkosi Nzimele, Leader of the National House of Traditional Leaders, declared: 'When it comes to decisions about women and children I know best because I am a man.' A teenage girl retaliated, asserting her right to speak for herself. At the same hearing, a group of 'virgin maidens' from the Transkei opposed the proposed ban on virginity testing on the grounds that it would prevent them from practicing their culture. Here a formally constituted deliberative arena stages the performance of three micro-narratives about the position of children and young people, namely: the reclamation of patriarchal authority and 'keeping women and children in their place'; the assertion of young people's citizen rights; and, in the case of the 'maidens', what Appadurai (1996) would term a micro-narrative of cultural boundary-maintenance.

In addition to inclusion in legislative debates, the national and provincial legislatures have established sectoral parliaments for children and youth. However, these are not separate institutions but days dedicated to involving children and young people in the work of the legislature. For example, the Gauteng Youth Parliament is used as a forum for young people to give provincial MPs an insight into their concerns and challenges.

In a changed state architecture, local governance structures are the main officially sanctioned arenas for citizen participation. Decentralized governance provides a structural arrangement – through ward committees – intended to empower local communities, including children and young people, to participate in identifying problems, strategies and plans and to mobilize resources (Nomdo and Roberts, 2011; Roodt and Stuurman, 2011). Findings from two small-scale studies of children and young people's experiences of local government present contrasting attitudes: cynicism and disaffection, on the one hand; optimism and a sense of empowerment, on the other.

A study conducted with Grade 12 students (aged 17 to 19 years) at a Rhini township school in Grahamstown in the Eastern Cape (Stuurman, 2009) points to their disillusionment with the promise of participation in local governance. These young people regarded ward committees as dominated by self-interested older adults with no concern for issues important to youth and politicians as corrupt and nepotistic; what is more, they did not believe that their own participation in the system could change anything (Roodt and Stuurman, 2011).

By contrast, in an NGO-led initiative, children and young people were able to participate meaningfully in an assessment of the National Budget of 2006–2007 and contribute to a plain language budget brief. Typically, the young participants in this budget assessment expressed hope and confidence in the possibilities for children to participate in significant social dialog and be heard. Following their experiences in the budget project, some of the participants successfully advocated for a child-friendly Integrated Development Plan in one of the municipalities in KwaZulu Natal (Nomdo and Roberts, 2011).

School governance structures constitute another legally defined public space in which children and young people can participate in deliberative decision-making procedures. Formally, the school as an institution is a regulatory space constituted by the education laws and policies of the country; informally, it is a participatory space 'whose affordances and patterns of inclusion/exclusion' are shaped by school culture and the diverse lives and experiences of the students (Carrim, 2011, p. 75). Such patterns of inclusion/exclusion appear not only in curriculum practices but also in school governance.

The Schools Act, as already mentioned, provides for secondary school learners to participate in school governance through election to the Representative Council of Learners (RCL) and for RCLs to elect learner representatives to the SGB. Intergenerational power relations, attitudinal obstacles and tokenism within SGBs may preclude learners' meaningful engagement in decision-making and frequently mute the young people elected to serve on them (Carrim, 2011; Heystek, 2001). A case study by Phaswana (2010) shows how intergenerational power relations in SGB meetings were being played out through a politics of language, rooted in South Africa's multi-layered history of colonialism, one of whose educational legacies is that the most children and young people continue to be schooled in a language other than their mother tongue. Learner representatives in a focus group described how teachers used English as a silencing device in meetings – whenever the young people raised critical comments in the vernacular in which they were most articulate, teacher representatives insisted upon English as the language of deliberation. If, as can be inferred from the context of Phaswana's study, this occurred in a school where teachers themselves speak one or more local languages as their primary medium of social interaction, then there is an irony in their deploying the dominant colonial language to keep young people in their place (Pendlebury, 2011).

Part V: Protest and performance: constituting new publics

Beyond the formally constituted spaces for public deliberation, different sites and modes of participation may open possibilities for transformative learning and a transgression of the power relations that obstruct participatory parity for children and young people. Teamey and Hinton (Chapter 2) suggest that sites of transformative participation rarely emerge directly within policy-making processes but rather emerge through various modes of expression in political actions, social movements and cultural events. Protest and performance are two such modes of expression.

In South Africa, protests initiated by children and young people, as well as organized campaigns in which they take the lead, provide alternative and historically familiar forms of 'speaking out' against the poor quality of education, authoritarian school management and inadequate facilities at schools (Bray et al., 2010; Moses, 2008). In urban pockets of the country, ad hoc protests about the poor quality of education have led to a coordinated social movement under the banner of a community-based organization, Equal Education, established in 2008 through the action of school-going youth in Khayalitsha on the outskirts of Cape Town. High school students who call themselves 'Equalizers' have spearheaded a campaign to compel the national education authorities to address the appalling facilities in most of the country's public schools, where fewer than ten percent of schools have stocked libraries and laboratories. In March 2011, Equalizers mobilized an estimated 20,000 young people to participate in a march to Parliament, where they handed over a memorandum calling on the Minister of Basic Education to build libraries in every school as required by the norms and standards for school infrastructure (Equal Education, 2011). Later in the same year, 60 Equalizers camped outside Parliament to demand a ministerial response.

Forms of improvization enable children and young people to portray their everyday lives in a lively manner through mirroring the bodily comportment and styles of speaking of different kinds of people within their communities (Henderson, 2006, 2011a, 2011b). Plays that they produce about problems they have defined within their communities demonstrate that children and young people are wry commentators on the social worlds in which they find themselves. Such performances of public commentary are examples of popular culture as an 'entertaining, serious game', where praxis involves 'contradiction, contestation, and experimentation' (Fabian, 1998, p. 32).

To illustrate, we draw on the example of a group of young performers from the African suburb of Khayelitsha in Cape Town. After school everyday, the *Kasi* Group met to rehearse their ongoing performance repertoires: including 'traditional' dance, the creation of short plays around topical issues that concerned them and the creation of what they termed 'images' – recited poems whose content is mimed. The *Kasi* Group regularly performed in street parades and during cultural festivals in the township in which hundreds of children and young people participate. One of the group's performances, filmed by Henderson and Moses of the Children's Institute at the University of Cape Town, was a poem written in response to the 2008 xenophobic attacks by South Africans, against African immigrants from other countries. At least 40 immigrants from different African countries, who had sought refuge in South Africa, were killed. Attacks on non-South Africans occurred especially in the poorest neighborhoods, where local people resented 'foreigners' whom they said were taking away their jobs.

The poem refers to how South Africans who had joined the armed wings of the liberation movements, and others who had gone into exile, were supported by other Africans from neighboring countries. Given this fact, it is a tragedy that Black South Africans today do not return the favor. The poem also refers to people being questioned in local South African languages to see whether they were South African. If they did not reply in a South African language, they were often killed or badly beaten. In some instances, South Africans who did not speak the same language as the attacker were also killed.

We reproduce extracts from this poem to demonstrate how children and young people often express their views most forcefully within parameters of their own choosing.

The 'image': November 2009

The *Kasi* Group began their performance singing, with their backs to the audience. A person emerged from the back line, running between two people and looking extremely perturbed. She was thrown to the ground and 'stabbed to death' by one of those running alongside her. The group began to recite:

I am black, My skin is the same as yours, My colour is the same as yours, My genes are African, nothing but African. When your leaders were beaten by whites, I was there to shelter them. Although I am not South African, I was patient. I offered them food, shelter. Most of all I offered them protection. I might be a South African, I can't speak Zulu, because I am from Venda, I can't speak Zulu, because I am Shangaan, I don't know how to say 'elbow' in Zulu. Most of all, it is not my language.

Since when was Zulu the only South African language? Yes, I am not from Gauteng [Johannesburg]. I was not born here, but I am South African. Where should I go if you beat me? I am not beating your father, your mother, your brother ... I am not calling them Makwerekwere [a term used to refer to refugees from other African countries], though they can't speak my language.

I might be dark in complexion, I might be dark with a foreign look, I might have a foreign body structure. Now instead of going to the only place I call home, I am scared of walking down the street without my I.D. [identity document].

Whites taught me to do that, centuries ago, But now my black brother is acting white, Why should black South Africans do this to me? ...

If I have to go back to Venda, Let all the Pedis go back to Pediland, Let all the Sothos go back to Lesotho, Let all the Tswanas go back to Botswana, Let all the Xhosas go back to the Eastern Cape, And let all the Ndebeles go back to KwaNdebele. Is this not ignorance?

Your unemployment is your responsibility. You, with intellect, get up and work, Let education empower you ...

Before 1994 you were blaming whites, Now you are blaming me, Who are you going to blame after chasing me away? Who are you going to blame after killing me? All we need is peace, unity and rights.

As the poem demonstrates, children and young people often live beyond the conceptualizations adults have developed of their lives and their place within society. They may thus be occupying public spaces, and expressing their critical views, in ways that are broader than conceived by adults who initiate formal processes for including children and young people in governance and planning.

Conclusion

In the context of political, everyday and creative practices, we have sought to unsettle notions of children and young people's public participation, and to show how in South Africa these vary across time and across different sites of activity. Where adults set the terms of engagement – whether at home or in institutionally defined public spheres – entwined practices of power and culturally inflected forms of respect may affect whether and how children and young people are heard. Where children and young people assert their claims to public space and political commentary, they may transgress the boundaries of their stipulated 'proper place' and so begin to dislodge taken-for-granted certainties and thus transform themselves, their relationships and – in the case of the struggle against the apartheid state – the social order. As the next chapter illustrates, there are also more subtle ways in which children and young people may begin to transform everyday relationships. In it, Meintjes describes how a radio project has enabled children and young people to speak respectfully with adults about topics normally muted through local forms of a culture of respect and thus to reconfigure the space in which their interactions with their caregivers unfold.

Acknowledgments

This chapter draws from papers presented by Patricia Henderson and Lucy Jamieson at international seminars held in South Africa (2009), Brazil (2010) and India (2010) as part of a series conducted under the auspices of the Leverhulme Trust Academic Collaboration Network on Theorising Children's Participation. We thank Helen Meintjes for helpful comments on earlier versions of the chapter.

Bibliography

Agamben, G. (1998) *Homo sacer: Sovereign power and bare life*, trans. Daniel Heller-Roazen, (Stanford: Stanford University Press).

Appadurai, A. (1996) *Modernity at large: Cultural dimensions of globalization*, (Minneapolis: University of Minnesota Press).

Arneil, B. (2002) 'Becoming versus being: a critical analysis of the child in liberal theory', in D. Archard and C. M. Macleod (eds) *The Moral and Political Status of Children*, (Oxford: Oxford University Press).

Bozalek, V. (2004) 'Recognition, Resources, Responsibilities: Using Students' Stories of Family to Renew the South African Social Work Curriculum', http://igitur-archive. library.uu.nl/dissertations/2004-1203-094505/index.htm.

Bozalek, V. (2011) 'Judging Children's Participatory Parity from Social Justice and the Political Ethics of Care Perspectives', *Perspectives in Education*, 29(1), 56–65.

Bray, R. (2010) 'Analytical review of literature, thinking and practice towards child and youth participation in east and southern Africa' in R. Bray and G. Clacherty (eds) *Child and Youth Participation in East and Southern Africa: Taking stock and moving forward*, (Pretoria: Regional Inter-Agency Task Team on Children and AIDS (RIATT) Eastern and Southern Africa).

Bray, R. (2011) 'Effective children's participation in social dialogue' in L. Jamieson, R. Bray, A. Viviers, L. Lake, S. Pendlebury and C. Smith (eds) *South African Child Gauge 2010/2011*, (Cape Town: Children's Institute, University of Cape Town).

Bray, R. and Brandt, R. (2007) 'Childcare and Poverty in South Africa: An Ethnographic Challenge to Conventional Interpretations', *Journal of Children and Poverty*, 13(1), 1–19.

Bray, R. and Moses, S. (2011) 'Children and Participation in South Africa: Exploring the Landscape', *Perspectives in Education*, 29(1), 6–17.

Bray, R., Gooskens, I., Kahn, L., Moses, S. and Seekings, J. (2010) *Growing up in the New South Africa: Childhood and adolescence in post-apartheid Cape Town*, (Cape Town: HSRC Press).

Bray, R., Moses, S. and Henderson, P. (2009) 'Children and Participation in South Africa: Exploring the Landscape'. Unpublished paper presented at the first international seminar on Theorising Child Participation: Learning across Disciplines and Countries (Cape Town, South Africa, 6–8 April 2009).

Budlender, D., Proudlock, P. and Jamieson, L. (2008) 'Formulating and Implementing Socio-economic Policies for Children in the Context of HIV/AIDS: A South African Case Study', *IDS Bulletin*, 39(5), 62–70.

Carrim, N. (2011) 'Modes of Participation and Conceptions of Children in South African Education', *Perspectives in Education*, 29(1), 75–83.

Cornwall, A. (2011) 'Introductory overview: buzzwords and fuzzwords – deconstructing development discourse', in A. Cornwall and D. Eade (eds) *Deconstructing Development Discourse: Buzzwords and Fuzzwords*, (Rugby: Practical Action Publishing in association with Oxfam GB).

Das, V. (2007) *Life and word: Violence and the descent into the ordinary*, (Oxford: Oxford University Press).

Dawes, A. (2008) 'Political transition and youth violence in post-Apartheid South Africa: in search of understanding' in J. Hart (ed.) *Years of Conflict: Adolescence, Political Violence and Displacement*, (Oxford and New York: Berghann Books).

Du Plessis, L. M. and Corder, H. (1994) 'The genesis of sections entrenching specific rights' in L. M. Du Plessis and H. Corder (eds) *Understanding South Africa's Transitional Bill of Rights*, (Cape Town: Juta).

Ehlers, L. and Frank, C. (2008) 'Child participation in Africa' in J. Sloth-Nielsen (ed.) *Children's Rights in Africa: A legal perspective*, (Aldershot: Ashgate).

Equal Education (2011) '20,000 March for minimum norms and standards!', http://www.equaleducation.org.za/article/20000-march-for-minimum-norms-and-standards.

Fabian, J. (1998) *Moments of freedom: Anthropology and popular culture*, (Charlottesville: University of Virginia Press).

Fraser, N. (2009) *Scales of justice: Reimagining political space in a globalizing world*, (New York: Columbia University Press).

Hall, K. (2013) 'Analysis of the General Household Survey 2011', analysis prepared for http://www.childrencount.ci.org.za/

Hall, K. and Wright, G. (2011) *In Brief: A Profile of Children Living in South Africa using the National Income Dynamics Study*, (Cape Town: Children's Institute, University of Cape Town, in collaboration with the Centre for the Analysis of South African Social Policy, Oxford University).

Hansard (2012) *Minister of Social Development response to Question 2023 or written reply, August 2012*, (Cape Town: Parliament of the Republic of South Africa).

Henderson, P. C. (2006) 'South African AIDS Orphans: Examining Assumptions around Vulnerability from the Perspective of Rural Children and Youth', *Childhood*, 13(3), 303–327.

Henderson, P. C. (2009) Unpublished fieldnotes.

Henderson, P. C. (2011a) 'Theorising Creative Expression in Children's Participation', *Perspectives in Education*, 29(1), 18–26.

Henderson, P. C. (2011b) *AIDS, intimacy and care in rural KwaZulu-Natal: A kinship of bones*, (Amsterdam: Amsterdam University Press).

Heystek, J. (2001) 'Learner Representatives in the Governing Bodies of Secondary Schools', *Acta Academica*, 33(3), 207–230.

Hyslop, J. (1988) 'School student movements and state education policy: 1972–1987' in W. Cobbett and R. Cohen (eds) *Popular Struggles in South Africa* (London: James Currey).

Jamieson, L. (2008) 'Involving Children in the Development of Child Protection Legislation in South Africa' Paper presented at the XVIIth ISPCAN International Congress on Child Abuse and Neglect, Towards a Caring and Non-Violent Community: A Child's Perspective. Hong Kong, Republic of China, 7–10 September.

Jamieson, L. (2010) 'Law Reformers' Views on Child Participation: Strategic Ally or Liability?' Paper presented at the third international seminar on Theorising Child Participation: Learning across Disciplines and Countries (Delhi, India 12–17 December 2010).

Jamieson, L. (2011) 'Children's rights to participate in social dialogue', in L. Jamieson, R. Bray, A. Viviers, L. Lake, S. Pendlebury and C. Smith (eds) *South African Child Gauge 2010/2011*, (Cape Town: Children's Institute, University of Cape Town).

Jamieson, L., Bray, R., Viviers, A., Lake, L., Pendlebury, S. and Smith, C. (eds) (2011) *South African Child Gauge 2010/2011*, (Cape Town: Children's Institute, University of Cape Town).

Jenks, C. (1996) *Childhood*, (London: Routledge).

Jonker, I. (2001) 'The child who was shot dead by soldiers in Nyanga' in Collected Works, trans. Jack Cope and William Plomer (Cape Town: Human & Rousseau).

Leal, P. A. (2010) 'Participation: The ascendancy of a buzzword in the neo-liberal era' in A. Cornwall and D. Eade (eds) *Deconstructing Development Discourse: Buzzwords and Fuzzwords*, (Rugby: Practical Action Publishing in association with Oxfam GB).

Marks, M. (2001) *Young warriors: Youth politics, identity and violence in South Africa*, (Johannesburg: Witwatersrand University Press).

Meintjes, H. (2011) 'Unsettling the status quo: children's challenges to adult perceptions and practices', in L. Jamieson, R. Bray, A. Viviers, L. Lake, S. Pendlebury and C. Smith (eds) *South African Child Gauge 2010/2011*, (Cape Town: Children's Institute, University of Cape Town).

Meintjes, H. and Hall, K. (2011) 'Demography of South Africa's children', in L. Jamieson, R. Bray, A. Viviers, L. Lake, S. Pendlebury and C. Smith (eds) *South African Child Gauge 2010/2011*, (Cape Town: Children's Institute, University of Cape Town).

Mniki, N. and Rosa, S. (2007) 'Heroes in Action: A Case Study of Child Advocates in South Africa', *Children, Youth and Environments*, 17(3), 179–197.

Moses, S. (2008) 'Children and Participation in South Africa: An Overview', *International Journal of Children's Rights*, 16(3), 327–342.

Ndebele, N. (1995) 'Children in South African national reconstruction', in S. Stephens (ed.) *Children and the Politics of Culture*, (Princeton: Princeton University Press).

Ngomane, T. and Flanagan, C. (2003) 'The Road to Democracy in South Africa', *Peace Review*, 15(3), 267–271.

Nomdo, C. and Roberts, H. (2011) 'Children's involvement in government policy and budget analysis', in L. Jamieson, R. Bray, A. Viviers, L. Lake, S. Pendlebury and C. Smith (eds) *South African Child Gauge 2010/2011*, (Cape Town: Children's Institute, University of Cape Town).

Pendlebury, S. (2011) 'Children and school governance: representation, participation and power', in L. Jamieson, R. Bray, A. Viviers, L. Lake, S. Pendlebury and C. Smith (eds) *South African Child Gauge 2010/2011*, (Cape Town: Children's Institute, University of Cape Town).

Phaswana, E. (2010) 'Learner Councillors' Perspectives on Learner Participation', *South African Journal of Education*, 30, 105–122.

Portfolio Committee on Social Development (2007) 'Children's Amendment Bill [B19B-2006] Report', http://www.pmg.org.za/docs/2007/071024draft.htm.

Reynolds, P (2008) 'On Leaving the Young out of History', *The Journal of the History of Childhood and Youth*, 1(1), 150–156.

Reynolds, P. (2012) *War in Worcester: Youth and the apartheid state*, (New York: Fordham University Press).

Roodt, M. and Stuurman, S. (2011) 'Participation, Local Governance and Attitudes of Youth: A Grahamstown Case Study', *Perspectives in Education*, 29(1), 66–74.

Ross, F. (2003) *Bearing witness: Women and the truth and reconciliation commission in South Africa*, (London: Pluto Press).

Seekings, J. (1993) *Heroes or villains? Youth politics in the 1980s*, (Johannesburg: Ravan Press).

Seekings, J. (1996) 'The "Lost Generation": South Africa's "Youth Problem" in the early 1990s', *Transformation* 29, 103–125.

Seekings, J. (2006) 'Beyond Heroes and Villains: The Rediscovery of the Ordinary in the Study of Childhood and Adolescence in South Africa', *Social Dynamics*, 32(1), 1–20.

Sloth-Nielsen, J. (1996) 'Chicken Soup or Chainsaws: Some Implications of the Constitutionalisation of Children's Rights in South Africa', *Acta Juridica*, 6–27.

Skelton, A. and Proudlock, P. (2011) 'Interpretation, objects, application and implementation of the Children's Act' in C. J. Davel and A. Skelton (eds) *Commentary on the Children's Act* (Claremont: Juta).

Straker, G. (1992) *Faces in the Revolution: The psychological effects of violence on township youth in South Africa*, (Cape Town: David Philip).

Stuurman, S. (2009) 'The Role of the Ward Committees as an Interface between Local Government and Community: A Case Study of Makana Municipality'. Unpublished MA dissertation (Grahamstown: Rhodes University).

UN Committee on the Rights of the Child (CROC), (2009) 'General Comment No. 12: The right of the child to be heard, 20 July 2009', CRC/C/GC/12.

Woodhouse, B. B. (1999) 'Recognising Children's Rights: Lessons from South Africa', *Human Rights*, Spring 1999, 15–18.

Young, I. M. (2002) *Inclusion and Democracy*, (Oxford: Oxford University Press).

9

Growing Up in a Time of AIDS: The Shining Recorders of Zisize

Helen Meintjes

Introduction[1]

As the HIV epidemic increasingly took hold across South Africa during the 1990s and early 2000s, images of destitute young orphans left to fend for themselves by overburdened kin support systems proliferated. Depictions of helpless children prone to hunger, school dropout, exploitation and sexual debut at a very young age, and predisposed to future criminality were repeated, over and over, in local and international media (Meintjes and Bray, 2005) as well as in international aid agency, government, donor and non-government organization (NGO) publications (Meintjes and Giese, 2006). Rapidly growing in number, orphans were stereotyped as both the quintessential victims of the epidemic and a significant social threat in South Africa (Meintjes and Bray, 2005; Meintjes and Giese, 2006).

Children and young people were seldom engaged as sources in media reports about their circumstances (Media Monitoring Project, 2004; Meintjes and Bray, 2005). Analyses of South African media reporting critique a tendency to 'use the voices of children' to support preconceived stories rather than to inform the account: 'Children ... are enlisted as characters to enrich and confirm the journalist's stake on the situation, rather than brought in as active participants in creating their own representations' (Bird and Rahfaldt, 2011, p. 54). Initiatives to involve children and young people directly in producing media, including producing media for children, were similarly limited and present only in a handful of urban community media settings.

It is against this backdrop that the *Abaqophi BakwaZisize Abakhanyayo* children's radio project was first established at Okhayeni Primary School in rural KwaZulu-Natal, South Africa in 2005. It was initiated by Zisize

Educational Trust, an NGO working through schools to provide a range of support services in the area, and the Children's Institute, a policy research and advocacy unit based at the University of Cape Town. *Abaqophi BakwaZisize Abakhanyayo*, the name given to the project by its young participants, translates from isiZulu into English as the Shining Recorders of Zisize.

Colleagues in the collaborating institutions were troubled by international and South African representations of the experiences of children and young people growing up in the context of AIDS. As researchers, service providers and teachers, we were struck by the disjuncture between our direct observations of children with whom we worked and popular images of children affected by HIV. The almost exclusive focus on orphaning, and the nature and extent of stereotype present in depictions, masked the diverse repercussions of the epidemic for children. They also obscured the variety of children's and families' experiences, concerns, responses and achievements. The collaborating team was concerned by the ways in which we observed these popular understandings to be shaping funding, policy, interventions and even South African law (see also Meintjes and Giese, 2006).

The radio project thus set out to provide children in a remote, severely HIV-affected district in South Africa with the skills and support to develop their own narratives for radio broadcast. What kinds of images of childhood would children growing up in these contexts present? What aspects of their lives would they choose to highlight, given the opportunity? Would these representations differ from those produced by adult journalists and others? Through child-directed storytelling and public broadcast of the material, the project aimed to nuance depictions of children's experiences growing up in a context of poverty and the AIDS epidemic, and to encourage adults to consider and appropriately address their needs and experiences.

Over 60 children aged nine years and above have been involved in the project since it first began, most of them on an ongoing basis. During weekly after-school sessions and intensive holiday workshops, the young participants have been trained and supported to produce broadcast-quality radio programs in a variety of formats including personal radio diaries, commentaries and features. In addition to distributing their programs via the web (www.childrensradioproject. ci.org.za), the children host a monthly show on the local community radio station, where they air their pre-recorded and edited programs, facilitate live discussions in studio and with listeners and report on news collected from schools in the area.

The project is unusual in South Africa for its remote rural location, as well as the opportunity for children and young people to be involved for multiple years in an initiative aiming to both build their skills and extend their voice.

This chapter considers some of the transformative effects of the children's participation in the project, with a particular focus on shifts observed at the local level. It examines the method, nature and content of the radio program production, and the way in which participants have made use of the process to open up spaces for expression and communication that are not generally available to them in their everyday lives. It considers the effect of the program production process on the participants and on their relationships with adults, arguing that an initiative like this, in a context in which child-adult communication is constrained in a number of ways, enables important, if small, shifts to occur in the ways in which adults view and engage children. Throughout, I refer to the participants as 'children': In the region in which the project operates, young people of school-going age (and beyond) are considered to be 'children', and would generally identify themselves as such.

The chapter is based on: notes from after-school and holiday workshops, team reflection meetings, and consent sessions and other meetings with caregivers; transcripts of recorded material and final radio programs; field observations since the start of the project; and data generated at a participatory evaluation workshop facilitated with all children participating in the project in September 2009.

Context

The rural expanse of Ingwavuma, in the far north-eastern corner of Kwazulu-Natal, South Africa, stretches across the Lebombo mountains and the Pongola river flood plain, sharing its borders with south-eastern Swaziland and southern Mozambique. Umkhanyakude district, into which Ingwavuma falls, is one of the poorest districts in South Africa (Day et al., 2011). Like other ex-Bantustans, the area was strategically underdeveloped during apartheid and remains severely under-resourced even today (Noble et al., 2006). Homesteads – some constructed from wooden poles, stone and wire-mesh, others from cement blocks – are scattered fairly uniformly across the countryside, with some clustering at transport and service nodes. Homes near the main roads increasingly have access to electricity but the vast majority of households do not. Almost two-thirds of households in the district rely on candles for lighting and wood fires for cooking (Statistics South Africa, 2008), and 30 percent of households report having no access to any form of toilet facility (Statistics South Africa, 2009). Few have water piped to their houses or yards (approximately 30 percent) and most residents collect water from erratically operating public water pumps and the nearby river. One-fifth of adults aged between 20 and 59 years old were recorded as having no formal schooling in 2007, while a further 57 percent had not completed school. Access to work opportunities in the area is limited and the vast majority of households rely heavily on social grants provided by the State for children and the elderly. Over half of households have a total monthly income (including social grants) below R2210 (in 2012 values, and equivalent to £286 per month, using Purchasing Power Parity [Statistics South Africa, 2008]).

Here children (who constitute half of the population) grow up not only amidst extensive poverty but also with a legacy of under-resourced or absent service provision and a burgeoning HIV epidemic. Forty-one percent of pregnant women in the district are infected with HIV (Department of Health, 2012), a statistic that places the area firmly at the epicenter of the epidemic in South Africa.

Newspapers are available only in larger towns. Most are published in English, thereby excluding the majority of the isiZulu-speaking population. Limited access to electricity in the area constrains television ownership and usage: approximately 36 percent of households reported owning a television in 2007 in contrast to extensive radio ownership (73 percent) (Statistics South Africa, 2009). For the vast majority of residents in the area, the only regular access to the media is through radio. In this regard, Maputaland Community Radio station, a community station based in one of the small towns in the district, plays a central role alongside the State-owned isiZulu-language station Ukhozi FM.

As is the case in many parts of southern Africa (and outlined in the previous chapter), interactions between children and adults in the area are shaped by deeply entrenched customary practices associated with respect (see also Argyle and Preston-Whyte, 1978; Krige, 1950). A series of practices of avoidance connote children's respect for elders: rules of engagement in general require them to avoid eye contact with unrelated adults and not to approach adults unless spoken to first. Responses to adults' questions are ideally kept short, and their instructions obeyed immediately. There is little inter-generational dialog about issues in the home or community. Children make a substantial contribution to sustaining family and community life (through sharing responsibility for domestic and agricultural work, provision of care for the very young, the elderly, and the sick, and so on) but they seldom participate in decision-making processes, including those that have important implications for their own lives.

Project design

Children between 9 and 18 years are grouped by age and location into five groups that meet for weekly after-school sessions and intensive holiday radio training and production workshops. Each group is at a different level of technical skill, depending on the length of their involvement in the project. Participants are supported through a series of training and production processes.

The first is a series of art workshops in which children produce individually illustrated personal accounts that document a 'journey' through their lives. Once this 'foundation phase' is complete, they learn how to record personal radio diaries about aspects of their lives. Adult facilitators use interactive, practical methods to train them in storytelling and narrative, question formulation, interviewing, the components of radio program production as well as the technical aspects of audio recording. Over time the children progress to other formats and to producing and presenting the live show. Each year the facilitators attempt to expand and consolidate the participants' radio skills: locally based Zisize-employed facilitators support the ongoing training and production from week to week; Children's Institute facilitators design and lead the facilitation of skills-building workshops during school holidays (held as frequently as funding permits).

The children identify the topics for their programs. This they sometimes do individually, sometimes collaboratively. In discussion with each other and the facilitators, they plan their narratives, who they would like to interview, what questions they will ask and the locations for recordings. Wielding recorders and microphones, they record interviews, narratives and soundscapes. Once recordings are complete, the more experienced participants script and narrate their programs, and finally agree on edits to complete the programs.

The facilitators' role is to enable skills development, support the program planning and production process, grasp what the children want to achieve with each program and enact this as best possible during the technical editing process. The task is to mediate in moments where teamwork fails, provide information where asked, keep a watchful eye on the participants and provide an avenue for them to access help when facing difficulties in their personal lives.

Figure 9.1 A boy from the *Abaqophi bakwaZisize Abakhanyayo* children's radio project in rural Ingwavuma, South Africa, records sound effects for his radio diary program
Photographer: Sue Valentine, 2007.

A crucial component of this initiative has therefore been to build the capacity of project team members in Ingwavuma to facilitate child- and youth-participatory processes in general, as well as more specifically in radio production. When the project was first initiated, this expertise was located in the Cape Town-based Children's Institute team and consultants: as a result of a variety of participatory training interventions, modeled practice and ongoing mentorship within the overall project team, the project facilitators based in Ingwavuma have learned to design and facilitate most of the necessary processes, as well as edit programs on site. However, building and sustaining a team of facilitators with a deep understanding of – and ease with – non-directive facilitation of children as well as technical media skill is one of the project's central challenges. Local facilitators find themselves in an ambiguous position that can be difficult for them to navigate: on one hand, their task is to enable and support participants to express themselves openly; on the other, they understand that within this context, parents and caregivers consider them to be parental stand-ins (with concomitant expectations of the exercise of authority and control) while their children are in their care.

Radio programs

Children have addressed a diverse set of experiences in their programs. These include their experiences of living with the constant presence of illness and death in their homes or neighborhood, of living amidst widespread and enduring poverty, in changing households and in an under-serviced and remote rural area. They tell stories of precious pet goats or favorite cows, of treasured gifts, of rare and exciting journeys to the nearest town or to visit relatives living elsewhere. They describe milestones and rites of passage: a first trip hitchhiking alone to the shop; participation in a virginity-testing ritual; meeting a father for the first time; a first day at school; learning to ride a bicycle; a first encounter with stairs, at an uncle's wedding at a nearby tourist lodge. They detail favorite activities: hunting birds, playing soccer, collecting honey from wild beehives, jumping elastics, or identifying cars as they drive past on the lone tarred road. They explore the local mythology of a two-headed snake living in the nearby dam; they question the Zulu king about the gendered nature of virginity-testing practices; and they interview grandmothers who play the ancient Jew's harp. They find out about fathers and mothers, absent and present. They describe seeking solace: at the river; in the bush while herding cows; with a beloved aunt. They story the emotion of the constant mobility of their and others' lives: adults and children moving from household to household, from caregiver to caregiver, from South Africa to Swaziland and back again; seeking employment or care or access to resources, to escape from abuse, for love. They detail their devastation: not being told about a father's imminent death; the slaughter of a pet goat; exclusion from a parent's funeral; or a mother's unexplained move out of a household. They share their deep knowledge of their environment, describing where to find bees and naming trees and plants that can be eaten or used in the treatment of illnesses. They describe their responsibilities: collecting water from the pump or river, or firewood from the bush; ensuring a spic and span house or yard; or checking that a grandmother took her tablets. They take listeners to their favorite places: a huge rock amongst the aloe plants on the hill; the river where there are always others keen to play; a mother's grave. They tell stories of caring for ill parents, elderly grandmothers and young siblings. Of adult care, kindness, neglect and abuse. Of memories, losses, wishes, courage, happiness and celebration.[2]

The programs repeatedly speak directly into silences in families and communities: silences about illness, death, abuse, absence, mobility, decision-making, (mis)communication and more. Children frequently use their program production process to draw attention to issues and experiences that trouble them, to ask questions they would like answered and to engage others for their perspectives. They do this through their choice of story, through the content of their narratives, through the questions they ask during interviews and through recording explicit messages to listeners.

Many of the children who produced these programs are orphans. All are affected in some way by the AIDS epidemic by virtue of the neighborhood in which they live. The diverse range of experiences, insights and concerns inherent in the depictions of their lives in their radio programs is in stark contrast to the depictions common in the mainstream media. In these brief audio-packages, the children capture not only extensive suffering and struggle but also their courage, creativity, dignity, curiosity and humor, as well as the remarkable extent of care provided by many adults in their communities. In so doing, they point to a broader (and in many respects more subtle) range of needs than is usually suggested in popular representations (a point discussed more fully in Meintjes, 2012).

Broadcast of programs

Captivated by the content and quality of the first set of radio diary programs recorded in 2005, the project team approached the national radio station catering for isiZulu speakers in South Africa to offer the programs for broadcast. After the team's repeated attempts to engage a number of producers, the station agreed to air the radio diaries during the current affairs slot on two consecutive days. The children and their families were elated at the prospect of the radio diaries being broadcast on a station with over 6.5 million listeners. However they were subsequently devastated at the outcome. Journalists at the station cut, spliced and reordered the content of the programs, each of which had been carefully edited in consultation with the participants and approved by their caregivers. Nuance was removed in a process that entailed selecting and merging only the elements of suffering and drama into two short inserts. The pieces that aired, to millions of listeners, presented an image of wretched destitution that angered and embarrassed families. Sensitive to the stigma associated with the HIV epidemic, parents complained that the broadcaster 'made it look as if there is nothing here other than AIDS' and were understandably reluctant to give permission for further broadcast of their children's programs until a clear code for their use in the media was in place.

Since this event, the programs have been broadcast primarily during the children's slot on the local community radio station, with the exception of special occasions such as World AIDS Day and the International Day of Children's Broadcasting. Despite the fact that the programs consistently astound adults who hear them, there has been little success in convincing journalists at this station or elsewhere of the value of inserting the programs into broadcasts targeting adults. Thus although the programs provide the possibility of alternative portrayals to those prevalent in the media, they fail to shift the dominant depictions provided to radio listeners either in the district or further afield.

Children and young people's sense of personal transformation

The children participating in the project have shown little concern about the limited reach of their programs. Their agenda is different: most joined the project to learn skills, make programs and have the opportunity to be on air. Their focus is on the local: for most, the chance to make radio of their choice, and thus have their experiences and perspectives heard by others in the district via the community radio station, is itself a valued achievement.

Reflecting on the project, they foreground the positive personal repercussions of their involvement. They highlight their appreciation of the useful skills they have learned and the pedagogical approach (involving participatory methods, so different to those that they encounter at school) used to achieve this. In particular, they celebrate their sense of increased confidence resulting from their experiences in the project, most of which are unusual in the context: the training and constant practice in asking questions and articulating their views; their exposure to English via contact with mother-tongue English speakers during holiday workshops; the development of a set of close-knit emotionally open peer relationships; the opportunity provided to talk publicly and privately about issues of importance or concern to them; and repeated positive interactions with adults who are responsive to their opinions and who value their perspectives. On one hand, participants describe their increased confidence to share their opinions, experiences and feelings in personal interactions. Nomfundo, aged nine when she joined the project, reflected at the age of 11:[3]

> Since joining this group, I am able to speak about things that have happened in my family. I'm not shy anymore ... I'm able to share my opinion. I don't keep it to myself ... I'm able to sit down with my parents and just talk to them. Sometimes I ask them to give me advice ... This has happened since I joined the project.

Hers is a repeated refrain. Similarly, participants repeatedly note the changes in their comfort with communicating in public spaces: in class, at meetings, at assembly and at other school and community forums. Commented Sabelo, renowned in the group for his turn of phrase (and aged 15 at the time):

> I'm no longer shy when I'm standing in front of people. I think I could speak in parliament without being shy! ... Because speaking has become a part of me. I am so happy that I can [now] express myself freely ... This is because I'm part of this project.

In other words, participants identify how shifts in their personal sense of confidence resulting from their participation in the project enable them to speak – and 'speak out' – more readily, and to positive personal effect, in both private and public domains.

Engaging across generations

In creating their programs, the children continually engage adults in inter-generational dialog of a kind that rarely occurs in this neighborhood.

For example at the age of 12, Mkhethi took the opportunity while making her radio diary to ask her mother about her father. She had never met him and had never been told about him. Slowly during the interview she gathered the courage to question her mother, and to reveal her desire for more information, at which point her questions flew out in quick succession:

> Mama, I want to know about my father, what was he like? ... Was he dark? How dark? ... Has he never seen me? ... Now would you like him to meet me? ... How can he meet me?

Her mother responded without hesitation, with clear and supportive answers, despite never having broached the issue with Mkhethi before.

Over the years there have been numerous other examples in which participants initiated powerful out-of-the-ordinary conversations with adults. An HIV-positive woman was asked to talk about her experiences of diagnosis, disclosure and raising a child. A doctor was asked to explain how children get infected with HIV and what treatment options are available. Nine-year-old Nomfundo confronted her father's alcoholism head on in conversation with her mother and together they detailed the ways in which life at home had improved since he stopped drinking in order to take tuberculosis treatment. Grateful that her stepfather took her into his home and loves her as his own child, Nothando (aged 11) reflected in dialog with her mother why this is frequently not the case for children in her neighborhood. Many children are born outside of marriage and long-term relationships. Perplexed by the practice of mothers leaving their children to live with other relatives when they marry a man who is not their children's biological father, she asked:

> Why do some mothers not live with their children when they have married into another family?

Her mother replied:

> I think it's because of the husband, maybe he says 'I only want you, I don't want the child you had previously, it's better you leave it behind'. But your stepfather told me that he loves me and my child.

Nothando grinned. This was something she knew. She believed her stepfather proved his love for her when he surprised her with a gift of a brand new bicycle, a rare and treasured item in the neighborhood. She continued the conversation with curiosity:

> How does that make you feel, mama?

And her mother explained:

> Ha! I saw that he really loved me because he did not treat you differently to the other children in the house.

Cognizant of the painful experiences of other children in her group, Nothando questioned her further:

What would your message be to those mothers [who leave their children upon marriage]?

Her mother hesitated briefly, before responding:

When a person loves you he should love you with your child, without discriminating against your child and separating you from your child.

Each instance of interaction, each moment of unusual communication, is striking because of the context in which it occurs and the way in which it transgresses the unspoken but widely understood limits of children's place in society. In each of these examples, children raise issues not usually discussed with adults, issues that in general are actively avoided by adults around them. With a microphone in hand, children have the pretext for asking pointed questions and, in so doing, many choose to initiate and direct conversation in ways not usually

Figure 9.2 A girl from the *Abaqophi bakwaZisize Abakhanyayo* children's radio project in rural Ingwavuma, South Africa, interviews her grandmother for her radio diary program
Photographer: Gabriel Urgoiti, 2007.

accessible to them. Faithful to their upbringing – and their training in the documentary interview – they approach their elders respectfully, without rebellion or accusation. Nonetheless, enabled by the format and method of the radio documentary, they unsettle conventional modes of communication and practice.

Throughout, adults have seemed at ease with participants' contraventions of convention and have often explicitly stated their appreciation of the outcome. Since the inception of the project, there has been only one instance of an adult complaining about a child's mode of communication. This occurred at an annual meeting of all participants in the project together with their caregivers. A representative from each of the five groups of participants presented an overview of what they had done over the course of the year. One of the children impersonated a popular radio disc jockey when he presented, using slang and speaking rapidly, with an accent. His jaunty performance was interpreted by adults present as inappropriately cocky and was immediately admonished at the meeting. The critique focused on the informality of his communication style as disrespectful. This was a rare instance of dramatic playfulness: there have been no similar examples from children when recording their interviews with adults.

Reaching adults, shifting practice

Jabu is a devoted son. In recording his radio diary at the age of 12, he surprised his mother with his clear memory of difficult times when he was a younger child. After his questions about the period when she left him in the care of his father's second wife while she travelled as a trader, she spontaneously reflected back to him the lesson she learned as a result of his inquiry:

> I never realized that [you], my child, felt the pain of what we were going through at that time in our lives. I didn't think children were aware of so much that is going on around them.

Another guardian, this time a grandfather and primary caregiver to his granddaughter Sibu (aged nine at the time), commented similarly after facing her questions about her mother's death six years previously:

> We sometimes think that our children cannot see what is going on. But they see! They just don't have the platform to ask.

Observations like these are a repeated refrain from those who encounter the children and the programs that they produce. School principals and teachers, parents, caregivers, and community members have all noticed – usually with surprise – that children are aware and capable of understanding their circumstances. Each instance is indicative of the extent to which children's capacity is concealed by dominant notions of childhood (including the need for children to be protected from emotional distress) as well as by local practices of respect that limit children's opportunities to communicate with adults. In transgressing social conventions of communication, the children who participate in the project dislodge adults' assumptions and nudge them to engage them differently. Many adults argue that having been exposed to children's ability and insight, they have changed their practices when communicating with children or plan to do so. As just one example, a school principal articulated the change in her view:

> What I have learnt is that we look at kids or think about kids as not being aware of issues, or of issues not affecting them. But after hearing the programs I've realized that children know about things we think they don't know about. I realized that they know, and if given a chance to speak about those things, they speak. I realized that they think deeply about these things and these issues that they raise … I no longer look at children as mere children who do not know anything. I look at them as people who know something and who have something to say to me, and who can speak freely and be just as confident as an adult.

A number of participants in the project have noted shifts in the ways in which certain adults treat them. They describe being consulted for their opinions more frequently by caregivers, as well as increases in the extent to which they are kept informed by particular adults. For example, Precious – who in her first diary program gently challenged her mother about failing to communicate properly with her about her father's death – observed changes in the ways her mother relates to her about her own illnesses.

> Now when she is sick she tells us. Before she did not because she thought we would be sad and be affected in our studies at school. Now she does not hide it. She tells us.

Zanele reiterated similarly:

> Some people hear our message just as we have said it [that is, take our messages to heart] ... In the past they did not consult us on what was happening: we would just see things happening. But these days they start by asking us what we think.

As children speak out, and speak directly to adults – asking questions, articulating concerns or desires – adults' notions of children and childhood are unsettled. Both children and adults gain new understandings of each other's perspectives through conversations facilitated by the program production process or through hearing the programs. Transgressions of social convention (from within a sanctioned frame) provoke important new insights for adults into children's lives. These enable small but significant shifts in their relationships and practices to take place.

This is not, however, a sea change: it is a series of isolated examples of transformative shifts in personal relationships, shifts that may or may not endure through time and changing contexts. A caregiver moves away – and a child again finds herself mistreated or unheard by the remaining members of the household. A mother dies – and a child is again kept away from death rituals by other adults, in the interests of protecting her. A child discovers that his father is comfortable – even values – being addressed or questioned directly in private but recognizes that he does not have the same latitude to upend deeply embedded cultural practices of respect with adults outside the home. Contraventions of communication norms while making radio programs are applauded by a teacher but disciplined when repeated in the classroom. In other words, shifts experienced by the participants are circumscribed by context, are time-specific and are located in individual relationships.

Conclusion

Despite substantial global shifts in concepts of childhood over the last two decades, dominant notions of children and childhood continue, on one hand, to limit the potential for community-based participatory interventions like the *Abaqophi bakwaZisize Abakhanyayo* children's radio project to achieve widespread and sustained transformative change. Although the programs produced by the participants in the radio project expand and nuance our images of children and young people growing up in a context of AIDS, they fail to intervene substantively in media (or broader public) discourses. This is arguably in part because programming produced by children is considered to be of interest only to their contemporaries (and thus broadcast is limited to children's programming slots) and in part because of the notions of newsworthiness that operate in the mainstream media in South Africa and beyond. Without changed priorities on the part of media authorities, or, alternatively, funds to pay for airtime on major stations, it is a challenge to secure broadcast slots for unconventional programming.

Paradoxically, however, it is also the nature and extent of narrowly circumscribed notions of childhood held in the neighborhood in which the project operates that enhance aspects of its transformative potential at a local level. In particular, the choice of radio as the vehicle for expression seems to enable children, in the expert role of reporter, to upend social convention intricately linked to customary practices of respect and the related 'place' of children in Ingwavuma. It permits children to say things they are not otherwise able to say, raise issues they are not otherwise able to address, to ask questions they are not otherwise able to ask and to speak to people they are not otherwise able to easily approach. Children lay before adults their capacity, expertise and insight by proficiently wielding microphones and recording equipment, formulating insightful questions, responding adeptly and asserting considered opinions. As reporters therefore, the children occupy a position of relative power: they set the agenda for communication, they ask the questions and in producing programs for radio broadcast they address a wider communal listenership. The approach limits opportunities for adults to patronize or dominate the children, clearly demonstrates their expertise and extends the possibilities for meaningful intergenerational interaction. The shared learning about each others' perspectives that is achieved through producing and hearing the radio programs has the potential to transform interpersonal relationships in ways that improve adults' understanding of children's capacity and enable more effective intergenerational communication to continue even in the absence of the microphone.

Participants' own views are that their experience in the project has also been personally transformative. At an individual level, the exposure to opportunities not commonly accessible to children and young people in the area – including access to particular kinds of skills, opportunities for expression associated with making radio, as well as unusual forms of intergenerational engagement – has shifted many participants' sense of self-confidence.

In the absence of more extensive broadcast of the children's programs, the impact of the project is thus largely through direct involvement. This is, however, limited by the project's scale, an issue difficult to address in a context of limited funding and, arguably more importantly, the challenge of identifying and sustaining facilitation teams with the appropriate philosophies and capacities to run a project of this nature.

Acknowledgments

This chapter benefits from the reflections of all the members of the Abaqophi project team since it began: Bridget Walters, Bongekile Mngomezulu, Sue Valentine, Gabriel Urgoiti, Andrew Sitima, Xolisile Mnyandu, Fana Matonsi, Gcina Mvana, Zakhele Msweli and Mbali Mthembu. A number of donors have supported the project: most recently, the DG Murray Trust, the Nelson Mandela Children's Fund and the Media Development and Diversity Agency. ELMA Foundation funding received by the Children's Institute is gratefully acknowledged for its contribution towards my time for writing. I am grateful, too, to Kath Hall, Shirley Pendlebury and Karen Tranberg Hansen for discussion of ideas and text.

Notes

1. This chapter is a substantially revised and expanded version of Meintjes, H. (2010) 'Unsettling the status quo: children's challenges to adult perceptions and practices' in L. Jamieson, R. Bray, A. Viviers, L. Lake, S. Pendlebury, and C. Smiths (eds) *South African Child Gauge 2010/2011*. (Cape Town: Children's Institute, University of Cape Town).
2. isiZulu audio and translated transcripts of the programmes can be downloaded from www.childrensradioproject.ci.org.za
3. All direct quotes throughout the chapter are translated into English from their original isiZulu.

Bibliography

Argyle, J. and Preston-Whyte, E. (1978) *Social system and tradition in Southern Africa*, (Cape Town: Oxford University Press).
Bird, W. and Rahfaldt, M. (2011) 'Children and the media: Voices worth hearing?' in L. Jamieson, R. Bray, A. Viviers, L. Lake, S. Pendlebury and C. Smith (eds) *South African Child Gauge 2010/2011*, (Cape Town: Children's Institute, University of Cape Town).
Day, C., Barron, P., Massyn, N., Padarath, A. and English, R. (2011) *The District Health Barometer 2010/11*, (Durban: Health Systems Trust).
Department of Health (2012) *The 2011 National Antenatal Sentinel HIV and Syphilis Prevalence Survey in South Africa*, (Pretoria: National Department of Health, South Africa).
Krige, E. (1950) *The Social System of the Zulus*, (London: Longman).

Media Monitoring Project (2004) *Media Wise: Children Make a Difference*, (Johannesburg: Media Monitoring Project).

Meintjes, H. (2012) 'Straight talk: Children's narratives of poverty'. Paper presented at the Conference on Strategies to Overcome Poverty and Inequality: Towards Carnegie III. University of Cape Town, 3–7 September 2012.

Meintjes, H. and Bray, R. (2005) '"But where are our moral heroes?" An analysis of South African press reporting on children affected by HIV/AIDS', *African Journal of AIDS Research*, 4(3), 147–159.

Meintjes, H. and Giese, S. (2006) 'Spinning the epidemic: The making of mythologies of orphanhood in the context of AIDS', *Childhood: A global journal of child research*, 13(3), 407–430.

Noble, M., Babita, M., Barnes, H., Dibben, C., Magasela, W., Noble, S., Ntshongwana, P., Phillips, H., Rama, S., Roberts, B., Wright, G. and Zungu, S. (2006) *The Provincial Indices of Multiple Deprivation for South Africa 2001*, (Oxford: Department of Social Policy and Social Work, Oxford University).

Statistics South Africa (2008) *Community Survey 2007*, (Pretoria: Statistics South Africa).

Statistics South Africa (2009) *Community Survey 2007: Basic Results – KwaZulu-Natal*, (Pretoria: Statistics South Africa).

10
Children Should Be Seen and Heard? Children and Young People's Participation in the UK

E. Kay M. Tisdall

Introduction

In their 2003 text book chapter, Kirby and Woodhead encourage readers to (re)consider their ideas about childhood by listing various proverbs. Some proverbs value children as a societal investment, such as 'Children are the wealth of the nation' (Tanzania), 'It is the young trees that make the forest thick' (Uganda) or 'Educate the children so you will not have to punish the men' (Brazil). Other proverbs take a developmental, disciplinary approach like 'A tree should be bent while it is still young' (South Africa) or 'When a child knows how to wash his hands he eats with his elders' (Ghana). The UK proverb does not even provide these levels of recognition; the proverb attributed to the UK is that 'Children should be seen and not heard'.

This proverb suggests cultural views, perceptions of children and childhood, which would not support children and young people's involvement at all in individual or collective decision-making. The participation rights of the United Nations Convention on the Rights of the Child (UNCRC), then, would be a particular challenge to policy, practice and lived realities within families, communities and public spaces. To realize children and young people's participation rights, major cultural change would be required.

In many ways, this cultural change is taking place. The UK Government ratified the UNCRC in 1991. Children and young people's rights to participate are now included in various legal and policy documents. A plethora of structures, activities and consultations has been funded on local and national levels, seeking to promote, recognize and hear children and young people's views. When the change over recent years is reviewed, a great deal can be celebrated. Yet, ongoing, significant challenges continue in ensuring such participation is meaningful to all those involved, sustainable and effective – particularly in terms of having an impact on decision-making.

This chapter begins by sketching out the context for children and young people's participation in the UK, from basic demographics to legal developments. Moving on from this largely descriptive account, the chapter looks more critically at children and young people's participation, considering how it has been promoted and the implications for 'transformative' participation as a result. It looks to recent examples that may create new spaces, languages and relationships for participation, to meet the challenges above and potentially lead to 'transformative' participation.

Part I: The context for children and young people's participation

Children and young people are a minority group in the UK, within an aging population: in 2010, 19 percent of the population were under age 16, while 20 percent were of pensionable age; by 2035, 18 percent are projected to be under the age of 16 while 21 percent will be of pensionable age (Office for National Statistics (ONS), 2012).[1] The fertility rate dipped considerably in the first part of the twenty-first century and now is rising slightly (in 2010, the total fertility rate[2] was 1.98 children per woman in the UK (ONS, 2012)). The population is becoming more diverse, in terms of ethnicity, culture, religion and belief, but not consistently across the UK. For example, 26.5 percent of pupils in England are classified as being of minority ethnic origin (Department for Education, England, 2011). This compares to 8.0 percent in Scotland, 7.4 percent in Wales and 2.6 percent in Northern Ireland (Department of Education, Northern Ireland, 2011; Scottish Government, 2011; Statistics for Wales, 2011). Families from certain ethnic and cultural groups are more likely than the white population to have children, and to have more children, which may well increase this diversity across time (ONS, 2004b).

The UK's population density is large for European countries but unevenly distributed, with significantly greater density in England than elsewhere in the UK. While one of the world's largest national economies, the UK has one of the highest rates of child poverty in Europe (3.6 million children in the UK lived in low-income households in 2010–2011[3] or around 27 percent of all children (Department of Work and Pensions, 2012)). The UK has fared badly in the index of children's well-being, being ranked last amongst 21 'rich countries' in the UNICEF

Innocenti Report (2007) – although it has risen to number 16 out of 29 in the 2013 report.

The UK has an extensive welfare state, ranging from a National Health Service ('free at the point of delivery', although somewhat qualified), to compulsory primary and secondary schooling, to a 'safety net' of means-tested benefits to provide a minimum living standard. The UK is a liberal democracy, with a strong adherence to the rule of law, and thus (officially) a separation between parliamentary, judicial and administrative powers. The UK has increasing diversity in governance and government, with devolution being introduced in the late 1990s. Northern Ireland and Wales each have their own Assembly and Scotland (re)gained the Scottish Parliament. While considerable commonality remains across the UK, much of children's policy is devolved. Differences are becoming more substantial between England, Northern Ireland, Scotland and Wales, particularly now that different political parties are in power in the different jurisdictions.

Certain trends and concerns came together in the early 1990s, which both influenced the drive for participation and helped formed it. On the negative side, the 1980s and 1990s saw a deep concern with the perceived disengagement of young people from formal democracy and political systems (Wilkinson and Mulgan, 2005). The democratic youth 'crisis' helped influence the growth of citizenship education in schools. It encouraged funding for youth work, particularly that which sought to engage 'hard to reach' young people, and helped (re)establish the local youth forums. It led to some interest in extending down the age for formal voting and standing for election: for example, young people at age 16 can be on Scottish community councils, which are a localized form of representative democracy. But the UK voting age otherwise remains at age 18,[4] despite young people's ability to leave school, take on full-time employment and serve in the military at age 16.

On the more positive side, non-governmental organizations (NGOs) in the children and youth sectors have enthusiastically promoted children and young people's participation. Such organizations have a long history, in the UK, and a long engagement with children, young people and their families (Hill et al., 1998). Many of the NGOs took up children and young people's participation as a lobbying issue, within legislative and other policy initiatives. Children and young people's participation became a funding stream for organizations and a source of policy and service leverage (Tisdall and Davis, 2004).

Other trends include extensive legislative change in children's services, which followed from ratifying the UNCRC (see below) and the rise of consumerism. The 1980s and 1990s Conservative governments introduced market ideas into public services, which included giving service users greater power. This extended service user choice (for example, parents can choose between state schools for their children to attend) and voice (for example, the 'Citizen Charters' that laid down what service users could expect and complaints mechanisms; the rise of service user forums). Those advocating for children and young people's participation pointed out that children and young people were service users too (for example, Fajerman et al., 2004) – in fact, children and young people are one of the groups most affected by the welfare state and the largest group using their services, when health and education are included.

Thus a range of positive and negative trends and concerns came together, supporting children and young people's participation.

Legislative and policy changes – towards children's participation?[5]

In the UK, ratification of international treaties has little direct and immediate impact on domestic law. International law requires the UK to comply with the UNCRC, since the UK ratified it, but the UNCRC did not become actionable in domestic UK courts. This would require 'incorporation' or bringing the UNCRC into UK domestic law.

Various options are available for such legal incorporation. The most common one in the UK is gradually including rights into legislation, as bills are put forward to legislatures over time (see examples below). Incorporation of various rights can also come indirectly, as domestic and European courts refer to them in their decisions. More radical forms of incorporation are currently being developed across the UK. For example, a private member's bill was put forward in the Westminster Parliament in 2009 (The Children's Rights Bill), which would have substantially brought the UNCRC into UK and English law. However, the Bill was neither accepted by the Government at the time nor ultimately successful. In Northern Ireland, attempts have been made to include the UNCRC in a general Bill of Rights. However, such bills have been controversial within Northern Irish politics and, at the time of writing, there is no current activity. The Welsh Assembly has continued with its leading attention to children's rights, with legislation requiring Ministers to give 'due regard' to Part I of the UNCRC (i.e. the substantive rights of the convention) when exercising particular functions, like devising new policy (from May 2012 to April 2014) and eventually all functions (from May 2014) (Rights of Children and Young Persons (Wales) Measure 2011). Such duties are supported by processes of consultation and publication, as well as training for all civil servants on children's rights. Thus, while of limited legal power ('due regard' requires a process of consideration, by Ministers, but ultimately children's rights can be overridden by other factors), the Welsh Assembly continues to consolidate its adherence to the UNCRC, using the legislation as a lever for change in political culture and ultimately more broadly. Considerably inspired by the Welsh Measure, the Scottish Government proposed new legislation (the Children & Young People (Scotland) Act (2014)) to underline their commitment. The Act however, creates vague and weak duties on Scottish Ministers and the public sector (Education and Culture Committee, 2013; Tisdall, 2013).

Children and young people's participation rights are scattered across various pieces of legislation. The children's legislation of the 1980s and 1990s was held up by the UK Government, to the UN Committee on the Rights of the Child, as the major means of bringing the UNCRC into domestic law (see UK reports to Committee in 1994, 1999 and 2008). These claims by the UK Government are overstated. While the legislation variously combined aspects of family and child care law (and in Scotland also adoption law), the legislation did not cover substantially other relevant policy areas like education, social security nor equalities. Children's rights are not systematically incorporated into relevant legislation: for example, scrutiny of the Scottish primary and secondary children's legislation and guidance found over 100 gaps (Marshall et al., 2002). Yet the children's legislation has been the legal cornerstone often referred to, to promote children and young people's rights to participate.

This has had a positive impact on other legislation[6] – more often in terms of participation in individual decisions but also for collective decision-making. For example, the Scottish Parliament proudly accepted some participation rights for children and young people in schools, in the very last parliamentary stage of what became the Standards in Scotland's Schools etc. Act 2000. Wales has required school councils (representative bodies of students) within all publicly funded primary, secondary and special schools (School Councils (Wales) Regulation 2005). In England and Wales, the Education Act 2002 requires local education authorities and governing bodies of maintained schools to have regard to any guidance about 'consultation with pupils in connection with the taking of decisions affecting them' (s176(1)). However, the current guidance consists of two pages (Department for Education, England, 2014). The 2002 Act was further amended for school-governing bodies[7] to invite and consider pupils' views, in matters to be prescribed by regulations – but this is not yet operational. Rights to be involved in service planning have come through a range of legislation, from preparing local antisocial behavior strategies in Scotland, to planning for early childhood services in England, to local children's services plans in Wales.

Policy has further promoted children and young people's participation, from a range of national initiatives (for example; 'Quality Protects', which sought to improve services for looking after children; 'Every Child Matters', a more general program in England to improve outcomes for all children; to the leading commitment in the Welsh Assembly to children's rights). In Northern Ireland, the human rights aspects of the Northern Ireland Act 1998 include the duty on specified public bodies to promote equality of opportunity based on age (s75(1)). Children's commissioners are now established in all parts of the UK. All are established by statute with certain powers and have the role to promote children's views being taken into account. The offices have taken children's participation seriously in their own agendas (for example; Children's Commissioner for Wales, 1994; Kilkelly et al., 2004; Scotland's Commissioner for Children and Young People, 2010; UK Children's Commissioners, 2011) and to promote such rights generally.

Participation activities have proliferated. Youth forums sprouted throughout the UK, typically covering local government areas. Youth Parliaments at a national level have been supported in Northern Ireland (the Northern Ireland Youth Forum), Wales (Funky Dragon), the Scottish Youth Parliament and a Westminster UK Youth Parliament. The Northern Ireland Youth Forum describes itself as 'a youth led organization that lobbies, advocates, promotes and fights for the rights of young people.'[8] The other Parliaments have similar, if slightly different, remits.

While differing in structure and selection/election procedures, all of these Parliaments seek to represent young people; representatives generally need to be between the ages of 11 and 25.[9] School councils have been the predominant formal mechanism for 'pupil voice' in schools, with Wales presumably having 100 percent coverage in state schooling and statistical evidence showing 85 to 90 percent in England and Scotland (Tisdall, 2007; Whitty and Wisby, 2007). Mapping exercises shows the considerable growth of activities within the voluntary and statutory sectors (for example, Davey et al., 2010b).

With all this activity, expertise grew in how to engage children effectively and creatively in various group activities, to develop and articulate their views on services. Consultation with children, in policy and services, became an expectation in many fields – and not to do so would lay an official body open to public and media criticism (Tisdall and Davis, 2004). Professional training was encouraged to incorporate some attention to children and young people's views, while 'participation workers' numbers grew to the extent that networks flourished across the UK (the largest being in England, with Participation Works[10]). However, with the UK's economic recession and intense budgetary cuts from the Conservative-Liberal Democrat coalition Government, such activities may not be sustained in times of financial cut backs, which are already besetting statutory services and NGOs.

Part II: Transformative potential?

In the UK, four types of arguments have been made to promote children and young people's participation (Tisdall et al., 2008; Tisdall, 2011). First, similar to the narrative described above, appeals are made to international obligations and ensuing legal responsibilities. Second, the consumer and service user involvement claims have been influential, with the idea that taking due account of children and young people's views will make services and policy more effective and efficient. Third, the perceived 'youth crisis' in formal political engagement led to renewed attention to citizenship education and youth involvement more generally. Fourth, arguments are made that participation increases children and young people's well-being and development.

These four types of arguments capitalize on the UK's political and service structures, on broader trends of legalism and consumerism, and on appeals to protecting children and human investment. The top-down bureaucratic approaches can be utilized by those who believe in children and young people's participation, such as Stirling Council's children's services in the 1990s (Kinney, 2005), community planning in Wales (Butler, 2005) or early years services in Newcastle City Council (see Newcastle City Council, no date). But top-down approaches can be set from on high by policymakers and politicians while front-line professionals and service providers, families and children and young people themselves remain uninformed, unpersuaded and ultimately unaffected. For example, surveys repeatedly show a minority of children and young people know about UNCRC and/or children's rights more generally (see UK Children's Commissioners, 2007). Worries about tokenism are frequently expressed: that children and young people may well be consulted but nothing happens with their views; consultation now needs to be seen to be done but not necessarily to have any effect

(Tisdall and Davis, 2004). As one young person said, about his consultation experience on school meals, 'Why consult us when the decision was already made?'.[11] Concerns continue about how children and particularly young people are depicted in the media, swaying uneasily from children as innocents and needing to be protected to young people who are antisocial and out of control. This has led to media campaigns to try and change social opinions.[12] In other words, top-down and bureaucratic approaches can create requirements that services must fulfill but these can be tokenistic and not change individual or cultural attitudes for children and young people's participation.

The 'spaces' of children and young people's participation – at least those officially supported, from school councils to youth forums, from a policy consultation to a consultative conference – are thus frequently initiated by adults and largely on adult terms. While concerns may arise from young people's disengagement with formal politics, there is an official apoliticalness expected of children and young people's participation activities. None of the national youth parliaments have formal political power nor substantial budgets that they can distribute; in practice, they largely work as lobbying groups (e.g. by providing manifestos, alongside other NGOs, to try and influence subsequent decision-making). Such projects are not known for their political resistance nor radical activities; instead, writes Milbourne (2009):

> recent projects may be confined to generating only new sites and forms for young people's accommodation of, and adaption to, normative models of social and political institutions. (p. 351)

Moreover, such youth forums are not necessarily inclusive of the diversity of children and young people's views. According to English research:

> I know that in my area there are gangs and whatever else you want to call it, trouble makers, but I think they just get shoved off rather than being listened to and they don't get consulted on anything and, yes, people come and talk to our Youth Parliament and they say, 'Yes, we're going to go and talk to this group and that group and that group' but I think that when you're in maybe a bit of a dodgy area, for want of a better word, I think that they don't really get much of a say and I know that sounds bad but I think that's the way it is. (Interview with a young person with experience of involvement, quoted in Davey et al., 2010a)

Youth forums may thus perpetuate the exclusion of marginal groups (see Marsh et al., 2007).

If children and young people want to participate in mass protest, when they should be on school premises, they risk being treated as truants – and thus disciplined – rather than as active political citizens. Cunningham and Lavalette (2004) write of this happening when children sought to march in the anti-Iraq war protests. Children and young people's participation activities tend to be separated off from other participation activities, with specialist participation workers and separate reports. Indeed, special support for children and young people's participation has been made politically in policy and legislation *because* children and young people lack formal political power (Scottish Executive, 2000).

Given the above trends, what alternative ideas, spaces and languages might transform UK children and young people's participation? Three are explored below, drawing on ideas from early years pedagogy, political science's policy networks and governance, and social science's recent concern with knowledge exchange. An example is given within each section.

Pedagogical – listening in early years settings

Younger children have been excluded frequently from UK participation activities and particularly from collective, strategic decision-making (Burke, 2010; Clark et al., 2003; Davey et al., 2010b; UK Children's Commissioners, 2007). With school so often a site for wide-spread engagement with children and young people, those under school age (that is, those under age 4 or 5) are frequently not included in large-scale activities. While there have long been exceptions of engaging with young children (see for example Alderson, 2000), more generally younger children are casually, and without extensive justification, excluded. Underlying such exclusion are ideas of younger childhood, remarkably similar to ideas of childhood that previously undermined older children and young people's involvement: ideas of dependency, of being in the private sphere of families and households, of being insufficiently competent to communicate and insufficiently rational (Alderson, 2000; Konstantoni, 2011).

A growing strand of early years literature and committed practitioners are countering such ideas (for example, Clark et al., 2003; Pascal and Bertram, 2009; Young Children's Voices Network, facilitated by the National Children's Bureau). With more children accessing early years settings (Phillips et al., 2010; Scottish Government, 2010), these institutional sites have provided opportunities to recognize and support children's rights to participate. A notable influence has been an emphasis on pedagogy, inspired by Reggio Emilia and similar approaches. Rinaldi, the former pedagogical director of the Reggio's municipal schools in Italy, describes the approach as:

> a body of pedagogical thought and practice, permeated by cultural values, making the early childhood centres into social and political spaces ... to take the image of the rich child, an active subject with rights and extraordinary potential and born with a hundred languages. (2005, p. 17)

Following from this, the 'pedagogy of listening' is central:

> If we believe that children possess their own theories, interpretations, and questions, and are protagonists in the knowledge-building processes, then the most important verbs in educational practice are no longer 'to talk', 'to explain' or 'to transmit' ... but 'to listen'. (Rinaldi, 2006, pp. 125–126)

Documentation is central to the listening relationship. A range of media can be used for documentation, from videos to written notes to audio recordings. Documentation helps ensure all are listening and being listened to, making visible this listening to the individuals involved and the group. It allows for reading, revisiting and assessment, as part of the knowledge-building process.

'Listening', rather than participation, is generally favored in this early years literature (Tisdall and Gadda, 2011). Moss and colleagues (2005) provide a provocative discussion of this. They first quote Rinaldi, who emphasizes listening as an approach rather than particular tasks or procedures:

> listening is not only a technique and a didactic methodology, but a way of thinking and seeing ourselves in relationship with others and the world. Listening is an element that connects and that is part of human biology and is in the concept of life itself ... [It] is a right or better it is part of the essence of being human. (2005, p. 6)

Participation, they write, is associated with 'influencing change and decision making'. Listening can be part of participation – but it also goes beyond, in terms of a way or 'ethic of relating to others' that is more than 'just about' decision-making (Moss et al., 2005, pp. 8–9).

Inspired by such approaches, examples abound of young children being deeply involved in deciding how to develop their indoor and outdoor spaces, with practitioners and research utilizing multiple methods (like photo tours, drawings, and observation) and then collectively deciding on change (see for example Clark, 2010, Gutteridge et al., 2007). Certain early years settings have embraced children's involvement, as central to how they work, and children influence the nursery's daily life, from the curriculum to what toys are bought (see Miller, 2009). Paisley Pre-Fives Centre, for example, meets with interested children every month to discuss what they want to learn. Using tactile objects to catalyze discussion, over time the children become increasingly communicative about their ideas. The ideas and conclusions are recorded, for all to see, and the staff return to the children, discussing what has happened and asking for the children's evaluation. Over time, the Centre has worked to engage and train all staff in such methods, so that it has become a way of being within the Centre (Gordon-Smith, 2011). Children's participation is thus embedded in the nursery, regularly having an impact on the everyday lives of children there.

Policy networks and governance

Political science has developed ideas of policy networks and then governance, to describe how government has moved from more vertical top-down relationships to more horizontal ones:

> 'Governance' is a descriptive label that is used to highlight the changing nature of the policy process in recent decades. In particular, it sensitizes us to the ever-increasing variety of terrains and actors involved in the making of public policy. Thus, it demands that we consider all the actors and locations beyond the 'core executive' involved in the policy-making process. (Richards and Smith, 2002, p. 2)

A policy network is a type of horizontal relationship, where various actors connect with government. With an exchange of information between them, the government recognizes that particular actors have an interest in a particular policy area and a policy network is formed (Smith, 1997).

Children and young people were traditionally excluded from being present in such networks – those under the age of 16 are not working as civil servants, they are not politicians and would seldom be the representatives from organizations consulted and attending network meetings. At best, organizations would seek to bring in children and young people's views to such networks (see Tisdall and Davis, 2004). More recently, a number of examples have sought to bring children and young people directly into policy networks and thus policymaking – from the Children and Youth Board within the (then) Department for Children, Schools and Families (DCSF), 'to advise Ministers and policy officials on the development of policy and practice that affects the lives of children and young people in England' (DCSF, 2009), to a group of young experts 'Voice against Violence' originally set up as part of the Scottish Government's delivery plan on the National Strategy to Address Domestic Abuse in Scotland.[13]

Another example is the year-long Youth Commission on Alcohol, funded by the Scottish Government and supported by the NGO Young Scot. Sixteen young people were appointed to the Commission through an open recruitment process. An Advisory Group was set up with members from the Scottish Government, media, business, education, health, police and NGOs. The contact with the Advisory Group proved pivotal, according to one of the Youth Commissioners:

> This face-to-face exposure helped us to not only gain an insight into the key issues, but also to interact throughout the process with greater confidence so that we could maximise the opportunities presented to us. (Paul, 2011)

The Youth Commission undertook consultations, surveys, investigations and study visits. After their report's launch, the Scottish Government supported several of the recommendations, which became part of the Government's policy agenda (see Young Scot, no date). The Youth Commission was intentionally only a year-long project and disbanded subsequently. This short-term project thus engaged with policy networks, through its advisory group, and had demonstrable policy impacts.

Knowledge exchange

As academic research has increasingly been expected to have economic and social benefits to broader society, in the UK, so the concepts of knowledge transfer and knowledge exchange have gained increasing currency. Gradually more sophisticated frameworks are being developed of how to understand the processes of knowledge exchange – and how to promote it (Boaz et al., 2009; Nutley et al., 2007).

This growing area of interest draws on ideas of policy networks and governance, adding in the additional factors of the flows and changes of knowledge and practice as well as policy. There has been ongoing interest in contribution analysis, in trying to look forward to predict change and then to demonstrate how it has happened (Mayne, 2008). Drawing on social network and complexity theory, it emphasizes the importance of relationships and networks, of contexts and change, of serendipity as much as predictability, in change happening (Morton, 2012; Walby, 2007, 2009).

The literature suggests ways to enhance the chances of positive change (for example, Nutley et al., 2007; Walter et al., 2003; Weiss, 1998). These include (initial and ongoing) relationships with the 'users' of knowledge. This not only improves the quality of the knowledge produced but users are more committed to, and more informed about, the research. Passive dissemination through weighty written reports is less likely to have impact than targeted communication, which involves deeper audience engagement – like interactive discussions. Knowing the contexts and capitalizing on them can mean that the research is made available when there are openings for it to be used.

The external-facing work of the Children's Parliament (see Chapter 11) capitalizes on such key recommendations of knowledge exchange. While written reports may be produced, disseminated in print and put on websites, the Children's Parliament's primary goal is for children to have direct engagement with the decision-makers. Activities are organized where decision-makers engage with children and young people, in face-to-face communications. In the case study, the children's model environment was presented locally and nationally in the Scottish Parliament. Staff in the Children's Parliament network across other children's NGOs, investing in this despite their small staff size, so that they know the context and thus know where there are potential openings for influence.

Looking across the three examples

The examples discussed here, and the theoretical resources behind them, have certain similarities. All seek deep engagement of those involved, in the processes and understanding of the issues. This intensity is for everyone involved, adults and children, policymakers, practitioners and service users. Ongoing engagement is preferred, to establish trustful relationships, to ease communication and to facilitate knowledge exchange. Part of this engagement is direct communication, supported by written documentation, with the latter primarily used to facilitate reflection and document the listening.

The examples aim to foster changed relationships from the traditional hierarchical ones. The pedagogy of listening seeks to create spaces of co-creation (Moss and Petrie, 2002). The Children's Parliament wants direct engagement with decision-makers, to promote the human rights of children. The Youth Commission for Alcohol uses the term 'co-production', to suggest cooperative means of forming policy. Language is important to this change, trying to move away from traditional relationships to more productive ones.

The examples thus seek to create revised and new spaces for children and young people's participation – relational spaces and physical spaces. Human geography's ideas of social spaces, that physical spaces impact on social relationships just as relationships impact on physical spaces, are useful (see Gallagher, 2006; Lefebvre, 1991; Tisdall, 2014). Changed spaces are evident in the Paisley Under-Fives' Centre, for example. The children's meetings have led to documentation, which has changed literally what is displayed and done in the setting, as well as the social relationships within it. The Youth Commission utilized residential weekends and the Children's Parliament had longer term engagements, sometimes with key decision-makers. Residentials serve the practical purpose of making the most of children and young people's available time and participation budgets, in bringing together people from diverse geographical areas. Longer term engagements also serve to create intensive spaces and times for discussion and development, in particular types of spaces that foster group work, informal as well as formal relationships. Spaces are being (re)created by these participation activities.

All three examples go beyond the written word as ways of working and communicating. Within the Reggio Emilio approach, the phrase 'the hundred languages of children' is frequently used, with the expectation that listening involves engaging with all the different ways that children communicate verbally and non-verbally, and can be understood through all the senses (see Clark, 2010). The Children's Parliament uses arts-based and/or 'creative' methods, for their potential to engage a diverse range of children and young people, in accessible forms of communication. The Youth Commission used social media and interactive websites: closed ones for the core group, to aid communication between them, and openly available ones to engage more widely. The Children's Parliament and the Youth Commission produced video footage for disseminating their messages. The spaces created are thus entwined with different communication methods.

The three examples try to change the culture of organizations, of policymaking, of decision-making, to inculcate values, ways of working and thinking, and of being that support and respect children and young people's participation. As such, they present particular ideas of childhood – the 'rich' child of Reggio Emilio, the asset-rich service user in co-production, the policy actor of policy networks, and the expert within knowledge exchange. These run counter to the traditional ideas of childhood familiar in the UK, of dependency, innocence, irrationality and incompetence. These are not the children and young people of the proverb 'Children should be seen but not heard'. Children definitely should be 'seen', their communications made visible, their presence welcomed and facilitated. But they also must be 'heard' in the widest sense of Reggio Emilio's listening, an ethic of respect and interaction in the co-production of knowledge. Thus, to use the terms of Chapter 3, children and young people are both present and have a presence.

Concluding thoughts

None of the three examples were undertaken due to and within a legal framework that required children and young people's participation. They arguably were supported by aspects of the law and policy, such as the inspection requirements on early years settings to involve children in decision-making or the general legislative promotion of children and young people's participation. The examples were initiatives based on key adults' values, who sought to create different ways of working, spaces and relationships. The chapter has documented the sea change in UK legislation and policy, so that the idea of children and young people's participation is more widely accepted, that there are expectations in at least certain spheres for some involvement of children and young people collectively on matters that affect them. But it also notes the particular challenges amongst the plethora of activities that have taken place.

If the biggest challenges are how to make participation meaningful, effective and sustainable, as suggested above, the examples are illuminating. All three seem to have made participation meaningful to those involved, from the children and young people, to the practitioners, to other decision-makers. They are apparently effective, in terms of the processes being highly appreciated and rewarding, in having impact and outcomes that are tangible and appreciated. Only the early years setting, however, has a long-term sustainable approach. The Youth Commission was not intended to have an open-ended future and thus was arguably sustained by its own criteria. But it was well-funded, staffed and supported, and the core young people themselves donated a great deal of their time and energies. The Children's Parliament has successfully managed throughout the years but it is dependent as a NGO on grants and commissions. Sustainability remains highly problematic, especially now that public sector budgets are becoming tighter and posts are being lost.

Is the participation transformative? All three examples notably stay within the neoliberal framework, so criticized by Leal (2010, see Chapters 2 and 8), within the particular policy or service settings and within the bureaucracy of the welfare state. Rather than celebrating liminality, all three examples seek to centralize the participation within the decision-making processes, to infiltrate the policy networks, and to make participation the way early years settings work. They certainly created paradoxes, they were not always comfortable and they catalyzed change.

Perhaps their most transformative potential lies in the future. As participation activities spread across early years settings, schools, community planning and even how high-level government decision-making is made, it will change children and young people's expectations and the relationships they have. It may change the future, if the children and young people take their experiences and learning into adulthood, to alter ways of working, cultures of participation and spaces of engagement. In due course, how children and young people are perceived will change even further in the UK and with it recognition of their rights to participate.

Acknowledgments

Thanks is given to Anne Crowley (Cardiff University) and Laura Lundy (Queen's University Belfast), who kindly provided comments on a chapter draft. The contribution of Sarah Morton (CRFR, University of Edinburgh) to the section on knowledge exchange is appreciated, as she drew my attention to these ideas and references.

Along with the Leverhulme Trust, research underpinning this chapter has been supported by the Big Lottery Fund, the British Academy, the Economic and Social Research Council (RES-451-26-0685, RES-189-25-0174), the European Research Council and the Royal Society of Edinburgh.

Notes

1. The UK resident population is estimated at 62,262,000.
2. The total fertility rate is the 'average number of children a group of women would each have if they were to experience the age-specific fertility rates of the year in question throughout their childbearing lives' (ONS, 2012, Chapter 3).

3. Using the definition of 60 per cent of contemporary median net disposable household income after housing costs.
4. Sixteen- and 17-year olds will be able to vote in the 2014 independence referendum in Scotland. In July 2012, the Welsh Assembly held a debate on lowering the voting age to 16 for all elections and referendums in Wales.
5. For a more detailed update of activities between 2008 and 2011, see UK Children's Commissioners (2011).
6. Certain participation rights existed prior to the 1980s: for example, in Scotland, the right of children aged 12 or over to refuse to be adopted.
7. Of 'maintained' schools, which are schools funded by the local education authority.
8. http://niyf.org/ date accessed July 7, 2012.
9. This age range comes from youth work, which works with this age range. Forums and Parliaments may have activities that reach out to younger children.
10. http://www.participationworks.org.uk/ date accessed July 15, 2011
11. Comment made at Think Tank 'Children and Young People's Participation in Policy Decision-Making in Scotland: Making it meaningful, sustainable and effective', June 16, 2011 part of ESRC Research Council-funded project RES-189-25-0174.
12. For example, Young People Now's Positive Images Campaign and the Youth Net and the British Council's Respect? Campaign.
13. http://voiceagainstviolence.org.uk/ date accessed July 7, 2012.

Bibliography

Alderson, P. (2000) *Young children's rights: Exploring beliefs, principles and practice*, (London: Jessica Kingsley Publishers and Save the Children).

Boaz, A., Fitzpatrick, S. and Ben, S. (2009) 'Assessing the impact of research on policy', *Science and Public Policy*, 36(4), 255–270.

Burke, T. (2010) *Anyone listening? Evidence of children and young people's participation in England*, (London: Participation Works).

Butler, V. (2005) Research Report of Phase One of the Generation 2020 Project, http://tiny.cc/wnwsh.

Children's Commissioner for Wales (1994) Lifting the Lid, http://new.wales.gov.uk/ecolidocuments/ncp/ncp.00566.pdf.

Clark, A. (2010) *Transforming children's spaces: Children's and adult's participation in designing learning environments*, (London: Routledge).

Clark, A., McQuail, S. and Moss, P. (2003) *Exploring the field of listening to and consulting with young children*, (London: Department for Education and Skills).

Cunningham, S. and Lavalette, M. (2004) 'Active citizens or irresponsible truants? School student strikes against the war', *Critical Social Policy*, 24(2), 255–269.

Davey, C., Burke, T. and Shaw, C. (2010a) *Children's participation in decision-making: A children's views report*, (London: Participation Works).

Davey, C., Lea, J., Shaw, C. and Burke, T. (2010b) *Children's participation in decision-making: Survey of participation workers*, (London: Participation Works).

Department for Children, Schools and Families (DCSF) (2009) DCSF are Recruiting for the Children and Youth Board 2009–2011, http://www.participationworks. org.uk/news/dcsf-are-recruiting-for-the-children-and-youth-board-2009-2011

Department for Education, England (2011) Schools, Pupils and their Characteristics January 2011, http://www.education.gov.uk/rsgateway/DB/ SFR/s001012/sfr12-2011.pdf.

Department for Education, England (2014) Listening to and Involving Children and Young People, https://www.gov.uk/government/uploads/system/uploads/ attachment_data/file/271814/Listening_to_and_involving_chidren_and_ young_people.pdf.

Department of Education, Northern Ireland (2011) Enrolments at Schools and in Funded Pre-School education in Northern Ireland 2010/11 (Revised), http://www.deni.gov.uk/enrolments_at_schools_and_in_funded_pre-school_ education_2010_11__revised_.pdf.

Department of Work and Pensions (2012) Households below Average Income, http://statistics.dwp.gov.uk/asd/index.php?page=hbai, date accessed July 6, 2012.

Education and Culture Committee, Scottish Parliament (2013) Official Report 1.10.13, http://www.scottish.parliament.uk/parliamentarybusiness/28862. aspx?r=8536&mode=pdf.

Fajerman, L., Treseder, P. and Connor, J. (2004) *Children are service users too: A guide to consulting children and young people*, (London: Save the Children).

Gallagher, M. (2006) 'Spaces of Participation and Inclusion?' in E. K. M. Tisdall, J. Davis, A. Prout and M. Hill (eds) *Children, young people and social inclusion: Participation for what?*, (Bristol: Policy Press).

Gordon-Smith, P. (2011) 'EYFS best practice: All about ... listening to children', *Nursery World*, February 2, 2011.

Gutteridge, S., Legg, J. and Wharton, P. (2007) *Inside out and outside in*, 2nd edn (Stirling: Stirling Council).

Hill, M., Murray, K. and Tisdall, K. (1998) 'Children and Their Families' in J. English (ed.) *Social services Scotland*, (Edinburgh: Mercat Press).

Kilkelly, U., Kilpatrick, R., Lundy, L., Moore, L., Scraton, P., Davey, C., Dwyer, C. and McAlister, S. (2004) Children's Rights in Northern Ireland, http:// www.qub.ac.uk/schools/schooloflaw/research/researchprojects/childhood transitionandsocialjusticeinitiative/filestore/filetoupload,179673,en.pdf.

Kinney, L. (2005) 'Small Voices ... Powerful Messages' in A. Clark, A. T. Kjørholt and P. Moss (eds) *Beyond listening: Children's perspectives on early childhood services*, (Bristol: The Policy Press).

Kirby, P. and Woodhead, M. (2003) 'Children's Participation in Society' in H. Montgomery, R. Burr and M. Woodhead (eds) *Changing childhoods: Local and global*, (Chichester: John Wiley & Sons and Open University).

Konstantoni, K. (2011) *Young children's perceptions and constructions of social identities and social implications*, PhD Thesis (Edinburgh: University of Edinburgh).

Leal, P. A. (2010) 'Participation: The Ascendancy of a Buzzword in the Neo-liberal Era' in A. Cornwall and D. Eade (eds) *Deconstructing development discourse: Buzzwords and fuzzwords*, (Rugby: Practical Action Publishing in association with Oxfam GB).

Lefebvre, H. (1991) *The production of space*, (Oxford: Basil Blackwell).

Marshall, K., Tisdall, E. K. M. and Cleland, A., with Plumtree, A. (2002) 'Voice of the Child' under the Children (Scotland) Act 1995: Giving due Regard to

Children's Views in all Matters that Affect Them, Volume 1 Mapping Paper, http://www.scotland.gov.uk/Publications/2002/09/14905/6733.

Marsh, D., O'Toole, T., and Jones, S. (2007) *Young People and Politics in the UK: Apathy or Alienation*, (Basingstoke, Palgrave Macmillian).

Mayne, J. (2008) *Contribution analysis: An approach to exploring cause and effect, Briefing 16* (Italy: Institutional Learning and Change Initiative).

Milbourne, L. (2009) 'Valuing difference or securing compliance? Working to involve young people in community settings', *Children & Society*, 23(5), 347–363.

Miller, J. (2009) *Never too young: How children can take responsibility and make decisions*, 2nd edn (London: Save the Children UK).

Morton, S. (2012) *Exploring and assessing social research impact: A case study of a research partnership's impacts on policy and practice*. PhD thesis (Edinburgh: University of Edinburgh).

Moss, P., Clark, A. and Kjørholt, A. T. (2005) 'Introduction' in A. Clark, A. T. Kjørholt and P. Moss (eds) *Beyond listening: Children's perspectives on early childhood services*, (Bristol: Policy Press).

Moss, P. and Petrie, P. (2002) *From children's services to children's spaces: Public policy, children and childhood*, (London: Routledge/Falmer Press).

Newcastle City Council Stop (no date) *Look and listen to us: A toolkit for involving children in choices and change*, (Newcastle: Newcastle City Council).

Nutley, S., Walter, I. and Davies, H. T. O. (2007) *Using evidence: How research can inform public services*, (Bristol: Policy Press).

Office for National Statistics (ONS) (2004a) Ethnicity & Identity: Geographic Distribution, http://www.statistics.gov.uk/cci/nugget.asp?Id=457.

Office for National Statistics (ONS) (2004b) Ethnicity & Identity: Households, http://www.statistics.gov.uk/cci/nugget.asp?Id=458.

Office for National Statistics (ONS) (2012) National Population Projections, 2010-based Reference Volume: Series PP2, http://www.ons.gov.uk/ons/rel/npp/national-population-projections/2010-based-reference-volume--series-pp2/results.html#tab-Age-structure, date accessed July 6, 2012.

Pascal, C. and Bertram, T. (2009) 'Listening to young citizens: The struggle to make real a participatory paradigm in research with young children', *European Early Childhood Education Research Journal*, 17(2), 249–262.

Paul, T. (2011) 'Youth Commission on Alcohol', *Children and Young People's Participation in Policy-Making*, http://www.crfr.ac.uk/reports/Participation%20briefing.pdf.

Phillips, R., Norden, O., McGinigal, S., Garnett, E. and Osemarn, D. (2010) 2009 Childcare and Early Years Providers Survey, https://www.education.gov.uk/publications/eOrderingDownload/DFE-RB012.pdf.

Richards, D. and Smith, M. J. (2002) *Governance and public policy in the UK*, (Oxford: Oxford University Press).

Rinaldi, C. (2005) 'Documentation and Assessment: What is the Relationship' in A. Clark, A. T. Kjørholt and P. Moss (eds) *Beyond listening: Children's perspectives on early childhood services*, (Bristol: The Policy Press).

Rinaldi, C. (2006) *In dialogue with Reggio Emilia*, (London: Routledge).

Scotland's Commissioner for Children and Young People (2010) A Right Blether, http://www.arightblether.co.uk/, date accessed October 26, 2010.

Scottish Executive (2000) *Child strategy statement*, (Edinburgh: Scottish Executive).

Scottish Government (2010) Pre-School and Childcare Statistics 2010, http://www.scotland.gov.uk/Publications/2010/09/28130623/29.

Scottish Government (2011) *Statistical Bulletin: Summary Statistics for Schools in Scotland, No.1 2010* Edition: December 1, 2010 (amended June 13, 2011), http://www.scotland.gov.uk/Publications/2011/03/04154230/11.

Scottish Government (2012a) Your Scotland, Your Referendum, http://www.scotland.gov.uk/Resource/0038/00386122.pdf.

Scottish Government (2012b) A Scotland for Children, Consultation on the Children and Young People Bill, http://www.scotland.gov.uk/Resource/0039/00396537.pdf.

Smith, M. J. (1997) 'Policy Networks' in M. Hill (ed.) *The policy process: A reader*, (Wheatsheaf Hertfordshire: Prentice Hall/Harvester).

Statistics for Wales (2011) Schools' Census 2011: Final Results, http://wales.gov.uk/docs/statistics/2011/110906sdr1532011en.pdf.

Tisdall, E. K. M. (2007) *School councils and pupil participation in Scottish secondary schools*, (Glasgow: Scottish Consumer Council).

Tisdall, E. K. M. (2010) 'Governance and Participation' in B. Percy-Smith and N. Thomas (eds) *A handbook of children and young people's participation*, (London: Routledge).

Tisdall, E. K. M. (2011) 'Taking Forward Children and Young People's Participation' in M. Hill, G. Head, A. Lockyer, B. Reid and R. Taylor (eds) *Integrated working in children's services*, (Harlow: Pearson).

Tisdall, E. K. M. (2013) 'The potential for children's rights in Scotland: Learning from the UNICEF UK report on legal implementation of the UNCRC in 12 countries', *Scottish Human Rights Journal*, 60, http://scottishhumanrights.com/publications/journal/article/featureuncrc.

Tisdall, E. K. M. (2014) 'Addressing the Challenges of Children and Young People's Participation: Considering Time and Space' in T. Gal and B. F. Duramy (ed.) *Promoting the participation of children across the globe: From social exclusion to child-inclusive policies*, (Oxford: Oxford University Press).

Tisdall, K. and Davis, J. (2004) 'Making a difference? Bringing children and young people's views into policy-making', *Children & Society*, 18(2), 131–142.

Tisdall, E. K. M. and Gadda, A. M. (2011) *Early Years Practice – Consulting with Children. Discussion Paper*, (Edinburgh: Scotland's Commissioner for Children and Young People).

Tisdall, E. K. M., Davis, J. M. and Gallagher, M. (2008) 'Reflecting upon children and young people's participation in the UK', *International Journal of Children's Rights*, 16(3), 419–429.

UK Children's Commissioners (2007) Children's Commissioner Report to the UN Committee on the Rights of the Child, http://www.niccy.org/uploaded_docs/UNCRC_REPORT_FINAL.pdf.

UK Children's Commissioners (2011) UK Children's Commissioners' Midterm Report to the UK State Party on the UN Convention on the Rights of the Child, http://www.childcomwales.org.uk/uploads/publications/277.pdf.

UNICEF Office of Research (2007) Child Poverty in Perspective: An Overview of Child Well-being in Rich Countries, http://www.unicef-irc.org/publications/pdf/rc7_eng.pdf.

UNICEF Office of Research (2013) *Child Well-being in Rich Countries: A comparative overview, Innocenti Report Card 11*, (Florence: UNICEF Office of Research).

United Kingdom (1994) Initial Reports of State Parties due in 1995: United Kingdom of Great Britain and Northern Ireland, http://tinyurl.com/2weg82p.

United Kingdom (1999) Periodic Report United Kingdom of Great Britain and Northern Ireland, http://daccessddsny.un.org/doc/undoc/gen/g02/405/43/pdf/g0240543.pdf?openelement.

United Kingdom (2008) Periodic Report United Kingdom of Great Britain and Northern Ireland, http://www2.ohchr.org/english/bodies/crc/docs/advance versions/crc_c_gbr_4.doc.date.

Walby, S. (2007) 'Complexity theory, systems theory and multiple intersecting social inequalities', *Philosophy of the Social Sciences*, 37(4), 449–470.

Walby, S. (2009) *Globalization and inequalities*, (London: Sage).

Walter, I., Nutley, S. and Davies, H. (2003) Research Impact: A Cross-sector Literature Review, http://www.ruru.ac.uk/PDFs/LSDA per cent20literature per cent20review per cent20final.pdf.

Weiss, C. H. (1998) 'Have We Learned Anything New about the Use of Evaluation?', *American Journal of Evaluation*, 19(1), 21–33.

Whitty, G. and Wisby, E. (2007) Real Decision Making? School Councils in Action, http://www.dfes.gov.uk/rsgateway/db/rrp/u014805/index.shtml.

Wilkinson, H. and Mulgan, G. (1995) *Freedom's children: Work, relationships and politics for 18–34 year olds in Britain today*, (London: Demos).

Wilkinson, H. and Mulgan, G. (2005) Freedom's Children, http://www.demos.co.uk/files/freedomschildren.pdf.

Williams, A. (2010) Comment – Is Co-production Taking Youth Participation to a New Level? Children and Young People Now, http://www.cypnow.co.uk/news/1045146/National-Youth-Agency-Comment–co-production-taking-youth-participation-new-level/?DCMP=ILC-SEARCH.

Willow, C., Franklin, A. and Shaw, C. (2007) Meeting the Obligations of the Convention on the Rights of the Child in England: Children and Young People's Messages to Government, http://www.nspcc.org.uk/Inform/policy-andpublicaffairs/CYP_Msg_to_Govt_wdf48658.pdf, date accessed October 24, 2007.

Young Scot (no date) *Building the boat: Young people as co-producers of policy*, (Edinburgh: Young Scot).

11
Transforming the Urban Environment: The EcoCity Project

Colin Morrison, Cathy McCulloch, Drew Mackie,
Sandy Halliday and Howard Liddell

Introduction

The EcoCity was created by Gaia Planning and the Scottish non-governmental organization (NGO) Children's Parliament. The process was conceived during a conference that brought together educationalists and architects to look at children's potential involvement in developing the built environment. The EcoCity process was created as a tool for engaging with children both in redesigning an existing community and in creating a 'fantasy' landscape. The EcoCity process integrates learning and engagement around three key themes of children's human rights, ecological design and urban design.

EcoCity projects have since been delivered in a number of UK cities. This chapter will consider the EcoCity process in terms of children's participation and transformational change. It will also focus on the experience of the 2011 Dunfermline EcoCity project[1] (which engaged children in the city of Dunfermline in the region of Fife, Scotland) to explore relevant issues. To begin some contextual information is given about the Children's Parliament and the EcoCity process; this is followed by children's and adult participants' views on participation in EcoCity. Some reflection is given on what factors facilitate children's involvement and what facilitates stakeholder's interest and ability to use children's participation to influence change. The chapter will conclude by considering the question: is the EcoCity process transformative?

The Children's Parliament[2]

The idea, and name for the Children's Parliament, came from children attending the first-ever EcoCity project that the authors facilitated in 1992. Children aged between 10 and 13 years old from Norway,

Germany, Denmark and Scotland spent a week together in Edinburgh, Scotland, living together and discussing, planning and building a large-scale model of their vision of an environmentally friendly city of the future. At the center of their city the children placed a children's parliament. Their view was that children need to come together to talk about what matters to them. The children identified that adults need to understand that children's views are important and worth listening to. For the children the word parliament meant a place to talk and to listen, and meeting in the environment of a parliament signified the importance of what children had to say. This exciting idea has been developed by a small team of adults who having established Children's Parliament as a Scottish NGO now deliver a range of initiatives across the country. Rather than a building, the Children's Parliament has become a way of working and our 'parliament' is convened in any place, at any time, with any group of children who want to have their say.

The Children's Parliament today works with children in the context of family, school and community. In our projects, consultations and community program children learn about their human rights whilst acquiring knowledge, skills, behaviors and values for citizenship. Our work connects children with each other, with adults, with their communities and with policy development and services. Because we know that children engage and learn best when they are being creative and active, our whole approach is based on using the creative arts; using model building, drama, sculpture, photography, poetry or any other art form provides a 'safe' way in to a wide range of issues making it possible for children to feel comfortable sharing their views and concerns with others. Our ways of working make it possible for us to embark on a fast track to feelings and give permission to challenge, in a safe environment, standard sets of ideas, beliefs and ways of behaving. The legacy for children and adults who participate is a sense of having fun together but also the possibility of identifying new ways of being together that are mindful of and informed by everyone's human rights.

We have developed a thematic and holistic approach which underpins our work and reflects the interests of the United Nations Convention on the Rights of the Child (UNCRC). The Children's Parliament themes are: Who we are, Where we live, Freedom, Health and happiness, Feeling safe and being cared for and Having our say. Whilst children have the rights articulated in the UNCRC from birth, in terms of participation rights or opportunities to 'have a say' the experience of rights is often more explicit in their teenage years. With this in mind much of the work of the Children's Parliament has focused on middle childhood. We see this as a time to engage children as they become increasingly aware of the world around them, when there is an interest in exploring that larger social world and an openness to learning the skills, values and behaviors that will equip them for an adult life where participation is a habit of a lifetime. Middle childhood is also a time where there are concerns about vulnerability as independence grows and so Children's Parliament promotes awareness of rights as a way of helping children keep themselves safe, while highlighting the role adults have in ensuring children experience the protective rights to which they are entitled.

Our approach is based on developing open and honest relationships with children, on valuing their worth and their views and on committing to creating a space within which they feel safe, challenged and trusted. This means valuing the participation process as a means of learning and gaining skills, as well as valuing the products of that process. A particular focus is on including all children, prioritizing engagement with children deemed to be 'in need' in terms of Scottish legislation. While the Children's Parliament is focused on direct engagement with children we do understand and articulate connections with policy, which in the Scottish context has seen an increasing commitment to children's participation, to recognition and implementation of the UNCRC in the context of community life and the design and delivery of children's services.

The EcoCity process

EcoCity allows a group of around 40 children (between 9 and 11 years old) to create, over a five-day period, a large-scale, 3-D environment that reflects the kind of community/city they want to grow up in: a place where the needs of all citizens are taken into account. The process takes account of all aspects of people's lives – physical, emotional, creative, spiritual and intellectual – and encourages children to respond to worries and concerns with creative solutions.

The EcoCity process provides a useful support tool for planners and others responsible for supporting the development of inclusive, sustainable and engaged communities. While creating streets, play areas, transport and energy systems, children also consider the qualities they need from adults in their lives. The process encourages them to think about what needs to happen in relation to their issues or concerns; for example, how to create play areas within communities that allow children an essential level of freedom as well as keeping them safe.

Figure 11.1 'Random Town': children work early in the process to consider key aspects of urban design; here they use blocks to begin to create streets and public spaces
Photographer: Howard Liddell.

The EcoCity process requires a minimum five-month timeline. This leads the children, their families, classmates and the local community through workshops and information-gathering processes, culminating in the final 'build week'. Stakeholders from the statutory, voluntary and private sectors then have the opportunity to use the EcoCity model and all the elements leading to its creation, to inform their planning and decision-making processes.

The children's model-building team usually has children from a number of local schools within the communities of interest. Prior to the five-day build a number of workshops are run in the schools, which highlight the key themes of children's human rights, ecological design and urban design. Children from each school are then nominated to become model-builders who will join the five-day 'build' aspect of the project where initial ideas are developed. These children also take part in advance 'site' visits, exploring their own communities with a fresh perspective, identifying in their real environment what they value and what they want to change. The criteria for selection of children to join the build team are described to schools as 'choose children who have something to contribute and who will get something out of their engagement'. In addition, the EcoCity team actively encourages school colleagues to nominate children who may be considered vulnerable or marginalized or who may otherwise not be considered in opportunities to represent other children or their school. The participation of these children demonstrates that it is possible to create an environment where they can succeed and develop self-confidence and self-esteem. Frequently, the views of these children are the ones that go to the heart of some of the more endemic community problems and their ideas to help solve these issues are often illuminating and impactful.

Participating schools are expected to provide a teaching staff member for the model-building week in order that the knowledge and effort can be built on and sustained for a larger number of children back in their own schools. Often, during the model-building week the other children back in the participating schools will create a forest of trees, which can be used to surround the EcoCity and which capture key messages and aspirations from a larger number of children.

The EcoCity process also offers the opportunity for cross-generational interaction. In addition to their own needs, the children are prompted to consider the needs of others around them. Through direct engagement children learn about their elders' childhoods and life experiences and use these to inform their own planning and design. By providing a creative approach to working with the wider community, the city the children construct is a tangible model of an environmentally friendly space that meets the needs of everyone who lives there.

The EcoCity team (Gaia Planning[3] and Children's Parliament) prepares and oversees each EcoCity but the process relies on a supportive and dedicated team of local adults who commit themselves to the process, particularly during the week-long 'build'. A successful EcoCity should involve local town planners, those with responsibility for green spaces and educationalists. The skills and knowledge of a wide range of professional disciplines such as water engineers, transport managers, police officers and others from the local community are also very useful to involve, to give advice and assistance to the children during the 'build'.

A final presentation is given by the children on Day 5 to which they invite their classmates, parents and family, local and national politicians as well as representatives of professional groups including those from architecture, urban planning, design and education. There is usually a high level of press interest.

Figure 11.2 Daily debrief: as their city emerges the children come together to explain developments and resolve issues
Photographer: Howard Liddell.

The colorful and imaginative model, which measures approximately 6m × 6m, is transportable in 1m × 2m sections, and can be displayed in different locations around the community. This is a key opportunity for local partners to build on the momentum of the EcoCity process and ensure the knowledge, commitment and understanding of the children are harnessed and developed. A final report on the process is compiled by the EcoCity team who then facilitate sessions with local commissioning agencies to ensure the key messages from EcoCity are understood and connected with the existing adult-oriented planning or regeneration processes.

Project profile: the EcoCity project in Dunfermline, Scotland 2010–2011

Dunfermline is a city of nearly 50,000 inhabitants in central Scotland. It is the birthplace of industrialist and philanthropist Andrew Carnegie, himself a figure in promoting early twentieth century urban renewal, whose legacy is evident in the city. This includes the city's western boundary, the 80 acre Pittencreiff Park.

The area has higher than the regionally average rates of households on low incomes, higher unemployment and lower educational achievement. Residents also report worries over crime and higher levels of dissatisfaction with the physical appearance of their local area. Local agencies, including Royal Dunfermline (a partnership agency which seeks to build upon the history and civic pride of the city), Carnegie Trust (with its headquarters in Dunfermline but working across the UK and Ireland on issues of civic society, rural development and democracy) and Fife Council (known in Scotland as the 'Local Authority', the local elected administrative/government authority) have embarked on a process of imagining Dunfermline in 2020 and beyond and sought to engage children in this process by commissioning an EcoCity project.

The EcoCity team engaged with five local Primary Schools with children in the target age range of nine and ten years old. Local professionals from a range of backgrounds were recruited and they attended a training session that provided detail on the initiative as well as the principles that underpin the project. The children and adult team followed the EcoCity process as described earlier and children identified the following issues that their city must address:

- Play and places to play are a strong theme across the project – from small children to teenagers, children want outdoor places to play.
- Transport is a major concern. The children decided cars/traffic should be kept away from people and children playing. Where there is traffic, it should be slow and for essential services like fire and police; in their model the children give limited access for deliveries to shops or houses. The view was expressed that all the traffic in the town center should be removed. To help people get around, the children developed a city-wide bike hire system and electric car club.
- Dunfermline is felt to be too gray: children said that everywhere should have more color.
- When it comes to infrastructure, the city needs to develop more park and ride facilities and make it easier to get to the railway station. Wind turbines could be located within the cartilage of the city and there should be more above ground water systems and features.
- In terms of layout, there is a need to create a new Town Centre square and to develop more shared space rather than closed gardens. The children saw opportunities for more urban gardens and some dedication of these spaces to growing your own vegetables and fruit (in the tradition of the UK use of unused urban spaces often by railway lines or near industrial sites called 'allotments').

- The city also needs more business, shopping, leisure and recreation activities. This must include a reinvigoration of Pittencreiff Park. The children saw the potential for making the park more accessible to people with disabilities and the location of animals and play facilities to attract children and families. The park sits alongside the historic Dunfermline Cathedral and the children proposed a new multi-faith center to draw people from many faiths to stay and study.

In his honor children created the Andrew Carnegie statue and slide – a structure with an internal sloping surface. Children climb up and enter through the head and on coming down the slide hear all about Andrew Carnegie's life.

The children also considered the needs of specific communities within Dunfermline. This included addressing how to link or improve connections between the city center and the peripheral housing estates through better transport, walk and cycle ways. The children commented that their engagement in the project meant they spent time with children from communities they did not necessarily know well enough, other than by reputation.

Children also discussed issues which could be categorized around the theme of 'relationships'. Although difficult to capture in the urban landscape, they wanted adults engaged in planning to imagine their city and their neighborhoods to be places where people are happier and friendlier, where children and adults play together, where adults make more time to spend with children, where people care for each other and no one is frightened, and where children are trusted and listened to. These hopes and aspirations were represented on 'aspiration' clouds that were hung over their EcoCity model.

Since completing their model environment the children have presented their work to members of the public in Dunfermline in local venues and have attended and presented at the annual Festival of Politics held in the Scottish Parliament in Edinburgh. A full report on the project was been submitted to funders. At the end of the process the EcoCity team present formally to stakeholders and other interested groups and individuals; in the context of our Dunfermline EcoCity project this saw the team present to a stakeholder event as part of a strategic day looking at the longer term regeneration of Dunfermline. Further, at the time of writing, a number of the children's ideas are in development and small groups have been established to consider the following:

- Using street and public art.
- Regeneration of the 'public park' as a key open space in the city.

- The possibility of a viewing platform on the Kingsgate shopping center, providing views across the historical city center.
- Pedestrianizing the High Street; responding to demands to take traffic out of the city center.
- Developing the Lynburn Corridor: an open space that currently separates peripheral communities from the center but could be used to facilitate access.
- A group has been established to look at setting up an 'all-faith centre'.

Children's views on participation in the project

Children are, almost without exception, thrilled to be part of such a multilayered project with the prospect of making a real contribution to the development of their community. In particular, children appreciate the fact that this is a serious process where their participation and contributions are sought and valued. Our experience of EcoCity projects is that children flourish in a setting where all behaviors are respectful; indeed where there is a stated expectation that the basic tenet of relationships is respect, from everyone to everyone. Specialist techniques have been developed to ensure that there are no raised voices. This creates a comfortable setting for many children, allowing for a creative buzz within a calm and semi-structured framework.

Children also greatly appreciate being valued for their own views. They soon realize that it is their own ideas and solutions that are to be incorporated into the model and they are keen to make sure their ideas are taken seriously. There is space to think imaginatively and they work hard on the thinking behind their ideas. Through gentle questioning by adult facilitators, the children themselves can analyze whether an idea is worth developing or not and they are free to make those decisions themselves. Children find this very rewarding. They tell us they feel that they are believed in and feel like their ideas could directly influence the positive development of their communities.

Overwhelmingly the children say it is great fun to be part of an EcoCity project. They love the freedom they have to be creative and to form new relationships with children from other schools and neighborhoods and with adults. They value the power to influence, to challenge adults' often negative attitudes and perceptions of children and young people, and they treasure the opportunity to make a difference. From the recent EcoCity Dunfermline project one child wrote:

I liked that we got to meet new people and get to know them. This was easy because building the model took a lot of teamwork. It was easy to show people around the model because I know the model so well and fun because I liked showing how much hard work was put into it.

Adult participants' views

Adults who directly engage in the EcoCity process tell us that they leave the project with a strong sense of the impact that participation has had on the children and the skills children learn. Adult members of the team have told us:

> J [a participating child] said he would only work in my group at the beginning of the project. By the second day he had volunteered to go to another group where he fully took part in all discussions, adding a lot to the discussions that took place. Each child has gained self-belief, confidence and have become responsible citizens.

> They gained experience in collaborative working, listening and talking skills, mixing with new people and public speaking. Those who might not normally volunteer for these types of activities were having a go with brilliant results. They also gained a great sense of pride in their achievement and were given the opportunity to celebrate their hard work with friends, family and many others.

> They have a clearer link to how their learning can be applied to real life situations, a greater understanding of the importance of considering the point of view of others and an idea of some of the careers/jobs they could have in the future which they may never have thought about.

In addition to the positive impact on the children, adults also report the potential impact that EcoCity has on their own practice in relation to community engagement and how they might undertake this work in the future. Again from the Dunfermline EcoCity project colleagues report as follows:

> Importantly, this type of process appears ideally suited to facilitating and capturing the ideas of the younger generation who will go on to live in the places we're currently trying to improve. The future Scottish planning system may well have found its process for engaging children in planning.

Those adults who had the good fortune to listen to the children discussing their ideas will attest to the value of the learning and thinking which the children engaged in during building the model. As a means of engagement it must be hard to beat. The longer term impact on the young people is likely to be significant.

Finally, although not directly involved in the delivery of the EcoCity project, parents who have come to see the work and have it described to them by their child, have also provided feedback on the project and its benefits. These echo those positive outcomes identified above.

She is much more confident with people not well known to her. She was always fairly sure around people she knew well but this tended to evaporate with anyone unfamiliar. She displays a far greater knowledge and understanding (and empathy) with Dunfermline itself.

The children will remember the experience for the rest of their lives and I know it has changed attitudes and I would say that the children have grown up quite a bit having been given the responsibilities. They are much more aware of the environment around them.

This was a fantastic opportunity for him. I have never seen him as enthusiastic about a project before. He was also very proud of the result.

This was definitely one of the best learning weeks of our child's education. She has been inspired and encouraged by the experience. It is good to see continued communication with yourselves after the project and a desire to continue and improve what you do.

Factors that facilitate children's involvement

The EcoCity team has adult facilitators who have a range of professional experience in direct work with children in formal and informal learning environments. The local team is also made up of adults with a wide range of professional skills able to offer advice and guidance on any issue that might arise in the context of (re)designing their city. As a result, children quickly understand that adult facilitators are listening, they are respectful, they have something to offer in support of the task children are set and they take children seriously.

As described earlier, the EcoCity process is also built around a 'learning by doing' approach so that there is rarely too much sitting in one place or listening passively to adults talk. Instead there is activity, interspersed with actively listening to others, dialog and debate, communication between teams and negotiation about what happens next. In this sense there is always something to do and be done; even when children are given the space to mull something over quietly away from the frenetic activity of building the model. This way of working is adopted in all contact with children, including in the initial preparatory workshops we undertake in schools before children are identified for the core week-long build element of the EcoCity process.

In preparation for delivery of an EcoCity project there is a need to explicitly address adult behaviors; it is made clear that adults ought to be respectful of children's views, that they will listen and help children think through their options and the consequences of their decisions and that where the behavior of a child is interfering with another child getting the most out of the experience this is discussed openly and honestly with the child causing concern. In such circumstances there is a focus on solving problems and on making the experience better for everyone.

In initial engagement and preparation work, there is also a need to convince and engage education professionals and parents by describing children's participation in the EcoCity process as a learning experience and to address any initial concerns that there might be about this being a distraction from 'real' learning that can only take place in a school/ classroom. To do this we are able to talk about the experiences and outcomes we seek to deliver and relate these to the stated purposes of Scottish education/school provision.

Factors that facilitate stakeholders' interests and ability to use children's participation to influence change

In the most recent EcoCity project, profiled earlier in this chapter, stakeholders have included Royal Dunfermline, Carnegie Trust and a wide range of departments and services within the Local Authority Fife Council. However, whilst this coming together of partners is essential for EcoCity success over the past 20 years, EcoCity commissions have always begun with one individual – perhaps an officer in a Planning Department or an elected member in a Local Authority, or a senior staff member within a partnership agency charged with community regeneration, who has seen what the project can do. From this initial spark, the EcoCity team is able to visit a locality and talk with interested individuals and organizations to plant a seed that in some circumstances leads to delivery of this significant multi-agency, community-based initiative. The benefits that come from showing what we do rather than (just) talking about it are a common experience for the Children's Parliament (whatever the focus of our work), where it is often easier to model the work than to describe what we do and why it makes an impact. As we have stated earlier, we focus on 'learning by doing' for the children and adults seem to be no different.

Stakeholders who benefit most from an EcoCity project are those who are open to different approaches and those who make a commitment to the time that is required to embed the project in the community. In this sense, EcoCity is not a quick fix or an exercise that allows a commissioning agency to tick the community engagement box; rather it is a new start that refocuses partners on how seemingly intractable issues can be understood and addressed.

EcoCity projects work best when there is a willingness to challenge the assumption that as professionals we know best; this requires professional honesty and confidence. This is not to say that professional skills and experience, our 'know how' do not have value, but it locates the professional person in the role of serving the community rather than the community finding itself as the passive recipient of distant decision-making. In this approach, professionals are encouraged to view those who live in target communities (including children) as being part of the solution rather than part of the problem.

To deliver an EcoCity project requires an investment from commissioning agencies in terms of both local professionals' time as well as direct funding to engage the EcoCity team and pay for the costs of children's participation, from transport to lunches to the materials needed for the EcoCity build. As facilitators of the process, the Children's Parliament and Gaia team need to be focused on delivering agreed outcomes and are literally 'hands-on' at all stages: ensuring relationships with every child, every participating professional and key officers from commissioning agencies are well supported. Commissioning agencies have always sought value for money from EcoCity projects but in the current funding climate this is perhaps even more of a necessity; our view is that investing in EcoCity as a model for community engagement invigorates local partnerships and engages families and communities often labeled as harder to reach by more traditional approaches. Where this works children, adults and local agencies feel that the EcoCity project is their project and when the EcoCity team moves on they feel they are able to use the learning which has taken place.

Whilst the EcoCity team strives to build effective partnerships and that stakeholders sustain their commitment, there have been occasions where this has not worked as successfully as we had hoped. On occasion, the opportunities for positive dialog were not sustained and old conflicts re-emerge; partners can find it difficult to maintain the staff/resource commitment that a continued engagement with the children requires; we have felt that on occasion the creativity of the initial EcoCity approach has been lost when stakeholders subsequently try to organize the children's work and ideas into adult structures and agendas (in which they deal with problems rather than holistic creative solutions). In order to mitigate such issues, we have learned over time to ensure that local partnerships include a wide range of agencies and professional groupings so that our focus on the principles of ecological design, urban design and the rights of the child is not lost.

Is EcoCity transformative?

The idea of transformative change is increasingly discussed and debated in Scotland. In terms of children's learning (in school and in informal/ community-based settings), the Scottish Government intends that learning is to be transformed by a commitment to a more coherent and flexible curriculum for 3- to 18-year olds called 'Curriculum for Excellence'.[4] In terms of broader issues of health and social care, other key policy drivers and impending legislation affirm Government commitments to improving outcomes for children and young people through new approaches to design and delivery of public services and a desire to improve UNCRC implementation.

Whether change in Scotland's schools or children's services is transformational remains to be seen but in considering the impact of EcoCity our reflection starts by drawing on the work of the After Now[5] project, an initiative based at the University of Glasgow that seeks to explore innovative responses to public health challenges in Scotland by discussing 'the ideas which shape and limit contemporary responses ... and look to a brave new future for public health' (University of Glasgow, 2012). Framing the challenges that Scotland faces through the lens of public health may in itself be transformational. While some societal concerns are evidently health issues (such as child obesity or sedentary lifestyles), others such as violence or poverty have not traditionally been viewed as such in the Scottish context. The usefulness of this perspective comes when we think of public health as having a concern for improving health and quality of life through approaches that are both preventative and reactive (treatment). It seems also that when we consider challenges as public health issues we are more able to draw on the range of professional perspectives and approaches which our responses require.

A key author of the After Now project is Professor Phil Hanlon, Professor of Public Health at the University of Glasgow. In the After Now initiative transformational change is defined, in terms of the individual and society, as 'change that brings about a better life'. More than this however transformational change requires us (drawing on Plato) to integrate 'the true, the good and the beautiful' understood as science, ethics and esthetics. The After Now project asserts that in contemporary Scotland we have allowed science (and particularly economics) to dominate the decisions of everyday life, so that 'the bottom line rules'. With this claim in mind, in terms of transformation of the urban environment here in Scotland, can we argue that EcoCity is a tool for transformation?

In earlier sections we have identified factors that facilitate children's involvement and factors that facilitate stakeholder's interest and ability to use children's participation to influence change. With these in mind we have chosen here to reflect on the potential that EcoCity has for transformative change; we may not have delivered one EcoCity project that has delivered every aspect now identified, but we have seen its potential across our 20 years of EcoCity delivery.

EcoCity changes how communities are viewed. For the most part, EcoCity projects are commissioned to engage children in communities viewed by formal agencies/services as problematic: perhaps in terms of indicators of deprivation, anti-social behavior or poor engagement with other participatory or planning processes. When a community is viewed as a collection of intractable problems, it is unlikely to be a place where local citizens feel able to identify or address issues. The EcoCity process does not reduce communities to a set of problems to be solved nor do we focus on the deficits. Instead we see communities in the round; we identify assets and explore ways to build these.

EcoCity reframes the negative: in our work with children we always pose questions positively. As an example, asking children to consider what would support implementation of their right to play encourages them to talk about friendships, the role of adults, excitement, fun, risks, being outdoors and indoors, rules, what children and young people of different ages want, to remember old games they have been taught, and to tell us about new games they have created. From this they can decide how a community supports play. On the other hand, asking children what we can do about the vandalized play park sees conversation stuck in complaints, fears and a continued view of children as passive users of a facility they most likely did not want.

EcoCity increases awareness and understanding of children's human rights. Awareness of the UNCRC amongst both children and adults in Scotland is poor. In considering the ways in which EcoCity can be transformative, our intention is to impact on awareness, learning and commitment to children's human rights. As described earlier, The Children's Parliament approach to this work adopts a holistic, thematic approach: rights are seen as protective, empowering and universal, they belong to everyone. Participation in EcoCity allows us to increase awareness of the challenges we face about implementation of the UNCRC here in Scotland where 'rights education' has often been somewhat paternalistic and distant, focused on the experience and lives of children in other countries affected by war, famine or drought. By encouraging children and adults to use the spaces for dialog, EcoCity contextualizes children's human rights and makes them relevant to Scottish children's experience at home, in school and in the community: these conversations change attitudes, expectations and behaviors.

EcoCity changes relationships and perceptions of children previously labeled as troublesome. EcoCity aims to give children who might not normally have the opportunity to represent their community or school to get a chance to participate, for example, children whose behavior is challenging in the classroom environment. Those who take part frequently surprise their parents and teachers because of their ability to engage positively and without disruption. Children tell us that, because the EcoCity adult team (which might include their own class teacher but working in a different context and in different ways) have positive expectations of them and do not treat them according to any previous labels attached to them, they feel like they have been given a fresh start. For many children, the experience is a turning point in their perception of who they are and what they can do. The parents of participating children can also be engaged afresh – there have been many occasions when family members who have never visited school or attended a school event have turned up to see what their child has achieved at the EcoCity project, with their engagement resulting from their child's enthusiasm and wish to share with their families. For all participating children, the EcoCity model provides an inspiring record of individual and group achievements.

EcoCity increases awareness and understanding of ecological and urban design. EcoCity shifts adult perceptions of children and their role in transformation of the urban environment. EcoCity taps into the fact that children think in a joined-up way. When we begin our program, we find that children value resources (energy, water, materials and people) and it is easy to get them to think about how we use these resources when designing things for the representation of their community on the EcoCity model. Building on this natural sense of ecological awareness does require some input and includes some explanation for example on how the principles of Earth (materials and landscape), Air (the local climate – sun and wind), Water (rain, water usage and sewage systems) and Fire (energy saving energy supplies) fit into the whole set of decisions to be made on the model. The sun sits above the model all week and the groups are reminded of the prevailing winds whilst they decide on the best way to shape their streets and squares. When adults in the team engage with children in this learning it becomes clearer to the adults that adult planning systems often treat sustainable design as an afterthought and not a fundamental principal running through the core. The children involved in an EcoCity project do not make that mistake.

In terms of urban design, through their participation children become very sensitive to the making of places – streets, blocks and squares – as they are encouraged to think about who uses them and how they change over time. This sensitivity is reinforced by the cross-generational sessions held in the schools before the model building. As a result in the latest Dunfermline EcoCity project, there was a general feeling that Dunfermline had no central gathering place and that this should be located at the lower end of the main shopping street. Across the group, there was a wish to reduce the effects of traffic and to restore places to the pedestrian.

With opportunities to learn about ecological and urban design, and in the belief that their views are being listened to, children begin to understand the legitimate and valuable role they have to play in the development of their own towns and local communities. By increasing their understanding of how communities work, alongside their own current knowledge of what works and what does not work for them, children become enthusiastic about making their towns and communities better. Given realistic boundaries (all the while remembering this is a children's project), the children are encouraged to be creative and use all their old and new knowledge and understanding to become engaged citizens.

Using the momentum and profile of the EcoCity, a significant opportunity arises at the end of the project for a local authority or other partner to support the EcoCity children's continued engagement in regeneration and development processes (see the earlier section 'Project profile: The EcoCity project in Dunfermline, Scotland 2010–2011' for examples from the most recent EcoCity). From transport and renewable energy systems to education and recreational amenities, children will have a valuable contribution to make in all aspects of their lives and in the lives of the wider community. In addition to this dedicated group of 40 or so children, there is potential for far greater numbers by involving friends and classmates of EcoCity children to ensure the views of children and young people, which are generally missed out of such processes, are embedded to usefully inform development work.

In conclusion

Others can decide if EcoCity is transformative but by describing and reflecting on EcoCity we intended to paint a picture of a vibrant and innovative approach that harnesses the imagination of children and provides a means by which we can hear and respect their contribution to changing our urban environments. Over 20 years, we have witnessed children identify and describe changes to the built environment and the interpersonal relationships that frame their lives which, if acted upon, will lead to a better life for them as a child, for their peers, families and neighbors. It seems to us that children have an intuitive sense of what is right and good, they are drawn to create communities that are beautiful and that minimize harm to our planet, they want to live in families and communities that are safe, healthy and happy. It is our responsibility as adults to help make this happen.

Acknowledgments

One of the co-authors of this chapter Howard Liddell died shortly after submission of the final text. His co-authors, colleagues and friends would like to pay tribute to him with a few words:

EcoCity was a major passion of Howard's and a project to which he devoted a great deal of time and often personal resources. In 1992, Howard had been the only 'green' architect who responded to an invitation to support a new built environment project for children that in time was to become 'EcoCity'. Those early days of EcoCity were a completely new venture for Howard but seeing the children's enthusiasm during discussion around ecological design and sustainability, he became an advocate for the involvement of children in planning and built environment processes. Howard was an inspirational architect, who touched and improved many people's lives. He was a brilliant communicator and his enthusiasm was infectious. He delighted in going against the flow of general opinion and he was usually at least one step ahead of everyone else. We will miss him.

Notes

1. For more detail on the Children's Parliament EcoCity work and the Dunfermline EcoCity project, including a full report on that project, go to: http://www.childrensparliament.org.uk/projects/eco-city.
2. For further information on the Children's Parliament go to: http://www.childrensparliament.org.uk.
3. For further information on Gaia Planning go to: http://gaiagroup.org.
4. For more detail on the Curriculum for Excellence, go to: http://www.ltscotland.org.uk/understandingthecurriculum/whatiscurriculumforexcellence/index.asp.
5. For further information on AfterNow project go to: http://www.afternow.co.uk.

Bibliography

University of Glasgow (2012) College of Medical, Veterinary and Life Sciences: Educational resources, http://www.gla.ac.uk/colleges/mvls/learningandteaching/educationalresources/resourcesbycategory/schoolofmedicine/afternow/ date accessed 27 February, 2012.

12
Conclusion: Unlearning Participation

Udi Mandel Butler and Kelly Teamey

This book originated with the challenge of how we could further our thinking and exploration of children and young people's participation by engaging with practices and perspectives emerging from different countries. The network discussions opened up spaces for us to see beyond dominant tendencies in this field that have emerged in Europe and North America. The bringing together of academics from a range of disciplines and continents made us reflect on the different trajectories and practices (past, present and future) of children and young people's participation. What are the possibilities of children and young people's voices being heard and their contributions to society being acknowledged in a world largely shaped by adults? How has the concept of participation itself suffered from being co-opted by agendas that have drifted a long way from the roots of the concept as revolving around individual and collective transformation? How does the spread of the notion of children and young people's participation, with associated policies, practices, concepts and language, interact with different country and cultural contexts? What other ways of understanding and practicing children and young people's participation can we learn from these different places and contexts? It is our suggestion, that as adults interested in understanding, writing about and encouraging children and young people's participation, we ought to learn to listen deeply (not just 'better' but to listen fully in an open and present way) and make space for listening in our writing, our inquiry and our thinking and analyses about such practices of participation.

In this concluding chapter we will attempt a brief synthesis of some of the key contributions to the questions raised in the previous chapters. Here we wish to point to some emerging common themes across the different countries, whilst also reflecting on the challenge of comparing and overgeneralizing in any attempt to bring together distinct historical, political, social and cultural settings through the topic of children and young people's participation. We wish to draw attention to the importance and innovation of the debates found in this book that illustrate the links between national history, politics and culture and an international network of organizations, and sets of ideas surrounding children and young people's rights and participation.

As we discuss here, although the chapters articulate distinct histories and political processes, they all converge around the significance of the United Nations Children's Rights Convention (UNCRC) of 1989. The chapters here acknowledge the importance of this historical marker in thinking about and catalyzing policies, programs and projects for children and young people's participation. At the same time, the authors also provide examples of participation and theorizing that reach beyond the centers traditionally related to the sources of ideas and practices often associated with the UNCRC, particularly from Europe and North America.

In the second part of this chapter we raise further questions on theorizing children and young people's participation, asking how this field suffers from institutionalized biases in its orientation, objects of inquiry and theoretical framework. We argue that, although important and innovative in its cross-national scope, there are missing forms of theorizing and inquiry that could (and should) be taken further. Here we suggest other bodies of theories, especially those linked to unlearning, decolonizing and indigenous forms of knowledge, that could also be drawn from and offer possible avenues of inquiry. Some of these are touched on in the previous chapters and they open up the field to other forms and spaces of participation with which children and young people engage.

We conclude this chapter by returning to, or re-affirming, the importance of transformative learning and listening as key ingredients in the field of participation. We also argue for the importance of understanding and practicing these processes more rigorously and reflexively in our theorizing, inquiry and day-to-day practices alongside and with children and young people.

Common themes and the challenge of comparisons

The previous country chapters offer a range of locally distinct social, economic, political, historical and cultural conditions within which participation occurs in the worlds of children and young people. The UNCRC is repeatedly referred to as an almost globally recognized and, to a certain legal extent, agreed-upon set of standards concerning the rights of children to participate. However, the Convention interacts with particular social, economic, political and cultural conditions in each nation. These interactions included each country's own traditions of children and young people's participation as well as, significantly, their own cultural meanings and practices associated within their populations and historical contexts.

The nature of this interaction between national, regional and local conditions and practices associated with children and young people, and a set of ideas, policies and practices coming from networks that are heavily influenced by the agendas of international organizations and donor agencies, is clearly different from place to place. The case studies provide a flavor of the multiplicity of situations, community projects, nongovernmental organizations (NGOs), social movements and government initiatives that have taken on board children and young people's participation, both as a result of this UNCRC environment, as well as through their own internal logic, political agendas and priorities of development.

As outlined in Chapter 4, in Brazil we saw how the ratification of the UNCRC coincided with a process of 're-democratization' following the end of a long period of dictatorship (from 1964–1985) and a struggle to reclaim rights and civic participation that had been severely repressed. The new constitution of 1989, and the Child and Adolescent Statute a year later, considerably transformed the rights of children from previous legal incarnations towards a more participative nature. These new laws had already been in development for several years in the debates, practices and mass mobilizations in civil society and community organizations. International bodies such as UNICEF, which were heavily involved in the drafting of the UNCRC, helped to energize these debates and practices. However, the main inspiration for the new laws in Brazil comes from the long Latin American tradition of civil society activism that can be traced to mass social movements, such as the Movement of Popular Education and Liberation Theology.

Similarly in South Africa, the post-apartheid government from 1994 onwards also took inspiration from the UNCRC in their drafting of the new Constitution. As Chapter 8 illustrates, the new Constitution and the political and cultural climate following the end of apartheid were progressive and attentive to the rights of participation for children and young people in some ways but in other ways (re)confined the space for children and young people's engagement. This was despite the role children and young people had played, politically, in the struggle against the previous racist and oppressive regime.

As described in Chapter 10, the UNCRC has also inspired greater attention to involving children and young people, in legislation across the UK and policy initiatives. A rights-based rationale came together with others – like service user involvement and training children for democratic citizenship – to create a plethora of participation activities. Yet the often top-down, bureaucratic approach to children and young people's participation in the UK has led to repeated concerns about tokenism and lack of impact. Potentially transformative activities are arguably supported by aspects of law and policy, but the activities were dependent on key adults' values, who sought to create different ways of working, spaces and relationships.

These dynamic relations between national history, politics and culture and a shifting international set of conventions, discourse and practices around children's rights to participation can be seen across all country chapters. Indeed, within the country chapters, a key focus is on the political and policy environment that either hinders, or worse, oppresses children and young people's participation or else provides conditions for it to flourish.

The 'formal' and the 'everyday'

Alongside the above dynamics of 'local' contexts interacting with 'globalized' practices and discourses, another key thread found in the country chapters and the case studies is the tension between institutionalized, or 'formal', and non-institutionalized, or 'everyday', spaces of participation. Chapter 8 addresses this tension directly:

> Children and young people, collectively and individually, contribute to the unfolding of everyday life in multiple ways, many of which are inadequately described, or ignored and dismissed within adult society.

Whilst on the other hand, there are:

> The ways in which children are called to participate, often through brief commentary in formal governance and policy formulation, [that] may be formulaic and may miss the manner in which children engage in the minutiae of local politics in their lived environments, as well as the terms and language they bring to bear on these processes. (Chapter 8)

Many formalized forms of participation may be understood as 'transitive', 'forced' and 'manipulative' as Rahnema (2010) describes (see

Chapter 2 for further explanation), rather than 'intransitive', 'free' or 'spontaneous' (that are more congruent to the 'unfolding of the everyday'). The tension and distinction between these two domains – children and young people's contribution to the 'unfolding of the everyday' and their formulaic involvement in more formalized spaces of deliberation or collective action – are significant. They highlight the different meanings that can be attributed to 'participation' and to understanding what constitutes 'political' or 'transformation' and 'transformative' action, as discussed across Chapters 1, 2 and 3. 'Real' participation is often perceived as occurring in more visible public spaces of collective deliberation and action rather than the myriad other spaces that contest or reproduce the 'everyday' (see Butler and Princeswal, 2010).

Some local cultural meanings and social practices can be difficult to reconcile when they challenge personal ideas and theories framing what we believe participation ought to look like. Chapters 6 and 7 (on India) and Chapters 8 and 9 (on South Africa), for example, point to deep traditions of inter-generational hierarchy where children and young people have very clearly defined cultural norms of obedience to their parents and Elders. As discussed in Chapters 1 and 2, minority world models of 'normal' childhood emphasize individual protection and empowerment, while other constructions of childhood often assume obedience to older people alongside greater degrees of responsibility and independence amongst peers.

There is a modernist or modernizing thread of thinking permeating the theorization and practice surrounding children and young people. These modernizing sets of ideas and behavioral changes associated with the rights of children to participate are seen as empowering or even emancipatory (see Prout, 2005, 2011; Tisdall and Punch, 2012). This is not to deny that there are countless 'traditional' or 'cultural' practices that can be described as being highly oppressive to children and young people across the world. However, it must be remembered that culture, amongst other things, is a contested domain where different groups or individuals struggle for power, resources, privilege and the assertion of their sense of identity. We might engage with the concept of 'culture' as a process (verb) rather than a static 'thing' (noun) to support us in understanding this contested domain more clearly.

The discourse and practice of rights have undeniably been an important and powerful instrument in providing a language and set of institutions – as well as policies and practices for redressing a number of these forms of oppression and imbalances of power. At the same time, we need to be mindful of how the discourse of rights, with particular constructions of childhood, might blind us to what the above (first) quote points to, the day-to-day contributions of children and young people to the 'the unfolding of everyday life'.

In researching and writing about children and young people's participation, we often pay little attention to the contributions of children and young people in day-to-day life in particular social and cultural contexts. Instead, the bulk of our attention and the catalyzing of participation focus more on formalized and public spaces of participation. Such spaces are in most cases the embodiment of practices, discourse and institutions associated with 'rights'. These have been designed and created by adults and their own sense of what constitutes collective action and deliberation (whether for transformation or social reproduction) – again for a set of instrumental outcomes that adults tend to decide according to their view of what will be of benefit to children and young people.

As Chapters 1 and 2 illustrate, we have come to understand participation as part of a linear process that is aimed toward some kind of utilitarian goal prescribed for an instrumentalist outcome. Along these lines, White (1996) has outlined a list of four different forms of participation, one of which she calls 'instrumentalist participation'. Such participation seeks to achieve a particular predefined 'useful' or utilitarian end, that is typically defined through a 'top-down' mechanism with little or no representation from those the participation is supposed to help (see Chapter 2 for further information on White's classification). In this way the 'formal' instigations to participate, which are almost always catalyzed and framed by adults, often adhere to this 'global' discourse and understanding of both 'participation' and 'childhood'.

A consideration of what we can perceive as spaces of participation – as well as how those spaces are playing out different attributes of participation – is key here. Reading across the book's chapters, children and young people's participation happens across a plurality of spaces and takes on a variety of forms. The questions 'participation in *what*?' and '*how* is participation occurring?' always need to be asked.

In the previous chapters the 'what' has included projects developed by local NGOs: in rural South African villages involved in different forms of communication and storytelling through radio; across Scotland in sustainability and urban planning; or on the streets of urban India concerned with the capacity building, organization and collective action of street and working children. The 'what' has also included local, regional and national rights councils, assemblies, clubs, parliaments and policy networks facilitated by the state, and the non-governmental sector, in

Brazil, India, South Africa and the UK. In most cases, these spaces are constructed by adults themselves from within the state, NGOs, local organizations and so on, which provide the space and often define the 'how' – the parameters for the participative involvement of children and young people. Perhaps this is inevitable given the extreme imbalance of power and resources between adults and children more generally. At the same time, however, we should always try to be mindful of the values, motivations and ways of thinking and knowing that inform the creation and encouragement of spaces and practices of participation.

The value(s) of participation

Whilst the origins of participation may have been more radical (see Chapter 2), the call for participation these days, as many authors in the previous chapters point out, has been a mantra of neoliberal political economy. Participation has become a ploy for the empowerment of consumers to participate in making rationalist and materialist choices helping those who provide service or goods to acquire greater profit and efficiency. As Chapters 2 and 3 discuss, what began as an aspiration for participation to be used as a means for social transformation itself morphed into a series of ideas and practices used by key powerful institutions to maintain the status quo and gain legitimacy (Cooke and Kothari, 2004; Leal, 2010; Rahnema, 2010; White, 1996). Rahnema (2010) expands on a list of six reasons explaining the 'unprecedented interest governments and development institutions have recently taken in the concept of participation' (p. 129):

- The concept is no longer perceived as a threat;
- Participation has become a politically attractive slogan;
- Participation has become economical, an appealing proposition;
- Participation is now perceived as an instrument for greater effectiveness as well as a new source of investment;
- Participation is becoming a good fund-raising device;
- An expanded concept of participation could help the private sector to be directionally involved in the development business.

Most of the book's chapters critically engage with the range of meanings and histories that lie behind the various calls to participation at a local level. Yet more research is still needed to unearth the values, practices, discourses and knowledge systems embedded within the broader (global) architecture of political and economic power to determine *how* these influence local practices and experiences. In addition, the complex histories of each context, often distorted through years of colonial power, have created legacies of social and cultural inequalities, directly and indirectly impacting on children and young people's participation. Framed in a language of rights, questions of the 'what' and 'how' of participation are often answered in connection to voice, to an acknowledgment of the subjectivity (individuality, emotions, motivations, thoughts and desires) of the child or young person. This acknowledgment relates to questions of personhood, of who is considered a full person in society, especially societal laws and its cultural practices. At the same time, the role of adults, in either assisting or blocking children and young people's participation, emerges strongly in the examples given across the previous chapters. As discussed in Chapter 1, participation is often said to be about changing patterns of relations between adults and children and also between children themselves, in terms of the roles and expectations of them. Such shifts, at least ideally, imply a transformation toward the redistribution of resources too, for if we are really supposed to hear what children and young people say, such listening ought to prompt us to do things differently.

These dimensions of power and distributions of resources recur through the previous chapters, as we see many examples of the tensions and challenges inherent in the shifting of relationships between adults and children and young people. For example, Chapter 8 articulates a triad of necessary conditions (or consequences) of participation with reference to Fraser (2009) as involving *redistribution, recognition* and *representivity*. Fraser writes of participatory parity, which entails the redistribution of resources for fair and equal entitlement and access by all participants. Through this parity, the recognition of the value of each member of the polity and representivity, are manifested, in that each participant's voice be heard and valued as legitimate. To recapture 'participation' in its earlier and more truly democratic meaning (as linked more closely with transformation), there is the urgency to unlearn how and where 'participation' has been colonized by various neoliberal institutions as well as to consider various perceptions of 'transformation'.

Participation as learning and transformation

Participative situations for children and young people are typically framed, explicitly or implicitly, as pedagogical processes. That is, children and young people in participative situations come to acquire cognitive, emotional, social and practical competencies, skills and confidence to be contributors to society, the community or another collective. Yet, if learning is to be considered one of the most important aspects of participation, why is this not explored in more depth in theory and in practice – outside of the education field? Where are the key learning theorists, especially the transformative learning theorists, in the literature on children and young people's participation?

What the previous chapters suggest is that the transformative and pedagogical aspects of participation are deeply enmeshed within nuances emerging through extended periods of time – pointing again to the significance of the 'unfolding of the everyday'. Projects for children and young people's participation are often limited in time, with predefined linear, utilitarian and instrumentalist tools for implementation and analyses. Restricted time frameworks tend to miss or ignore the spontaneity that is often core to deep and transformative learning inherent within participative processes. These shortcomings tend to characterize the formal and institutionalized spaces adults design for children and young people's participation. In contrast, deep and transformative learning that might come to characterize participative situations is often unforeseen, unintended and nuanced. Such learning might then be invisible, without focused forms of listening and participation, particularly from outsiders.

Writings on indigenous ways of knowing and learning, addressed in Chapters 2 and 3, provide additional perspectives on valuing the everyday and deep learning which describe transformation as a holistic participative process. To understand this is to engage with what 'indigenous ways of knowing' actually means. Arbon, an Aboriginal scholar in Australia, provides a succinct and clear explanation. Indigenous ways of knowing is not about only knowing something with your mind, in an intellectual capacity. Rather, 'to know' is also 'to do' (to practice and take various forms of action) as well as to 'be', or to cultivate what is being learned into everyday life. The 'unfolding of the everyday' in this case reflects the depth and complexity of indigenous ways of knowing – the inseparability of 'knowing-being-doing' (see Arbon, 2008). Thus the process of knowing through an indigenous perspective is a lifelong journey of continual transformation that is connected to everyday life (see Peat, 1996).

To cultivate the social practices required in particular participative settings, say a radio project or a debating and collective action group, requires a gradual learning of the milieu, its social, cognitive, emotional and embodied nuances. The example of the collective of the Landless Children in Brazil organizing themselves and challenging the adults in their camp who had canceled their trip seems comical, in Chapter 5: especially the moment when the adult camp leader addressed the leader of the children's collective as 'my son' only to be told that in that role he was not his son but a representative of the children's collective. Such self-control, confidence and courage of the young activist show a remarkable competency in the social practices of collective organization and facing up to injustices, which living and being within the Landless Movement world taught him.

Chapter 7 gives us the opportunity to learn from the longer term impact of participation: the three interviews with former participants of the children's *sangam* in India for a number of years, show how being part of participative spaces can lead to deep transformations and confidence. In turn, this can prompt a drive for greater engagement and leadership within civic and community life (see also Butler and Princeswal, 2010 and CIESPI, 2007). Yet these moments of, for lack of a better word 'socio-political-cultural-spiritual awakenings', are little understood or explored. In an attempt to explain, Rahnema expands on participation as 'inner' and 'outer' transformation:

> to participate means to live and to relate differently. It implies, above all, the recovery of one's inner freedom – that is, to learn to listen and to share, free from any fear or predefined conclusion, belief or judgment. As inner freedom is not necessarily dependent on outer freedom, its recovery is an essentially personal matter ... it enables one not only to acquire a tremendous life power for the flowering of one's own life, but also to contribute, in a meaningful way, to everyone else's struggle for a better life. ... To live differently implies, that change be perceived as a process which starts from within, and defines as one pursues one's creative journey into the unknown. (Rahnema, 2010, p. 140–142)

The implications of institutional biases

The above discussion brings us to the question of – *What is missing in inquiry and theorizing around children and young people's participation?* We have suggested that most spaces and practices of children and young people recognized and/or labeled as collective or public 'participation' occur in specific and often institutionalized spaces (for a similar point, see also Clark and Percy-Smith, 2006; Percy-Smith, 2010). The key question that emerges therefore, is – *How are institutional biases implicated*

into the thinking, practices, discourses and inquiry on children and young people's participation?
This complex question has a range of possible threads. Firstly, concerning the spaces of participation, we need to ask how, particularly through empirical work, we might be missing entire domains of children and young people's participation. *Where else can we engage (and subsequently challenge) our own understanding in the worlds of children and young people's participation that we have not considered? What are our blind spots?* It is imperative for the field to bring forth the broad understandings of participation as transformation whilst at the same time emphasizing listening, deep learning, and the redistribution of roles and resources as integral to participation. Further we also need to acknowledge how participation is present not only in institutionalized and policy settings but also in the 'unfolding of the everyday'.

From the experience of bringing together this book, we identify five domains that would merit further attention, as spaces for (potential) transformative participation:

- Social, political and cultural movements, transgressions and transformations;
- Information and communication technologies;
- Our relations to the non-human world;
- The worlds of colonized peoples; and
- The institution of schooling.

Social, political and cultural movements, transgressions and transformations

First to clarify, the meaning of 'transgressions' here refers to the act of going beyond accepted boundaries – to transcend institutional norms, rules and expectations. It is undeniable that children and/or young people do take part in a number of political settings: children or youth parliaments, student councils, children's clubs, policy networks and so forth. Yet, 'the political' is also situated in diverse non-formal, non-institutional and oppositional spaces and practices that can transform the very institutions of politics and social and cultural practices by providing transgressive and imaginative possibilities and examples.

Examples of this in the book go from more playful protest movements such as the *Kissathon* started as a Facebook group by a young protester in South Africa against the government's clampdown on children and young people's display of affection and, other historically impactful examples, such as young people's (especially school children's) involvement in the anti-apartheid struggle through diverse and often creative ways. Similarly, in Chapter 7, Prem's protest against the lack of privacy in school toilets transgressed hierarchical adult-child relations, but ultimately was successful in initiating change. Other recent examples include young people's creative occupation of public space and attempt to create a new form of collective debate: the global Occupy Wall Street movement that started in 2011; the highly successful movement started by school children themselves, the *Movimento Pinguin* and its after-shoot, and the current Chilean student movement opposing privatization of the public education system.

What is significant about these examples is how such activities are generated through the worlds of children and young people themselves. While children and young people engage with the political machinery of the adult word, they also innovate, often in playful and creative ways. Countless examples of such movements and transgressions exist, although their various and often meaningful contributions to societal transformation often go unacknowledged, unnoticed or are downplayed. What some of the chapters show is that when transgression occurs, both at a larger societal level (such as in the case of the anti-apartheid struggle and the post-apartheid era) or in more localized scale (such as in the radio project transforming the relationships between children and adults in South Africa), any change in relations of power is at best situated and precarious. Whilst personal transformation might be enduring, as illustrated in Chapter 7, wider societal transformations instigated by these processes of participation are often short-lived and fragmented.

Entrenched power differentials between adults and children and young people tend to reassert themselves with transgressions and transformations that are confined to periods of social and political upheaval, or to particular spaces or brief moments. Longer term transformations, such as within more deeply institutionalized spaces (for example the school classroom or the public meeting forums in the village), do not tend to be sustainable. The quandary is that these transgressions rarely transform deeply engrained and entrenched values, habits and institutions; they engage and transform small spheres that tend not to have much lasting or influential effect, in terms of broader societal change.

Holistic transformation most often fails in spite of the success of transgressions within specific spheres. What might holistic transformation look like and how might it be brought about? Chapter 8 articulates a triad of necessary conditions (or consequences) of participation, as involving *redistribution, recognition* and *representivity* (Fraser, 2009).

Fraser writes of participatory parity, which entails the redistribution of resources for fair and equal entitlement and access by all participants. Through this parity, the recognition of the value of each member of the polity, and representivity, are manifested, in that each participant's voice is heard and valued as legitimate

The role of adults, in either assisting or blocking children and young people's participation, emerges strongly in the examples given across the previous chapters. As discussed in Chapter 1, participation is often said to be about changing patterns of relations between adults and children and also between children themselves, in terms of the roles and expectations of them. Such shifts, at least ideally, imply a transformation in the redistribution of resources too; if we are really supposed to hear what children and young people say, such listening ought to prompt us to do things differently. These dimensions of power and resource distribution recur through the previous chapters, as we see many examples of the tensions and challenges inherent in the shifting of relationships between adults and children and young people.

These are timeless questions that are associated with different ideas and practices related to social change and revolution. The significance here is for a wider engagement and understanding of the learning and experiences of transformation (inner and outer) that children and young people experience within and through social, political and cultural movements, transgressions and transformative processes. The book has a number of examples, such as the *children's sangam* in Chapter 7, *Abaqophi BakwaZisize Abakhanyayo* children's radio project in Chapter 9 and Paisley Pre-Fives Centre in Chapter 10, that point to the benefits of incorporating adults – adult facilitators, adult decision-makers, parents and other community members – into the transformative processes in practice and the analysis in terms of theory and research. While recognizing that these examples in themselves are still in progress and imperfect, they show how participation has altered certain practices, changed attitudes and at least begun to change local cultures. In the examples, adults were a targeted and recognized part of transformative participation.

Information and communication technologies

Various examples in this book hint at the growing need to understand information and communication technology (ICT) in regards to children and young people's participation: the use of social media by the Youth Commission on Alcohol, in Chapter 10, or the *Kissathon* and Occupy Wall Street Movement mentioned above. Kahn and Kellner

(2007, p. 433) describe our current society as 'undergoing the most dramatic technological revolution in history' centered on computers, information, communication and multimedia technologies that are 'outmoding' and imploding traditional forms of social organization, culture and politics. The ways in which technologies such as mobile or smart phones and the Internet are reshaping children and young people's identities, competencies and relations of power *vis-à-vis* the adult world are an important question. ICTs are quickly and radically reshaping social practices, language, literacies, meaning and relationships by offering multiple opportunities for online communities, social media, new forms of organizing, communication, political action, consumption, cultural production and learning. How the key ingredients of participation noted above are reflected in these newly created territories and practices surrounding ICTs is an open question that merits more investigation.

Kahn and Kellner (2007) also describe our current historical period as the age of 'technocapitalism': modernist and corporate forces of science and technology have created a techno-cultural-industrial complex that is driven by the forces of current forms of capitalism more broadly identified as neoliberalism. Important questions concerning this techno-cultural-industrial complex in regards to the topic of participation include:

• Whose interests are being served by emergent technologies and the media?
• Who is being excluded and why?
• How is the social order merely being reproduced rather than transgressed and transformed through different forms of media?
• How are ICTs enhancing or distorting possibilities for transformative participation?
• How are ICTs part of a greater ecology of learning?

A final question ICTs have prompted us to ask is the extent to which they immerse us ever more into a technological world at the expense of realizing our embeddedness and dependence on the non-human world. For example, in his 1997 book, *The spell of the sensuous: Perception and language in a more-than-human world*, Abram argues that technology, particularly written literacy, has separated us as human beings from the non-human world. Furthermore, it is through this process of separation that the current social, cultural and ecological crises that we find ourselves in can be explained. Abram argues that we have forgotten how to 'read the non-human world' and to form reciprocal relationships with the beings that dwell within it. Through our perpetual dependency on human technological tools, we must critically investigate how we are simultaneously opening up new spaces whilst closing down others – how we are curtailing other forms of participation, social relationships, community relatedness and relationships to the non-human world.

Our relations to the non-human world

This takes us to a third and often missing domain of participation, involving the relationship of children and young people to the non-human world, particularly with reference to indigenous ways of knowing. This domain is not typically associated with the notion of 'participation', yet considering the challenges we all face through increasingly tangible issues such as climate change, environmental destruction and over-consumption, it is a key space to be attentive to. Chapter 9 provided a beautiful glimpse into this world of children's participation in the non-human world through the radio interviews carried out in the community project. Here we hear about children's:

> deep knowledge of their environment, describing where to find bees, and naming trees and plants that can be eaten or used in the treatment of illnesses. They describe their responsibilities: collecting water from the pump or river, or firewood from the bush; ensuring a spic and span house or yard; or checking that a grandmother took her tablets. They take listeners to their favorite places: a huge rock amongst the aloe plants on the hill; the river where there are always others keen to play; a mother's grave.

Learning to live in harmony with all beings in the non-human world involves learning to enter into relationships with all the cognitive, emotional and embodied awareness and skills that this entails. Here we can again refer to Arbon's (2008) indigenous cosmological description of *being-knowing-doing*. Participation, in the context of such a cosmology (that is, the way in which we make sense of our place in the universe), means something altogether different to what might be understood within a tradition of democracy and civil society that originated the meanings and practices commonly associated with 'participation' (see Chapters 2 and 3).

The worlds of colonized peoples

A fourth domain of participation addresses the worlds of children and young people who come from indigenous and/or marginalized populations and who have been (and often continue to be) adversely affected by colonial and post-colonial forces. As stated earlier, the center of gravity of the discourse and practice surrounding children and young people's participation, at least as commonly understood by academics, governmental, international agencies and NGOs, originates in the UNCRC. The discussions to produce this document involved a number of countries and drew on divergent cultural understandings of children and young people's roles and responsibilities (see, for example, the discussions instigated by African delegates on the importance of respect to elders in African cultures). Yet debates around cultural understandings of children and young people and the spaces of participation they had in society also need to explore the cultural contexts that have been destroyed or aggressively dismantled and weakened by long histories of colonialism and post-colonialism.

Chapter 3 provides an example of the *ghotul*, a children's domain amongst the Koitors an *Adivasi* (or First People) community in the Chattisgarh State of India. The *ghotul* is a sphere of children and young people's participation before the imposition of British colonial structures of governance and schooling, which were subsequently taken on by the Indian government. A *ghotul* is an age set group where children and young people enter to learn and be amongst their peers. *Ghotul* members organize all festivals, prepare food for marriage, help families in a village in different stages of cultivation, and sing and dance to keep the cultural traditions alive but also participate in political discussions. The *ghotul* shows a sphere of children and young people's participation and contribution to community life in a society long before the imposition of state institutions through either British colonialism or Indian nationalism.

Given the modernist tendencies of children and young people's participation, both in theory and in practice, much could be learned from seeking out places and spaces where indigenous practices continue – despite colonial expansions – or are being rejuvenated. Examples of such cultural reclamation abound in many parts of the world today as we witness a resurgence of indigenous, First Nations, Native American, Maori and Aboriginal communities reconnecting with their cultural practices and pedagogical traditions. In these, children and young people can have key roles and responsibilities within their communities. Furthermore, reclaiming such indigenous cultural and spiritual practices can helpfully influence non-indigenous communities, particularly those communities that place a spiritual value on the non-human world in which we are all a part.

The institution of schooling

The last domain, that is often and paradoxically unproblematized in the international development literature on participation, is that of the institution of schooling. Education and schooling, which are often conflated as being the same, has become central within children and young people's lives around the world, especially as encouraged by such international agendas as 'Education for All' and the Millennium Development Goals. Many educationists have noted that the vast majority of learning takes place *outside* of schools. Yet it is currently *within* the walls of schools where a substantial percentage of childhood now tends to be experienced.

One of the most critical thinkers pertaining to the institution of schooling was Illich (1970, 1973). His views created such a stir that in academia he is most often denounced as professionally illegitimate (Kahn, 2009). In some ways this is a source of irony as Illich described himself as a 'de-professional'. Illich aimed to push us all to engage critically with the industrialized model of schooling as a deeply engrained and entrenched institution of society (as embedded within a much broader political economy of power and social reproduction) that needs to be dis-established.

According to Illich (1970), institutions such as schools are de-humanizing because of how they force a set of controls onto our bodies and minds, conditioning us to become something other than our true selves. Participation within the spaces of schooling tends to be 'forced', 'manipulated' and 'transitive' (Rahnema, 2010) and without placing any value on the 'unfolding of everyday experience'. The rationale for schooling's continued forms of imprisonment (as referred to by Illich) is to prepare citizens for the work force, rather than as free and critical human beings that aim to live their lives to reach their true purpose and passions for themselves, each other and the world around them. Illich countered the idea that schooling could be reformed as a 'better' public good and instead called for vernacular values and skills and convivial tools that could meet people's needs. In other words, he advocated for people learning directly within their local contexts and pursuing their own passions of learning, through learning webs of people and communities of all ages rather than by entering the heavily industrialized and institutionalized learning environment that is schooling.

It is difficult to accept such challenging considerations. To be schooled is central to the cultural, political and economic construction of what it means to be an educated person. Schooling is so deeply embedded into childhood as part of our societal and life process that it is practically taboo to seriously consider otherwise. Yet, often ignored or discounted in academic literature are vast un-schooling and de-schooling movements of people and communities all over the world, young and old, who have attempted to create such learning webs within their local contexts and beyond.

A special kind of listening

A greater attention to these five domains of participation – social, cultural and political transgression, ICTs, the non-human world, the worlds of the marginalized and the territory of and alternatives to school – opens up important paths of enquiry. Attending to these domains draws on the literature of rights, policy, NGO work, governmentality and so forth, and casts its net further afield to political and social movement theories, writings on cultural resistance, theories of our relation to technology and the media, and to the non-human world, authors engaged with de-colonialism and indigeneity, un- or de-schooling and transformative learning. Research in these fields, as suggested in Chapter 3, ought also to draw attention to how we define theory to begin with, particularly by emphasizing the inseparable link between theory and practice.

Focusing on the diverse domains of participation pointed to here also entails a decolonizing and de-institutionalizing, an unlearning if you will, of our own engrained habits of thinking, doing, asking and listening. If we are to embark on any sort of decolonizing learning process within the field, we need to look (and to listen) to our own assumptions, our blind spots, about how we frame and understand processes of participation – and from where these assumptions and framings are coming. It requires an openness to the unknown and unfamiliar, *a special kind of listening.* Most of the chapters here suggested that listening is a transformative and crucial ingredient in this field of children and young people's participation. The question, then, is what are the qualities of such listening and how might we cultivate it in our day-to-day contributions to the 'unfolding of everyday life'?

Bibliography

Abram, D. (1997) *The spell of the sensuous: Perception and language in a more-than-human world*, (New York: Vintage Books).

Arbon, V. (2008) *Arlathirnda ngurkarnda ityirnda: Being-knowing-doing: de-colonising indigenous tertiary education*, (Queensland: Post Pressed)

Butler, U. M. and Princeswal, M. (2010) 'Cultures of Participation, Young People and Public Action in Brazil', *Community Development Journal*, 45(3), 1–12.

CIESPI (2007) *Nós: A Revolução de Cada Dia*, (Rio de Janeiro: CIESPI/PUC).

Clark, A. and Percy-Smith, B. (2006) 'Beyond Consultation: Participatory Practices in Everyday Spaces', *Children Youth and Environments*, 16(2), 1–9.

Cooke, B. and Kothari, U. (2004) (eds) *Participation: The New Tyranny?*, (Zed Books: London).

Fraser, N. (2009) *Scales of justice: Reimagining political space in a globalizing world*. (New York: Columbia University Press).

Freire, P. (1970) *Pedagogy of the oppressed*, (New York: Continuum Books).

Freire, P. (1973) *Education for Critical Consciousness*, (New York: Continuum).

Freire, P. (1976) *Education, the practice of freedom*, (London: Writers & Readers Group)

Illich, I. (1970) *De-schooling society*, (New York: Harper & Row).

Illich, I. (1973) *Tools for conviviality*, (New York: Harper & Row).

Kahn, R. and Kellner, D. (2007) 'Paulo Freire and Ivan Illich: Technology, Politics and the Reconstruction of Education', *Policy Futures in Education*, 5(4), 431–448.

Kahn, R. (2009) 'Critical Pedagogy Taking the Illich Turn', *The International Journal of Illich Studies*, 1(1), 37–49.

Leal, P. A. (2010) 'Participation: The ascendancy of a buzzword in the neo-liberal era' in A. Cornwall and D. Eade (eds) *Deconstructing Development Discourse: Buzzwords and Fuzzwords*, (Rugby: Practical Action Publishing in association with Oxfam GB).

Peat, D. (1996) *Blackfoot physics: A journey into the Native American Universe*, (London: Fourth Estate).

Percy-Smith, B. (2010) 'Councils, Consultations and Community', *Children's Geographies*, 8(2), 107–122.

Prout, A. (2005) *The future of childhood*, (London: Routledge/Falmer).

Prout, A. (2001) 'Taking a Step away from Modernity: Reconsidering the New Sociology of Childhood', *Global Studies of Childhood*, 1(1), 4–14.

Rahnema, M. (2010) 'Participation' in W. Sachs (ed.) *The Development Dictionary: A Guide to Knowledge as Power*, 2nd edn. (London: Zed Books).

Rickinson, M., Dillon, J., Teamey, K., Morris, M., Choi, M., Sanders, D. and Benefield, P. (2004) *A review of research on outdoor learning*, (London: National Foundation for Educational Research and King's College).

Tisdall, E. K. M. and Punch, S. (2012) 'Not So 'New'? Looking Critically at Childhood Studies', *Children's Geographies*, 10(3), 249–264.

White, S. (1996) 'Depoliticising Development: The Uses and Abuses of Participation', *Development in Practice*, 6(1), 6–15.

Index